Certainty, that thing of indefinite approximation: a quest through lives and literatures

Geoffrey Wilkinson

First published by Authors OnLine Ltd 2012

This reprint with corrections 2024

A CIP catalogue record for this book is available from the British Library

ISBN 978-1-9160622-3-8

Republished by Geoffrey M. Wilkinson
Franksbridge
Llandrindod Wells
Powys LD1 5SA
United Kingdom

for Susan

Contents

Special acknowledgements

I wish to express particular thanks to the following authors, editors, literary agents, trustees and publishers for allowing me to quote from their copyright material:

Rōshi Joan Halifax for excerpts from 'Old K"xau' in *Shamanic Voices: A Survey of Visionary Narratives*, which she edited in 1979; Faber and Faber Ltd for permission to reproduce the whole of Seamus Heaney's poem 'Postscript' from his collection *The Spirit Level*; The Wylie Agency (UK) Limited for permission to use extracts from two titles by V.S. Naipaul, *Finding the Centre* © 1984 V.S. Naipaul and *An Area of Darkness* © 1964 V.S. Naipaul; the trustees of the Owen family estate for an extract from Letter 578 in *Wilfred Owen: Collected Letters* edited by Harold Owen and John Bell (1967), reproduced by permission of Oxford University Press; Aitken Alexander Associates for excerpts from 'Sea-Room' by Jonathan Raban, first published in *Granta* Issue 10; Alan Teder for extracts from his translation of an interview with Arvo Pärt, originally published in 1998 in the Estonian-language newspaper *Postimees*; Professor Michael Walzer for excerpts from his essay 'The Argument about Humanitarian Intervention' in the Winter 2002 edition of *Dissent*; and Jessica Kingsley Publishers, London and Philadelphia, for extracts from *Nobody Nowhere* by Donna Williams (1999) © Donna Williams 1992 and 1999.

Further copyright acknowledgements, together with full publication details of the above and of all my other sources, can be found in the *Acknowledgements* and *Sources and notes* sections. Throughout I have followed the guidelines on 'fair dealing' suggested by The Society of Authors and I believe that I have secured permission from all the appropriate rights holders. If I have inadvertently overlooked any, however, I shall be happy to rectify the situation as speedily as possible.

I mean *Negative Capability*, that is when man is capable of being in uncertainties, Mysteries, doubts, without any irritable reaching after fact & reason ….

John Keats, letter to George and Tom Keats of 21, 27(?) December 1817 [1]

The rational man seeks the truth gropingly, he knows that his reasoning is only probable, that other considerations will arise to make it doubtful; he never knows too well where he's going, he is "open", he may even appear hesitant. But there are people who are attracted by the durability of stone. They want to be massive and impenetrable, they do not want to change: where would change lead them? This is an original fear of oneself and a fear of truth. And what frightens them is not the content of truth, which they do not even suspect, but the very form of the true – that thing of indefinite approximation. It is as if their very existence were perpetually in suspension. They want to exist all at once and right away.

Jean-Paul Sartre, *Portrait of the Antisemite* [2]

There is an intellectual function in us which demands unity, connection and intelligibility from any material, whether of perception or thought, that comes within its grasp; and if, as a result of special circumstances, it is unable to establish a true connection, it does not hesitate to fabricate a false one.

Sigmund Freud, *Totem and Taboo* [3]

1. PREFACE

Keats's man in uncertainties and Sartre's man in stone stand for two diametrically opposed states of being in the world. The first is a state that welcomes and accommodates uncertainty; the second, far from welcoming uncertainty, would have us suppress it and even deny its existence altogether. The essay that follows is an attempt to understand why, almost two hundred years after Keats's death, only small numbers of people – and they include poets, musicians, and quantum physicists – are *Negatively Capable*, while the rest of us are still all too familiar with the attractions of stone-like durability. Well, that is how it seems to me, and it is the premise of the whole essay.

The lives referred to in my title are the lives of all sorts of people, some historical and others, myself included, alive and kicking. They also include the lives of fictional characters and I make no apology for according these the same value as the lives of actual persons. The literatures range from the obvious (such as autobiographies and novels) to the less obvious (war crimes trial documents, non-mathematical scientific papers accessible to the general reader), and from the rarefied (metaphysical tracts, sacred texts) to the earthy (film scripts, lyrics of once popular songs). I have called it a quest *through* lives and literatures to indicate that, as far as possible, I try to let all this material speak for itself, or at least to speak before I do.

I would like to think that the essay makes meaningful connections across the boundaries of factual and imaginative reality, unconstrained by chronological time or the particularities of any one culture or language. But I am very aware, too, of the warning implicit in *Totem and Taboo* – that the mind's demand for unity and intelligibility in everything it grasps is an engine both of 'true connection' and of dreams, phobias, obsessive thinking, and delusions. So I begin by doubting my own quest, which, depending on your point of view, is either the worst thing I could do or the wisest.

2. THE STAY OF THE WHOLE WORLD

Wonted motions and the government of the universe

From the age of eight to thirteen I boarded at an obscure preparatory school, long since closed and demolished, in the northwest of England. The headmaster, Mr N, was a complex character. A disciplinarian with a ferocious temper, he once beat the entire school (more than sixty boys) in one morning because no one would own up to the alleged theft of a sixpenny piece. And yet this was the same man who would join us in the television room whenever *Batman* and *Top of the Pops* were on and who, as an end-of-term treat to the senior boys, would cancel his Latin lesson and instead read aloud from *Winnie-the-Pooh.* Of all Mr N's surprising characteristics, the one that has always puzzled me most was his preoccupation with bowel movements. On the door of every WC cubicle was a list of names and every morning, after breakfast, every boy named on the list was required to use that cubicle *in the prescribed order.* Alas, I no longer remember the organizing principle. Was it alphabetical order, Baker before Corbett, Richards before Stewart? Or was it date of birth, Johnson I before his younger brother Johnson II, and both before their baby brother Johnson III? In any event, we all made a show of complying with the regime, whether or not nature happened to call for it. We marched off purposefully to the designated place, counted to ten, pulled the chain and then, particularly when Mr N was within earshot, returned to summon the next person on the list: *Clarke, go! Pownall, go!* It would never have occurred to us to challenge the WC rota, precisely because it was part of the established and familiar routine of the school.

To the best of my knowledge, the orderly movements of bowels have never been the subject of much philosophical discourse or great literature. However, the orderly movements of stars and other heavenly bodies are a recurring theme in myth and legend, religion, philosophy and natural science. For example, among the sayings attributed to the

Greek philosopher-mystic Heraclitus, who lived around 500 BC, is this fragment: 'Sun [*Helios*] will not overstep his measures; if he does, the Erinyes, the minions of Justice, will find him out.' [4] There is an ambivalence in this saying. On the one hand, Heraclitus expresses his confidence in the regularity of the sun's motions. Day follows night. Always has done. Always will. On the other hand, he feels the need for magical-judicial sanctions, in the shape of the Erinyes, perhaps because he fears that without them Sun might do a jig across the sky and day *not* follow night. Or consider another example, this one from Richard Hooker's *Of the Laws of Ecclesiastical Polity* of 1593. Despite the huge differences of time and culture, Hooker seems to take up and elaborate on Heraclitus's anxiety:

> Now if nature should intermit her course, and leave altogether though it were but for a while the observation of her own laws; if those principal and mother elements of the world, whereof all things in this lower world are made, should lose the qualities which now they have; if the frame of that heavenly arch erected over our heads should loosen and dissolve itself; if celestial spheres should forget their wonted motions and by irregular volubility turn themselves any way as it might happen; if the prince of the lights of heaven, which now as a giant doth run his unwearied course, should as it were through a languishing faintness begin to stand and to rest himself; if the moon should wander from her beaten way, the times and seasons of the year blend themselves by disordered and confused mixture, the winds breathe out their last gasp, the clouds yield no rain, the earth be defeated of heavenly influence, the fruits of the earth pine away as children at the withered breasts of their mother no longer able to yield them relief: what would become of man himself, whom these things now do all serve? See we not plainly that obedience of creatures unto the law of nature is the stay of the whole world? [5]

Where Heraclitus appeals to the minions of Justice to discourage the sun from unruly behaviour, Hooker appeals to his contemporary readers' shared sense of horror, conditioned by the theology and world view of the time,[6] at an even larger vision of cosmic and earthly disorder. Hooker piles *if* upon *if*, calamity upon calamity, until at last it becomes intolerable: the alternatives to the world as we know it are all too awful to contemplate and therefore they cannot be.

It is time to take stock. I have assembled an unlikely company comprising a twentieth-century headmaster, a Greek Iron Age philosopher, and a sixteenth-century theologian. What all three have in common is a preoccupation with the orderliness, regularity and continuity of natural phenomena and processes. Could it be that Heraclitus echoes the concerns of early agrarian peoples for whom the sun provided diurnal assurance, and a cosmological prototype, of all their familiar realities – the progression of the seasons, their crops, their way of life and rituals, kin and community? Hooker's purpose is didactic: to enumerate the diverse laws (nature's law in this case, but also including a law of reason, human law and others) that flow from God's own eternal Law and protect the earth and the cosmos as a whole from disorder. Mr N's purpose remains a mystery but I suspect that it had something to do with the old motto *mens sana in corpore sano*, a sound mind in a sound body, with bowel regularity as the orderly – and, if Mr N had had his way, almost mechanical – means to *in corpore sano*.

Now it is all very well to guarantee orderliness, regularity and continuity by invoking a sort of cosmic probation service, as Heraclitus does, or by invoking a conventional dread of chaos, as Hooker does. But these seeming guarantees are vulnerable to doubt and objection. For instance, if the Erinyes monitor Sun, who or what monitors the Erinyes? And who or what monitors that monitor? And so on, ad infinitum. As for Hooker, all his wonderful rhetoric amounts to no more than saying that if something is unpalatable or disturbing or downright unthinkable, then it cannot be true. In the language of our time, that is a form of denial (or a form of magic) which banishes disorder from the mind's conception of the world without banishing disorder from the world itself.

To do the job properly, we need to lock orderliness, regularity and continuity into the fabric of the universe so absolutely that disorder is precluded, and not just in practice but *even in principle*. One man who attempted such a feat, through a system of metaphysics, was the German philosopher Gottfried Wilhelm Leibniz. His system consists of several principles, key among them sufficient reason. In its formal terms, which relate to Leibniz's definitions of truth and falsity, sufficient reason says that a proposition is only true if its opposite is a self-contradiction.[7] This may be of interest to a logician but is not enormously helpful for our purpose. In terms of its metaphysical implications, however, sufficient reason gets us off to a more promising start because it asserts that there must be some reason why everything is as it is (or exists at all) rather than otherwise (or not at all). Leibniz locates every such reason in an order of eternal truths, a 'metaphysical' necessity incapable of further explanation. The consequence is that this 'metaphysical' necessity (for which Leibniz has several other names, including 'logical' necessity) ultimately determines the existence, attributes and behaviour of everything in the world as we experience it, even if it seems to be a world that might never have come into being or that might have come into being differently. In other words, an order of metaphysically necessary reality determines our familiar and merely contingent order of reality.

'Besides the world or aggregate of finite things,' Leibniz wrote in 1697, [8] 'we find a certain Unity which is dominant … [in that it] not only rules the world, but also constructs or makes it; and it is higher than the world and, if I may so put it, extramundane; it is thus the ultimate reason of things. For neither in any one single thing, nor in the whole aggregate and series of things, can there be found the sufficient reason of existence.' He goes on to argue that the aggregate of finite things is derived from eternal truths by means of 'a certain Divine mathematics or metaphysical mechanics'. It soon emerges that the dominant Unity (or 'Being of metaphysical necessity') is God, who must exist to provide not only the ultimate reason of things but also the mechanism by which eternal truths can be actualized in the world as 'truths that are temporal, contingent, or physical'. God operates as this mechanism by choosing from among an infinite number of possible worlds and creating the best possible world, which, in accordance with Leibniz's definition of perfection, is the one 'by whose means the greatest possible amount of essence or possibility is brought into existence.' But notice the contradictory constraint that Leibniz has just imposed on his God: God is free to consider all possible worlds, but He is not free to choose (or create) a world other than the best. He cannot go for the second best, or the third best, or the ninety-fifth best. The constraint is embodied in Leibniz's principle of perfection or of the best (the principle parodied by Voltaire in *Candide* as Doctor Pangloss's doctrine that all is for the best in the best of all possible worlds), which exalts Leibniz's definition of the best possible world into an objective standard *independent of the will of God.*[9] This is particularly significant and I shall return to it later.

Leibniz's demand for order and consistency at every level and in every constituent of the universe has a further consequence: a preoccupation with gaps and leaps, or rather, with proscribing gaps and leaps under a law of continuity. 'Nothing takes place all at once,' Leibniz expounds in a commentary on John Locke's *Essay on the Human Understanding*,

> and it is one of my most important and best verified maxims that *nature makes no leaps.* ... the use of this law [of continuity] in physics is very considerable: it means that the passage from the small to the great and back again always takes place through that which is intermediate, both in degrees and in parts, and that a motion never arises immediately from rest, nor is reduced to it except through a smaller motion ....[10]

Discontinuity is precluded from creation and all the classes of beings that make up the universe are, Leibniz tells us, 'only so many ordinates of a single curve so closely united that it would be impossible to place others between any two of them, since that would imply disorder and imperfection.'[11] The world is derived precisely, reliably, reassuringly from an eternal order of metaphysical truth. Nature makes no leaps.

So far I have put Mr N in the company of Heraclitus, Hooker and Leibniz. I have one more name to add to the company: Albert Einstein. This may need some explaining. Einstein is perhaps associated most immediately with relativity. We tend to forget that he also made some of the earliest and most important contributions to the development of quantum theory, starting in 1905 when he proposed that the photoelectric effect could only be explained if light came in quanta of energy (later named photons). And yet, paradoxically, in this field he was a dissident pioneer who came to reject – almost denounce – the picture of the world that quantum physics produced. Philosophically as well as mathematically, the issue for Einstein came to revolve around one very fundamental question: how completely can we describe the physical world or, as he put it, 'physical reality'? Writing in about 1949, the Danish physicist Niels Bohr expressed this issue in terms of a choice between mutually exclusive alternatives:

> From the very beginning the main point under debate has been the attitude to take to the departure from customary principles of natural philosophy characteristic of the novel development of physics which was initiated in the first year of [the twentieth] century by Planck's discovery of the universal quantum of action. This discovery … has indeed taught us that the classical theories of physics are idealizations which can be unambiguously applied only in the limit where all actions involved are large compared with the quantum. The question at issue has been whether the renunciation of a causal mode of description of atomic processes … should be regarded as a temporary departure from ideals to be ultimately revived or whether we are faced with an irrevocable step towards obtaining the proper harmony between analysis and synthesis of physical phenomena.[12]

To the end of his life, Einstein stuck to the first view – that the renunciation of a causal mode of description should be seen as a temporary departure from the classical ideal – and maintained that the quantum description of the world is *incomplete*.

The whole business of renouncing causal description (and therefore causality itself, the principle that every event has a cause) arises because of the indeterminacy or uncertainty of the subatomic world, a world in which the observer can never know, even in theory, both the precise position of an object and its precise momentum simultaneously. This is the meaning of Werner Heisenberg's uncertainty relations, which, according to the equation he used in a lecture in 1929, say that the product of the uncertainties in the object's position and momentum cannot be smaller than Planck's constant of action, h (which is tiny, 6.626×10^{-34} joule-seconds). [13] In other words, the equation contains a minimum level of uncertainty that can never be eliminated. The experimental consequence of the uncertainty relations (which today are expressed in terms of a modified lower limit, Planck's constant divided by 2π) is that the more accurately the position of the object is measured, the less accurately its momentum is known, and vice versa.

The meaning of Bohr's reference to 'the limit where all actions involved are large compared with the quantum' is that only atomic and subatomic objects are small enough for it to be significant that the product of their uncertainties is always greater than or equal to h. In the everyday world, we are unaffected by Heisenberg's uncertainty relations only because actions (in the technical sense of joule-second units of energy) associated with macroscopic objects – toothbrushes, trees, elephants – are so large it is of no practical import that the product of their uncertainties cannot be smaller than h.

The uncertainty relations might seem to be an indictment of experimental deficiencies, as if implying that the right apparatus would be capable of measuring position and momentum at the same time. However, the message of the uncertainty locked into Heisenberg's equations is not that we need better apparatus, but that it is meaningless to describe an atomic object as though it had both a precise position and a precise momentum. As Heisenberg himself expressed it in the paper of 1927 in which he first formulated the uncertainty relations, 'Even in principle we cannot know the present in all [its] detail.' [14]

All of this was, and continues to be, profoundly at odds with classical Newtonian physics, which does allow a causal mode of description because it deals with precise and knowable information about objects in the macroscopic world. In the early years of the nineteenth century, the French mathematician and astronomer Pierre-Simon de Laplace had assured us that 'nothing would be uncertain' to an intelligence which knew at a given instant 'the movements of the greatest bodies of the universe and those of the lightest atom [including, by implication, the position and momentum of every particle in the universe] … the future, as the past, would be present to its eyes.' [15] That is, the intelligence would have all the information necessary to compute the past and future history of the universe. Since the early years of the twentieth century, quantum physicists have told us that, as a matter of principle, no intelligence could ever know both the position and the momentum of even *one* subatomic particle at the same instant in the present. The notion of predicting the precise future state of a single particle, let alone that of the whole universe, therefore has no meaning.

Some of the implications of quantum mechanics are so strange and counterintuitive that language struggles to convey them. It is no surprise, therefore, that terminology and semantics were among the topics debated by physicists at the conferences they held in Europe almost until the outbreak of the Second World War. At the Warsaw conference in 1938, for instance, Bohr warned his colleagues against phrases containing words such as 'phenomena', 'attributes', 'observations' and even 'measurements', which, he said, are apt to cause confusion because they are used in atomic physics 'in a way hardly compatible with common language and practical definition.' [16] New concepts and principles were called for. One of these was complementarity, which expresses, for example, the notion that a photon or a material particle (such as an electron) has a wave associated with it and exhibits wavelike behaviour. This apparent contradiction is now generally accepted to mean that 'wave' and 'particle' have to be regarded as two facets, not contradictory but *complementary*, of the same entity.

Complementarity is a key element in the Copenhagen interpretation, the body of ideas, elaborated collectively but identified especially with Bohr and named after his native city, that represents the standard or orthodox view of quantum mechanics. In terms of experimental observation, the Copenhagen interpretation has two particularly troubling implications for our supposed knowledge of the world. [17] Firstly, it requires us to accept that the act of observing an object *changes the behaviour* of the object. We cannot measure or validate a quantum system from any detached, 'outside' vantage point: we are inescapably part of the system, an observer-participant. In his lecture at the Como conference in 1927, Bohr had spoken of 'the impossibility of any sharp separation between the behaviour of atomic objects and the interaction with the measuring instruments which serve to define the conditions under which the phenomena appear.' [18] What this means is that complementary phenomena appear under mutually exclusive experimental conditions, which we arrange. If we choose an arrangement designed to detect a particle property such as position, we cannot expect to detect a wave property such as momentum in the same experiment, and vice versa.

The second troubling implication of the Copenhagen interpretation is that the results of observations are *all* that we can know. We may look at an atom, for instance, and detect an electron at energy level A, then look again and detect an electron at energy level B. We assume that it has been the same electron at levels A and B, but we cannot say what it was doing when we were not looking at it. What we deduce is the probability that if we look once and find state A, then next time we look we will find state B (and different probabilities for other states). In other words, the descriptions of quantum mechanics deal only with statistical likelihood, not with the determinacy and still less the certainty of classical Newtonian physics. Or, in Heisenberg's formulation again, we cannot know the present in all its detail.

Which brings us full circle. No, said Einstein, given a complete description, we *can* know the present in all its detail and probability will be restricted (to borrow Max Born's words [19]) to 'masking our ignorance of the initial conditions' of a system.

In 1935 Einstein published a paper jointly with two Princeton colleagues, Boris Podolsky and Nathan Rosen. As signalled by the rhetorical question of its title, 'Can Quantum-Mechanical Description of Physical Reality Be Considered Complete?',[20] the intention of the Einstein-Podolsky-Rosen (EPR) paper was to demonstrate that the quantum description cannot be considered complete. The question is easily answered, the authors say, 'as soon as we are able to decide what are the elements of the physical reality. … We shall be satisfied with the following criterion, which we regard as reasonable. *If, without in any way disturbing a system, we can predict with certainty (i.e., with probability equal to unity) the value of a physical quantity, then there exists an element of physical reality corresponding to this physical quantity.*' The crux of the EPR argument (which, as of 1935, stands or falls solely by the interpretation of a thought-experiment) is that it is possible to imagine a system such that an observer *could,* without disturbing the system, predict with certainty the value of a physical quantity and thus satisfy the 'reasonable' criterion of 'physical reality'.

Einstein, Podolsky and Rosen envisage two particles that interact with each other and then fly apart to form two systems. Even within the constraints of quantum mechanics, we will have been able to measure precisely the sum total momentum of the two particles and the distance between them before they interacted.[21] Hence if we later (that is, after the two particles have flown apart) choose to measure the momentum of the first particle, we will know, precisely and without disturbing the second system, the momentum of the second particle because the total must be unchanged. In accordance with the EPR criterion, therefore, the momentum of the second particle will be shown to correspond to an element of physical reality. Alternatively (not simultaneously), we could measure the position of the first particle and precisely deduce the position of the second, still without disturbing the second system and thus demonstrating that the position of the second particle *also* corresponds to an element of reality. To put it another way, we will have done something that quantum mechanics – which says that momentum and position cannot both be elements of reality simultaneously – is unable to explain. And this means, in turn, that something must be missing from the quantum description. It is incomplete.[22]

The authors end by rejecting the Copenhagen interpretation as an affront to reasonableness:

> One could object to this conclusion on the grounds that our criterion of reality is not sufficiently restrictive. Indeed, one would not arrive at our conclusion if one insisted that two or more physical quantities can be regarded as simultaneous elements of reality *only when they can be simultaneously measured or predicted.* On this point of view, since either one or the other, but not both simultaneously, of the quantities *P* [momentum] and *Q* [position] can be predicted, they are not simultaneously real. This makes the reality of *P* and *Q* [in the second system] depend upon the process of measurement carried out on the first system, which does not disturb the second system in any way. No reasonable definition of reality could be expected to permit this.[23]

According to the Copenhagen interpretation, in other words, for the second particle to have the reality of a precisely defined momentum, or the reality of a precisely defined position, it would somehow have to 'know' which measurement – momentum or position – we had chosen to carry out on the first particle. This was unconscionable for Einstein, Podolsky and Rosen because it would imply that the two systems influenced each other through action at a distance. There is an assumption, which goes by the name of locality (or separability), that there can be no such influence between spatially separated systems; in its most restrictive form, Einstein locality (or Einstein separability), it is underpinned by Einstein's special theory of relativity, which states that no signal of any kind can travel faster than the speed of light. [24] And yet, implies the Copenhagen interpretation, the two EPR systems would influence each other acausally and instantaneously no matter how far apart they might be, whether nanometres, kilometres or light-years. It is difficult to disagree with Einstein and his colleagues: no reasonable definition of reality would permit such a thing.

Leave nothing to chance

Where does it come from, this preoccupation with orderliness, regularity and continuity? Why have natural phenomena and the world in general been thought so unreliable, so untrustworthy, that they cannot be left to look after themselves but must be regulated in every conceivable respect and in the minutest detail? What was the impulse behind the metaphysical diktats that Leibniz imposed on the world (and on God)? And why was it so important for Einstein to pin down physical reality in a complete rather than an incomplete description? Why all this irritable reaching after fact and reason?

In Western cultures, traditionally we have looked for an explanation of everything that seems wrong with the world, and with ourselves, in the myth of the Fall. That is still a good place to begin, but not with the Fall to be found in the Book of Genesis. In this context it is more revealing to consider the Fall according to Plato: not the biblical story of man's fall from grace, but Plato's story of man's *fall into the world of change*.

Plato's Fall is a subtle business, encompassing the very nature of the physical world. For Plato the visible, tangible world is not 'fully real' because it belongs to the order of things that are each only a 'likeness' or 'moving shadow' of something else. That something else is the eternally unchanging, and therefore perfect, pattern or form that the divine creator had before him as he did his work. Unlike the form, which 'always is and never becomes', the likeness is 'always becoming but never is'. The form is imperceptible to the senses, 'uncreated and indestructible, admitting no modification'. But that which resembles the form is perceptible to the senses, which makes it an object of sensation and opinion; created and changeable, it is 'in constant motion, [and] comes into existence in and vanishes from a particular place'. [25]

Sensible things are objects of opinion and sensation, Plato repeats, 'and therefore change and come into being.' This particular translator's choice of the connecting word 'therefore' [26] is very interesting: while it makes good sense in the context, 'therefore' also results in a strange inversion of causality. We might expect to hear that things are objects of opinion because they are always changing, such that people may not agree about the significance or desirability of the change, for example. But to be told that they change *and come into being* because they are objects of opinion introduces a very peculiar dimension into our perceptions and our whole experience of the world.

Moreover, it is no trivial matter that the creator has made a world of change on the pattern of something eternally the same. They are chalk and cheese. The eternally perfect is just that, eternally perfect. But its likeness will change and, initially at least, that change can be in only one direction – away from perfection. And this is true of everything in creation:

> Change, ... except in something evil, is extremely dangerous. This is true of seasons and winds, the regimen of the body and the character of the soul – in short, of everything without exception ... [27]

As Plato immediately reiterates, change in an evil thing may be for the better. Elsewhere he even hints at the possibility of broader cycles of favourable change,[28] but his dominant message does seem to be that, in the world we inhabit, change is both unavoidable and bad.

The biblical Fall and Plato's Fall both convey a sense of lost perfection. The biblical version expresses it most explicitly as the banishment of Adam and Eve from Paradise. Meanwhile Plato has removed perfection to the far side of the yawning gap between an eternal pattern and its fleeting likeness; no matter how closely the likeness may resemble the pattern, it can never be the same thing. We are trapped in a world of imperfect look-alikes and moving shadows, the world of change.

Plato relegates the world of change to an inferior plane of reality, but at least he establishes *some* connection to link the world necessarily with its perfect form and thereby provide, in a phrase coined by the historian of ideas Arthur Lovejoy, 'a determining ground of concrete existence'.[29] Conversely, if the creator – through some unsuspected blemish in his perfection or, worse still, arbitrary whim – had established no connection at all to support concrete existence in the world of eternal forms, the world of change would be grounded in precisely nothing. 'Unless,' continues Lovejoy, 'the fact of existence could at some point be exhibited as a necessity subsisting in the world of essences [i.e., the Platonic forms or their theological equivalent, divine reason], the two worlds remained strangely unrelated; there was no bridge from one to the other; and the whole realm of the existent appeared given over to blank unreason.'

Back to Leibniz. From the perspective of Plato and his philosophical legacy, Leibniz's principles of sufficient reason and perfection represent an earnest attempt to bridge the two worlds, to ground the world of change in the world of eternal forms. 'Thus we now have physical necessity based on metaphysical necessity,' Leibniz concludes. 'For although the world is not metaphysically necessary, such that its contrary would imply a contradiction or logical absurdity, nevertheless it is necessary physically, that is, determined in such a way that its contrary would imply imperfection or moral absurdity.'[30] Or we might conclude that Leibniz's principles have now furnished both an argument for the existence of God and, through the actualizing mechanism that God provides, the required connection between the world of forms and the world of change. Lovejoy must be close to the psychological truth when he speculates that Leibniz is trying to ward off the intolerable conception that in fact we inhabit a world of *blind chance*. For to entertain any such notion even for a moment would mean placing Caprice on the throne of the universe:

> It implied that Nature, having no determining reason in it, flouts and baffles the reason that is in man. A world where chance-happening had so much as a

> foothold would have no stability or trustworthiness; uncertainty would infect the whole; anything (except, perhaps, the self-contradictory) might exist and anything might happen, and no one thing would be in itself even more probable than any other. [31]

In turn, we begin to see why Leibniz allows God only an ambiguous, conditional sort of free will. God cannot be permitted to define the bestness of the best possible world spontaneously because there is no guarantee that even He, God, may not have recourse to chance. Leibniz is quite blunt about this:

> If the will of God did not have for a rule the principle of the best, it would either tend towards evil, which would be worst of all; or else it would be in some fashion indifferent to good and evil and guided by chance. But a will which always allowed itself to act by chance would scarcely be of more value for the government of the universe than a fortuitous concourse of atoms, with no God at all. And even if God should abandon himself to chance only in some cases and some respects, … he would be imperfect, as would the object of his choice; he would not deserve to be wholly trusted; he would act without reason in those cases, and the government of the universe would be like certain games, half a matter of chance, half of reason. [32]

God is at the inexplicable apex of sufficient reason, the principle that says there must always be a reason why anything is as it is rather than otherwise. But God Himself must always have a reason why He wills as He does rather than otherwise and *that* reason is determined by a principle, Leibniz's principle of perfection, which is not of His own making. For it is inconceivable that the government of the universe should be in the hands (or the mind) of a God who played games of chance with it. Such a God *would not deserve to be wholly trusted.* Leibniz's insistence that God does not play games of chance strikingly illustrates his impulse to deny the slightest possibility of inconsistency, discontinuity or chance in creation or creator – all the more strikingly because it prefigures so exactly Einstein's protestation that he could not believe God played dice with nature.

Einstein's resistance to the implications of quantum physics surely had much to do with the philosophers who had influenced his thinking, the 'cast of characters who seemed to live within his cranium and counsel with him as he spoke', as the physicist John Wheeler puts it.[33] Benedict de Spinoza clearly was a major influence. Einstein explicitly named Spinoza when describing his own conception of God as 'a superior mind that reveals itself in the world of experience … [which] may be described as "pantheistic" (Spinoza)', and again in his reply to Rabbi Herbert Goldstein of New York: 'I believe in Spinoza's God who reveals Himself in the orderly harmony of what exists, not in a God who concerns Himself with fates and actions of human beings.'[34] Was Leibniz also among the cast of characters in Einstein's cranium? It may be significant that Bohr, who knew Einstein's thinking so well, associated Einstein's reluctance to renounce the idealizations of classical physics with his 'mastery for co-ordinating apparently contrasting experience *without abandoning continuity and causality*'.[35] *Continuity* suggests Leibniz's law of continuity, that statutory guarantee of smooth progression in every department of creation, while *causality*, the principle that every event must have a cause, suggests at least some aspects of sufficient reason.

Did Einstein, then, conceive of something akin to a law of continuity underlying the 'orderly harmony of what exists'? Does this help to explain his faith in the 'castle in the air'[36] of a unified field theory that would bring together all the laws and descriptions of nature, including gravitation and electromagnetism as well as quantum mechanics, into one perfect whole? On the evidence of correspondence with colleagues, Einstein's concern for uniformity and continuity even extended to a demand that the 'genuine' universal constants of a unified field theory must be rational numbers, which 'appear in some sense with necessity in the logical evolution of mathematics as unique individual formations'. While Einstein had no proof for such an assertion,

> he could not imagine a unified and reasonable theory explicitly to contain a number which the mood of the creator could just as well have chosen differently,

> whereby a world of a qualitatively different lawfulness would have resulted. [37]

Because this is a paraphrase rather than a direct quotation, it is not absolutely clear whether that phrase 'the mood of the creator' is Einstein's own. But in spirit it does recall Leibniz's stricture that God would not deserve to be wholly trusted if He allowed arbitrary whim and chance into the government of the universe. Within the context of quantum physics, it is not hard to see why Einstein was so offended by the Copenhagen interpretation's requirement that we jettison the classical reason for things, causality, and resign ourselves to tinkering with probability: it meant admitting that God *had* abandoned the world to chance. As early as 1917, Einstein had accused his own statistical description of radiation processes of 'weakness' on the ground that 'it leaves the time and direction of elementary processes to "chance" ["*Zufall*"]',[38] and no argument could persuade him to allow chance or probability a fundamental role in the universe. It was this attitude which later set Einstein apart in the 'aloof and sceptical' solitude that Born and other colleagues so regretted. As Einstein acknowledged in a letter to Born, 'In our scientific expectation we have grown antipodes. You believe in God playing dice and I in perfect laws in the world of things existing as real objects, which I try to grasp in a wildly speculative way.' [39]

If behind Einstein stood Leibniz, behind them both stood Plato. In Leibniz's case, Plato's influence is evident in the mechanism of 'Divine mathematics' by which Leibniz derives 'physical' necessity from 'metaphysical' necessity and grounds the world of change in the realm of eternal forms. In Einstein's case, perhaps it is evident in the EPR paper, which starts by declaring that the concepts of a physical theory are 'intended to correspond' with 'the objective reality, which is independent of any theory'. The aim of Einstein, Podolsky and Rosen, remember, was to demonstrate that the quantum description of physical reality is incomplete: their 'condition of completeness' for a description that would satisfy them was that '*every element of the physical reality must have a counterpart in the physical theory.*' [40] Correspond. Counterpart. This care to connect the world as we experience it (or as physicists measure and describe it) with an objective and eternal order of 'reality' is so reminiscent of Leibniz that it is at least plausible to trace it back to the same source – the impulse to bridge the gulf between Plato's two worlds.

Teetering on the brink of probability

Imagine that God has put Leibniz in a time machine and, by some particularly whimsical setting of the dial, landed him in the periodicals room of a Manhattan public library on 21 October 1986. Leibniz picks up *The New York Times*, which is open at the science pages, and begins to read of experiments that have been carried out independently and almost simultaneously in three separate laboratories. **Physicists Finally Get to See Quantum Jump With Own Eyes.** [41] An inelegant headline, but it gives Leibniz a nasty turn. What the physicists have seen is a single atom (trapped in an electromagnetic field within a vacuum chamber switching instantaneously between three discrete, quantized energy levels. They have observed these quantum jumps by monitoring the random on-off blinking of a laser-excited fluorescence, which is measurable by a photon-counting device and, in one of the experimental setups, even visible to the eye through a microscope. A steady fluorescence is the effect of extremely rapid (up to about 10^9 or one billion times per second and indistinguishable jumps up and down between the ground state of the atom and one of the two higher-energy excited states. The on-off blinking is the effect of the relatively long (more than 30 seconds in the case of a barium ion and detectable delay before the atom spontaneously returns to its ground state from the second of the excited levels; until it does so, the atom is not 'available' for the rapid kind of jumping and hence the fluorescence is quenched. Both effects derive from the emission or absorption of a photon, a quantum of light, that occurs with each downward or upward jump. The transitions from one energy level to another, Leibniz's passage from the small to the great and back again, do not take place through that which is intermediate. They take place all at once, discontinuously. This is because the transitions involve electrons, which can jump from one well-defined energy state to another but which cannot jump to any intermediate state. There are no intermediate states in the atom. Nature *does* make leaps.

Einstein died in 1955. It should be no great matter to requisition God's time machine, collect Einstein and whisk him forward twenty-seven years to the Institute of Theoretical and Applied Optics at the University of Paris-South, there to witness the tenth and (as of 1982) closest to definitive test *in the laboratory* of the EPR thought-experiment. [42] This test, the third conducted by Alain Aspect and his team, measures the polarization (a property of light analogous to the spin of a material particle) of a pair of photons as the experimental equivalent of measuring the position or momentum of a pair of particles. Its most significant technical improvement permits the experimental arrangement to be changed while the photons are in flight, and changed so rapidly that no influence could reach one part of the apparatus from another unless it travelled faster than light – the first laboratory challenge to locality (page 14 above) in its most restrictive form.

All three Paris experiments (and five of the seven earlier tests at other research centres) demonstrate a degree of correlation between spatially separated systems that exceeds the limit permitted by the EPR conception of physical reality but agrees well with the predictions of quantum mechanics. Other experiments that have been conducted since 1982, including one in 2004 involving two photons separated (via optical fibres) by a distance of fifty kilometres,[43] in effect continue to endorse the Copenhagen interpretation at the expense of the EPR conception. The reality of the second system *does* depend upon the measurements carried out on the first system, regardless of how far apart they are. Only two explanations seem possible. Either the two systems do indeed influence one another through instantaneous, acausal action at a distance (and, as suggested most starkly by the third Paris test, probably in violation of Einstein locality [44]), or in some sense they remain parts of an indivisible larger whole even after they have supposedly flown apart. Both explanations make a nonsense of any intelligible notion of locality, for action at a distance within an extended whole comes to much the same thing as action at a distance between spatially separated systems – a discontinuous leap that takes place all at once. On the experimental evidence to date, we have no choice but to drop locality from our assumptions about the world and adopt *non*-locality (or *non*-separability) in its place. [45]

Since locality is central to the EPR argument, it is hard to see how Einstein could regard either explanation of the experimental findings as consistent with any 'reasonable' definition of reality. Confronted with the compelling evidence of Aspect and his colleagues, would Einstein finally recant his faith in continuity and causality? Or would he shake his head and protest that the quantum-mechanical description of the world is still incomplete, refusing even from beyond the grave to forgo the search for a complete description?

What are we to make of it all? The answers are there, and have been for about twenty-four centuries, in Plato's myths and metaphors. The quantum physicist's pronouncement that we can never know the present in all its detail, and even that the act of observing an object changes the behaviour of the object, is analogous to Plato's pronouncement that all sensible things are objects of opinion and *therefore* change and come into being. Electrons, photons, tables and chairs, the solar system, galaxies – all things properly belong to Plato's world of change, coming to be and ceasing to be, but never fully real. You may protest that no quantum effects, least of all indeterminacy, trouble us in the world as we experience it from day to day. We can be certain that familiar macroscopic objects are where they are, and stay there, whether or not we happen to be looking at them. And we can predict with certainty where billiard balls, missiles and other moving objects will be after a specified time, for it is possible to measure simultaneously both the precise position and the precise momentum of bodies that obey Newtonian mechanics. Practically speaking, all this is true. Fundamentally speaking, however, the reassuring certainties of the everyday world are founded on no more than a convenience, and ultimately an illusion, of scale. Yes, actions associated with macroscopic objects are so large that the product of their uncertainties is insignificant relative to Planck`s constant, h (page 10 above). But the fact is that quantum uncertainty pervades all the matter and energy of the known universe at the subatomic level – a fact that does not change just because we may be unaware of (or choose not to scrutinize) nature's workings at the subatomic level.

That all matter and energy are implicated in quantum uncertainty means, in turn, that all matter and energy are implicated in chance-happening, the statistical probability that A will be followed by B, or C, or D. Now this is even worse than Plato had anticipated, for it amounts to saying that the creator (or God) had not, after all, made the world according to an eternal pattern or form (or divine reason). There was no perfect and unchanging form for a creator to work from. The attempt to bridge the world of change with the realm of eternal truths was doomed from the outset, for the simple reason that there was no world of eternal truths to bridge it with. It is all far worse than Plato could have foreseen. The world makes itself up as it goes along, and not according to a perfect pattern but according to chance. [46] Caprice *is* on the throne of the universe and we must accept that, at the quantum level, it is not meaningful to go on expecting a 'complete' description of the world. Instead we must reconcile ourselves to, in Bohr's words, 'a final renunciation of the classical ideal of causality and a radical revision of our attitude towards the problem of physical reality.' [47]

Einstein belongs within the tradition in natural science and philosophy that has sought to uphold the ultimate reasonableness of the cosmos. Einstein himself characterized this tradition as follows: 'Certain it is that a conviction, akin to religious feeling, of the rationality or intelligibility of the world lies behind all scientific work of a higher order.' [48] On the basis of our current knowledge, we have to say that quantum mechanics, which largely developed from Einstein's own contributions, has confounded Einstein and his philosophical antecedents. The rationality or intelligibility of the world can no longer be an article of absolute faith. As even Leibniz would be forced to admit, at its most fundamental level the government of the universe *is* left to a fortuitous concourse of atoms. Or as Sartre might say, it is not just the very form of the true but the very stuff of the cosmos that is a thing of indefinite approximation. If the sun is the cosmological prototype of all regularity, causality and continuity, the quantum jump is the physical prototype of all irregularity, acausality and discontinuity. There does not have to be a reason why anything is as it is or happens as it does rather than otherwise: a mere statistic will do. All things, and all beings, teeter on the brink of probability.

3. ALL THESE PASSIVE EXPECTATIONS OF THE REAL

The best building in Cambridge

It must have been 1972 or 1973. I was a student in Cambridge, England. One day, as I was walking round the corner from King's Parade towards the market square, I was stopped by a solitary, camera-equipped Japanese tourist. 'Excuse me,' he said in quite good English, 'what is the best building in Cambridge?'

'Pardon?'

'Excuse me, excuse me. What is the best building in Cambridge?'

'Um, well, er, I suppose some people would say that King`s College Chapel over there is one of the best. Personally I think …'

From the frown spreading across his face, I could see that this was not the answer he wanted.

'No, no, excuse me. What is the *best* building in Cambridge?'

'Oh. OK. King`s College Chapel. Over there.'

'Ah, thank you, thank you. … Excuse me, will you take a picture of me in front of King's College Chapel?'

I did so, though I recall that the only way I could get both him and the chapel into the viewfinder was to ask him to stand on a small traffic island in the middle of the road. Anyway, he seemed satisfied and I went over to return his camera. 'Thank you, thank you,' he repeated. But then:

'Excuse me, what is the *second best* building in Cambridge?'

I have to confess that at this point I thrust the camera into his hands and fled into the market. It was all too clear where the thing was heading and I had no idea how I would cope with the next four, five or perhaps even nine best buildings in Cambridge.

The incident made a big impression on me. Probably the tourist was on a flying visit and had very limited time for his souvenir photographs. Yet they had to be the right photographs, the ones everyone was expected to take, not a haphazard sequence of spires and gatehouses snapped at random. And the pressure of that trivial dilemma exposed something which was not trivial but, as I still feel, oddly disturbing. Here was man who cheerfully assumed that works of architecture – and presumably also art, literature, and who knows what else – were all ranked according to a hierarchy of value uniformly agreed and uniformly known within a particular society or place. As an outsider, he did not know the hierarchy that applied in this English university city and therefore, for the later purpose of arranging the photographs in his album, he needed to ask a local who would know. I was passing by, he took me for a local, and so he asked me. A very cogent chain of reasoning, if you accept the initial assumption. But was it just the reasoning of an eccentric individual, who might as well have been Brazilian or Estonian, or indeed British, for all that his nationality was involved? Or was there some significance in the fact of his Japaneseness? Was he *representative*, the product not only of individual circumstances but of a pervasive social and cultural conditioning? Was it the man or was it Japan?

Both man and Japan, I would say in retrospect, but mostly Japan. With one important caveat, I base this judgement on my own experience of living, studying and working in Japan for a total of about ten years at various times between 1979 and 1992. The caveat is that my chance encounter with the tourist in Cambridge happened almost forty years ago and, at the time of writing, I have not been back to Japan for over twenty years. In other words, Japan has moved on a generation or more and I have no direct, firsthand feel for how much – or how little – it has changed. For this reason, while I believe the observations that follow are true and valid, they are true and valid of a Japan that is already receding into history and not necessarily of the Japan of today. Whenever I use the present tense in connection with Japan, therefore, it is the stylistic device of the present historic and may not refer literally to the present.

Mostly Japan. I say that because the tourist's assumption that everything, including values, and everyone can be neatly categorized and ordered is so characteristic of Japan. It is an assumption that manifests itself, collectively as well as individually, in a myriad different ways. Anyone who does business in Japan, for example, sooner or later will experience a formal business dinner. And anyone who experiences a formal dinner will notice the seating plan: host senior director sitting opposite guest senior director, host departmental manager opposite guest departmental manager, and so forth, according to the titles on their business cards. It is all obvious enough and of course such conventions are not unique to Japan, although some of the attention to ritual detail (such as that the place of honour always has its back to the ornament alcove, the *tokonoma*) may be peculiar to Japan. But what about this curious event from around 1970, recounted by the Japanese social anthropologist Chie Nakane. [49] When six Chinese players of *shōgi* (a board game sometimes likened to chess) visited Japan for a tournament, Japanese observers were surprised and perhaps a little shocked at the order in which the six lined up at the welcoming ceremony at Haneda Airport and again at the reception party in Tokyo. Mr Wan, the youngest at age seventeen and formally only a second-rank player, stood in fourth place, while Mr Tsen, the eldest and doubtless a first-rank player, occupied the last place. The explanation is that the Chinese players had adopted the order that reflected the actual results of their last title matches, not the order of their nominal rankings. Had they been six Japanese *shōgi* players visiting China, on the other hand, they would have arranged themselves in order of seniority and formal rank, regardless of recent match results. The principle of determining precedence according to age and seniority is known in Japanese as *chō-yō-no-jo* ('elder-younger-order'). The irony is that it came from China, one of many Confucian precepts brought in on the flow of cultural borrowings that began early in Japan's recorded history. [50] As a ranking principle, however, *chō-yō-no-jo* is interpreted and applied in Japan more literally than in China, where it now seems to have the force of a generalized respect for age and seniority but not an absolute principle. Hence for the Chinese *shōgi* players it could give way to another ranking or differentiating principle, merit, which they evidently felt was better suited to their immediate circumstances. It was this capacity for adjustment that so struck the Japanese observers.

The significance of ranking order in Japan is that it determines not just seating plans but, to a large extent, the disposition of society as a whole. Modern Japan is not a class society in the familiar sense of one structured *horizontally* in more or less loosely bounded tiers. Instead, from the micro level to the macro level, relations are structured – ranked – *vertically*, and not so much in tiers as in compartments. This is Nakane's thesis, which she had first begun to develop while doing sociological field work in rural Japan. If the test of a good thesis is that it convincingly explains empirically observed phenomena (or, more prosaically, personal experience), then I can only say that Nakane's does an uncannily convincing job of explaining the semi-historical Japan I know. [51] I strongly suspect that it continues to explain many aspects of contemporary Japan.

Nakane makes the point that, as a mechanism for ordering a whole society, seniority is simpler and more stable than merit. That is, ranking by seniority can be applied universally whatever the circumstances and, once set in motion, operates automatically according to its own internal dynamic (or lack of dynamic). In sharp contrast, differentiation by merit has to be applied on a case-by-case basis and, precisely because it involves particular judgements of worth made in particular circumstances, offers no guarantees of consistency, predictability or, Nakane's term, stability. I would add that in Japan differentiation by merit has also tended to be regarded as divisive and *unfair* because it may elevate some individuals, and not others, in ways that are perceived to be arbitrary or 'unreasonable'. Conversely, ranking by seniority is a very transparent mechanism: it assigns places to everyone in ways which, however gratifying or frustrating for the individuals concerned, are at least readily understandable.

Unsurprisingly, the stability of a social order structured primarily by rank and seniority entails a lot of inflexibility and, at worst, institutionalized rigidity. Nakane again on Japan:

> There is only one ranking order for a given set of persons, regardless of variety of situation. No individual members of this set (not even the man who ranks highest) can make even a partial change. The only means of effecting change is by some drastic event which affects the principle of the order, or by the disintegration of the group. [52]

In other words, the very fact that it takes a drastic event or group disintegration to disrupt the workings of seniority-based ranking is a measure of how powerfully it functions under more usual circumstances as 'the principal controlling factor of social relations in Japan'. And under those more usual circumstances inflexibility and rigidity are everywhere to be seen. There is little or no capacity for adjustment. In the academic world, for example, an ossified ranking order is reflected in the terms of address that male scholars conventionally use to one other. An undergraduate, say with the surname Watanabe, plainly has a very junior status in relation to a professor, which is why he will address the professor impersonally as *sensei* (honorific for 'teacher') while the professor is likely to address him as Watanabe*–kun* (where *–kun* is a term, also used to small boys, that can be familiar, avuncular or patronizing depending upon the relationship and the intention of the user). But even if Watanabe is so successful in his later academic career that his nominal status comes to match that of his old professor, yet he will continue to address him as *sensei.* Likewise, fifteen or twenty years later and even in front of Watanabe's own students (to whom Watanabe is of course their *sensei*), the old professor may well continue to address Watanabe as Watanabe-*kun.* These terms are fixed right at the beginning of the student-teacher relationship and they are fixed for life. Moreover, I think the term *sensei* is particularly significant because it both reflects and helps to perpetuate a frame of mind that makes it difficult – sometimes excruciatingly difficult – to disagree with or be seen to disagree with a former teacher. In its most extreme manifestation it is a frame of mind which dictates that, however distinguished his own career, a former student does not have the *right* to challenge or openly criticize his old teacher because to do so would conflict with the seniority-based order into which they are both locked. [53]

Similar constraints operate in the business world, for similar reasons. As in a university department, elaborate gradations of seniority and rank are revealed in the terms of address and sometimes even in the register of voice (which may change depending upon the status of the person being addressed) used between employees in a typical Japanese corporation. What is more, in some corporations consciousness of rank is instilled and reinforced through the employees' own practice of forming themselves into 'year clubs' according to their date of entry into the company. The result is that, literally from their first day in the job, new recruits have a minutely calibrated sense of their lower ranking in relation to established seniors and, in time, their higher ranking in relation to successive new entrants. [54] Again as in the academic world, rank has a direct effect on behaviour and communication. In a meeting with foreign visitors, for example, generally a junior employee will not speak unless called upon to do so by a superior and, even then, will strenuously avoid expressing any opinion that might be construed as contradicting or embarrassing the superior in front of the visitors. At the end of the working day, the same consciousness of rank prevents the employee from leaving the office before the departmental manager even if, at eight o'clock at night or later, all the manager is doing is reading the sports pages of his newspaper. For his part, the manager (say in Marketing) is constrained – or, more to the point, constrains himself – in other ways: conditioned for years by the closed, vertically aligned ranking system, his own thinking may be so compartmentalized that he rarely communicates horizontally across functional or departmental boundaries, even with other managers (in Finance or Manufacturing, for instance) of equivalent status. [55]

My purpose in choosing these examples is to suggest that in Japan the whole process of categorizing and ordering everything and everyone tends to become an end in itself, detached from the content of what is being categorized and ordered. In particular, I am suggesting that the process produces (or is produced by: who can say which comes first?) a pigeonholing mentality that does not distinguish between things which lend themselves to ranking by objective, uniformly agreed criteria and things which do not. At the relatively harmless end of the scale, this mentality is typified by the Japanese tourist I encountered in Cambridge, for whom 'What is the *best* building?', a question to do with individual and subjective judgement, was no different in kind from 'What is the *tallest* building?', a question to do with factual information about the world. At the more pernicious end of the scale, the process as a whole not only detaches itself from content but threatens to deny or annul content. There is no need to invoke meritocracy, freedom of speech or other such abstractions here: even from a pragmatic or practical viewpoint, social stability comes at a disproportionately high price when it demands the stifling of spontaneous opinion, youthful energy and talent on the one hand and, on the other, the rewarding of unctuous decorum, age for age's sake and, all too often, mediocrity. Especially as my earlier examples have related primarily to men, now is the time to acknowledge that, historically at least, the categorization and ordering of women in Japan also belongs at the pernicious end of the scale. Below is an advertisement for a driving school which I saw in a Tokyo subway train in about 1980 (and hence, at the risk of labouring the point, which may give a misleading impression of Japan today). It is self-explanatory:

Tanaka Driving Academy [56]

All learners welcome. Special facilities for:

- *Elderly Persons*
- *Disabled Persons*
- *Women*

The story so far. Japan is a society that orders itself by hierarchical gradations, primarily seniority and rank. There is a place for almost everyone and almost everyone is in their place, not in the sense of being assigned to this or that social class (a categorization that generally has little meaning in modern Japan) but in the sense of having a minutely prescribed role in some collective endeavour (a company or school, for instance). And yet 'role' is an inadequate word because what I really want to say is that the place each person occupies, however grand or minor, is in effect a little universe of expectations and behaviours. Figuratively speaking, and probably literally, no one has to tell a junior employee not to speak out of turn, for not speaking out of turn is part of what it means to be a junior employee in Japan. It is in the nature of things or, in this case, in the nature of being a *sarariiman* (Japanese-English for 'salary man' but with the connotation 'company man'). Likewise, no one has to persuade the eminent academic or the political faction leader to sit in the seat of honour at a formal gathering; he will gravitate there of his own accord. If he proceeds to hold court, making pronouncements in weighty monologues, favouring one person with warm words, putting down another with a nicely barbed nuance, then he is only doing what eminent academics and factional leaders do. That too is in the nature of things. How people behave in Japan is largely synonymous with how they are expected to behave: their behaviour is *in* the expectations that envelop them from the outside. In turn, those expectations arise in the categorizing process that orders the society. Moreover, because it is associated with a habit of mind that seeks to pigeonhole everything, the categorizing process affects not only how people behave but also how they think, including how they conceive of values. In fact, it seems the pigeonholing urge is so strong that sometimes it closes off any awareness that values can be distinct from – and may be at odds with – the categories in which things and people happen to be arranged. While I have no objective evidence for what I am about to suggest, I wonder how few, not how many, of the Japanese women passengers on that subway train in 1980 would have been offended by the Tanaka Academy's advertisement. A driving school classifies women below the aged and the infirm? Well, what of it? It is in the nature of things.

That is the story so far, minus one aspect that I have not spelt out explicitly. Depending on your point of view, it is another negative aspect, or a positive aspect, or both. For all its unjust, wasteful and self-defeating consequences, the categorizing and ordering process results not just in stability at the social level but also in *certainty* at the individual level. I am not talking about *comfort* or *happiness*, which are not necessarily the same thing as certainty even for those who have an assured place in some collective endeavour. And now for sure I am speaking semi-historically because two decades of recession, corporate restructuring, the unravelling of lifetime employment and other changes in Japan are creating a new (or larger) category of unemployed and underemployed people who have no assured place and who, by definition, are therefore denied the sort of certainty that I mean.[57] But imagine ourselves back into Japan's postwar golden age – which I would locate symbolically between the 1964 Olympic Games held in Tokyo and the day (29 December) in 1989 when the Tokyo Stock Exchange's Nikkei 225 index peaked at an all-time high of almost ¥39,000 – and daily existence for a great many people is full of certainty and certainties. That is because each of the little universes of expectations and behaviours provides the constituents of someone's life, arranged programmatically in stages. Although the stages (some of which have names, such as *hankōki*, 'the [infant and adolescent] rebellion phases', or *kekkon tekireiki,* 'the optimum age [especially for a woman] to get married') all head into the future, the life-programme effectively operates in reverse, pushing itself backwards into each person's earliest experiences and education. The life-programme for a *sarariiman* may take him to respectable retirement, the joys of watching his grandchildren grow up, and perhaps a little foreign travel, hobbies or other modest self-indulgences. To get there, however, he has to spend decades progressing up the ranks in the right company; to get into the right company he has to go to the right university; to go to the right university he has to go to the right secondary school; and so on, all the way back to the first decisions made for him by his parents. As a boy, he will be introduced to the relentless pressure of expectations both at his regular school and at the private 'crammer' school he attends after hours. As a new entrant in his company, the stress of chronic overwork will be compounded by casually nasty bullying and the other ritualized humiliations inflicted by managers and seniors. Comfort and happiness, not obviously. Certainty, yes. From kindergarten to the boardroom and beyond, there will be a place for him at every stage and that place will also be the certainty of what and who he is.

Traditionally, the key stages in the life-programme of a Japanese woman transform her from a dutiful daughter into a wife and mother, the *okāsan* of her own family. She may have to put up with many things, including the calculated torments of her mother-in-law, more conducive to misery than happiness. But I maintain that she, too, has certainty – unless she does something to forfeit it, a catastrophe that I believe I have witnessed in my own chance experience. From late 1979 I spent ten months on a Japanese language course, one of about a dozen postgraduates at a specialist institute in Tokyo. In addition to the language instruction itself, the course included a number of field trips designed to deepen our cultural understanding of Japan. By far the most memorable was a visit to a local magistrates' court, where we observed a hearing from the public benches. Up before the magistrate was a young woman who had been caught shoplifting and who had, I think, admitted the offence. She was quietly weeping in the dock, head bowed, unable to meet the magistrate's stern gaze. I do not remember what punishment, if any, the magistrate meted out but I do remember very vividly his summing-up, which he addressed directly to the woman. This is the gist of what he said:

> 'You've let your teachers down. You've let your parents down. You've let your children down. You've let yourself down. Don't you see what a terrible thing you've done?'

In the charged atmosphere of the courtroom, the effect of these words was electrifying. No longer weeping quietly, the woman was sobbing uncontrollably. The clerk of the court was in tears. I cannot speak for my fellow observers, but *I* was in tears. There was an extraordinary intensity in that moment when the accused was confronted with the reality of her offence, which had very little to do with a breach of the law and a great deal to do with a breach of expectations. She had transgressed a whole hierarchy of expectations, which the magistrate attributed to the most important people in her life, enumerated in their proper ranking order. [58] With hindsight, I feel the most telling of his attributions was to the woman's former teachers. From their exalted position as *sensei*, they had devoted themselves to her education and bestowed their trust upon her, both as a pupil in their care and as a future member of adult society. That trust put her under a lifetime of moral indebtedness to her teachers, yet in an act of impulsive behaviour she had forgotten her debt and debased their trust. Her real offence was not shoplifting but, for want of a better word in English, *ingratitude*. It might all have been so different. If only she had behaved as a young woman with children was expected to behave, she would not have dishonoured the debt to her *sensei*, she would not have brought shame upon her parents and herself, and she would have remained a good *okāsan* to her children. Her sobbing was the sobbing of someone adrift in what had once been a world of certainties.

The doers and the done-to

'Uche mon [each man]' should keep to his 'owne state [own social order]', we are told in a carol by John Audelay, an English priest who probably died towards the middle of the fifteenth century:

> It is the best, erely and late,
> Uche mon kepe his owne state.
> In what order or what degree
> Holy Cherche hath bound thee to
> Kepe it welle, I counsel thee,
> Desire thou never to go therefro,
> I say algate. [59]

Audelay goes on to list four states (or *estates*, as the orders were known) to which men should keep, those of the priest, the friar, the old man and the knight. Even to Audelay's contemporaries, this list must have seemed unusual because, while it includes the conventional first estate (the knight) and second estate (the priest), it omits what they would have regarded as the third estate: the undifferentiated mass of commoners (everyone from destitute rural peasant to prosperous townsman) who constituted the vast majority of the population. But to say that Audelay's contemporaries would have been surprised by the omission is not the same as saying that they would have been troubled by it, for medieval Europe generally did not consider the third estate worthy of sympathetic attention. Still in the fifteenth century, Georges Chastellain, chronicler to the dukes of Burgundy, dismisses the common people as 'this low estate of Frenchmen [*cestuy bas estat de François*]' made up of labourers and merchants 'of a servile degree'. [60] His is not the universal sentiment, however, and there are some who regard the existence, and especially the misery, of the third estate as a proper subject for poetry, chronicles and sermons. Such people include Chastellain's contemporary Jean Meschinot, a Breton poet in the service of the dukes of Brittany, who appeals directly to God on behalf of the common people:

O Dieu, voyez du commun l'indigence,
Pourvoyez-y à toute diligence:
Las! par faim, froid, paour et misere tremble.
S'il a peché ou commis negligence
Encountre vous, il demande indulgence.
N'est-ce pitié des biens que l'on lui emble?
Il n'a plus bled pour porter au molin,
On lui oste draps de laine et de lin,
L'eaue, sans plus, lui demeure pour boire.

O God, see the indigence of the common people,
Provide for it with all speed:
Alas! with hunger, cold, fear and misery they tremble.
If they have sinned or are guilty of negligence
Toward Thee, they beg indulgence.
Is it not a pity that they are bereft of their goods?
They have no more corn to take to the mill,
Woollen and linen goods are taken from them,
Only water is left to them to drink. [61]

Audelay and Chastellain speak not only for the social ethics of feudal Europe but also for Europe's later class-based notions that there is a place for everyone and everyone should keep to their place. And Meschinot speaks not just for the wretched peasants and labourers of his own day but for those at or near the bottom of any of Europe's hierarchically-ordered societies who, if reckoned to exist at all, tended to be regarded as functions rather than human beings in their own right. From the hovels of fifteenth-century France to, say, the stately homes and town houses of Jane Austen's England, what connects the humblest member of the old third estate with a manservant in the household of Lady Catherine de Bourgh is not poverty – on the contrary, the servant's material conditions are probably relatively comfortable – but *invisibility*. While the servant in his fancy livery may be 'seen' by his masters and mistresses as a piece of furniture is 'seen', he is no more perceived as an animate and completely human being than a beggar in rags would be. In fact the livery adds a peculiarly grotesque insult to the injury and that is why, if I had to choose one image to convey this quality of invisibility, it would be the image of an expressionless, unseeing and unseen servant hidden in a corner of some late-eighteenth-century drawing room. The significance of invisibility? It is a sort of certainty, but the worst sort that an estate- or class-ordered society can provide because it is the certainty of being treated as a labour-providing, revenue-producing, cannon-foddering or other function in someone else's world, of peopling and serving that world without being fully of it. It is the certainty of being on the wrong side of the arbitrary line or below the arbitrary level which tells the minority, who decide and do, that they properly belong in the world and tells the majority, who are decided for and done to, that they do not properly belong. And it is the worst of worst certainties for those among the majority who collude in their own invisibility by believing that to be decided for and done to is their 'natural' condition in life, which turns 'Know your place!' into 'I know my place', or who, while not believing that it is their 'natural' condition, nevertheless resign themselves to it, which is an expression not of deference but of despair. In *The Road to Wigan Pier*, George Orwell invokes a verse from *Ain't We Got Fun*, an American vaudeville song popular in Britain in the years immediately after the First World War:

There's nothing sure but
The rich get richer and the poor get children;
In the mean time,
In between time,
Ain't we got fun? [62]

To Orwell the song is evidence of 'a turbulent feeling in the air' at a time when 'the English working class were in a fighting mood' and he associates it with the 'lawless' attitude to life of soldiers, particularly soldiers who had survived the trenches only to find that they had no jobs and nowhere to live when they got back to England. The mass unemployment of the inter-war years put an end to the fighting mood and, as Orwell speculates elsewhere, may even have increased 'the tendency towards servility' in the working class. [63] But before all that, isn't there already a note of hopelessness as well as turbulence in the song? To follow Orwell's train of associations, perhaps it is a hopelessness akin to that felt by common soldiers before an assault across No Man's Land in which, they knew full well, their function was to be deployed and expended as consumables of war, not individual human beings or even men in uniform but so many bayonets (or 'bayonet strength', a term still used to this day to count infantry). [64] In the instant when these men were summoned over the top by the officer's whistle, what greater force overwhelmed their 'lawless' attitude – patriotism, comradeship, the fear of being shot for cowardice, or some older despair that had come with them into the trenches and would accompany the survivors back into the world that Orwell was to observe?

That world (or its class system, at least) appeared to revert to business as usual after 1918 and the country houses, for example, bustled anew with the activities of valets, kitchen maids, grooms and a host of other retainers, all correctly differentiated according to their duties and rankings. This is the world vividly captured in the film *Gosford Park*, set in 1932, which depicts master-servant relations that seemingly have not changed since about 1832 and are not expected to change for another hundred years. [65] In reality, however, it was a world already nearing its end and the last hours before the midnight of its demise have been captured equally vividly, I think, in the film *In Which We Serve*. Made in 1942 under the direction of Noël Coward and David Lean, it tells the thinly disguised story of HMS *Kelly*, a destroyer captained by Lord Louis Mountbatten, which was sunk off Crete in 1941. The Mountbatten character, Captain Kinross (played by Coward himself), is portrayed as a charismatic aristocrat-commander who is revered by his men in spite of the harsh and uncompromising demands he makes of them. Given Mountbatten's ancestry (great grandson of Queen Victoria) and his other connections with the British royal family, and given the explicitly hierarchical nature of life on board the ship (renamed HMS *Torrin* for cinematic purposes), the film can be seen – and surely was meant to be seen – as an allegory of the realm and its social order at war with a foreign enemy. Its message could hardly have been clearer: in time of peril more than ever, look to your hereditary rulers, keep to your place, and do your duty. The action of the film is interwoven with wistful flashbacks to loved ones and home life (arranged by rank and class into the reminiscences of the captain, the chief petty officer,[66] and an ordinary seaman) and the flashback technique itself takes on an allegorical meaning: this is what we are all fighting for, the familiar world of yesterday and not some new and brutish reality that the enemy would force upon us. These strands come together most revealingly in the scene in which Kinross arrives at his country house on shore leave. His driver is Edgecombe (played by Frederick Piper), who evidently functions as the naval equivalent of a batman. 'Take the car round,' Kinross says to Edgecombe as they pull up in front of the house, 'and then give Ellen a hand with the dinner.' I have a fantasy that this line is a remnant of a longer scene which ended up on the cutting-room floor because it was deemed *too* explicit, a socio-political Freudian slip suggesting that preservation of the class order was a home-front war aim – which, for the deciders and doers represented by the Kinross/Mountbatten character, effectively it was. The screenplay would have gone something like this:

Kinross: Take the car round and then give Ellen a hand with the dinner.
Edgecombe: Aye, aye, Sir. … Excuse me, Sir, but there's something I'd like to ask you.
Kinross: What's that, Edgecombe?
Edgecombe: Well, Sir, what's in this war for the likes of me?
Kinross: Ah, I'm glad you asked that, Edgecombe. You see, I want you to know that there'll still be a vital role for you when this is all over.

Edgecombe: You mean helping to build a better country with equality and prosperity for all?
Kinross: No, Edgecombe. I mean helping the cook in my kitchen.

On the other hand, *In Which We Serve* is so pregnant with dramatic irony that, had it been made three or four years later, there could have been an additional scene or even an alternative ending to the whole film. No dialogue, just a few extra directions in the screenplay:

> *It is 5 July 1945. Edgecombe, who has borrowed Captain Kinross's car* [Without permission? Appealing but implausible because Edgecombe would worry that it might be misunderstood as theft, which is not in his character and would make a nonsense of his action], *arrives outside a bomb-damaged village hall. He parks the car and strides with quiet resolve past the POLLING STATION sign and into the hall, where the camera looks over his shoulder as he writes a firm black cross against the name of the Labour Party candidate.*

'It is time for *the people* to define their war aims,' Orwell had written in 1941, and he tried to assist by outlining a six-point programme of action aimed 'quite frankly at turning this war into a revolutionary war and England into a Socialist democracy.' [67] For all its landslide magnitude, Labour's election victory in 1945 did not herald the socialist revolution of Orwell's programme. In a mood of war-weariness and political apathy, a predominantly working-class majority – 'the big masses', as Orwell put it – voted for something more modest and, in every sense of the word, more domestic: 'family allowances, higher old age pensions, houses with bathrooms, etc.' in the belief that a Labour government would make them 'more secure and, after a few years, more comfortable.' [68] Yet in a non-ideological sense, and despite the weariness and apathy of the electorate, it *was* a revolution and one that did result from the 'real shove from below' that Orwell had called for back in 1941. [69] The date 5 July 1945 (more correctly 26 July, the day of the count, delayed to allow for the return of ballot papers from service personnel overseas) marks the end of the ancient spell that had induced countless generations of the decided-for and done-to majority to accept, and sometimes to believe, that they did not fully belong in the world made by and for their 'natural' superiors. By voting for decent housing and a greater degree of social justice 'the big masses' signalled, less dramatically than if they had taken to the barricades but no less momentously, that they had woken from their long trance and were demanding to be treated as human beings, no longer mere functions, and to be recognized as properly part of the world, no longer consigned to its disregarded or unseen peripheries. Perhaps it could only have happened under the novel and extraordinary conditions of egalitarianism enforced by rationing, food price subsidies, redistributive tax measures and the other instruments of Britain's wartime command economy. Whether or not that is so, it seems that the spell was broken, finally and irreversibly.

The spirit of the age

In pre-1945 Britain, certainty for the lower orders, and especially the lowest of the low, the invisible people, was a baleful sort of certainty because it derived from the rigid class gradations that had evolved over centuries, compounded by an industrial revolution that had filled grimy towns and their factories with vast numbers of invisible men, women and children to serve as the consumables of mechanized production. However, history suggests that within societies sometimes there is an ethos or mood or spirit – let's call it the spirit of the age – that seems to have a life of its own and, potentially at least, may be a threat to the outward order socially, politically and in other ways. There was such a spirit of the age in nineteenth-century Britain, a spirit of certainty in an age of certainty. Society offered the certainty of being on the right side or the wrong side of the line dividing doers from done-to, determined historically by the class order of the pre-industrial past and increasingly by the efficient division of labour and other demands of the industrialized present. But the spirit of the age offered the certainty of knowing that everything and everyone – which, taken to its logical conclusion, meant everyone regardless of class or status – was progressing inexorably towards *a different and better future*. The spirit owed much to the Enlightenment of eighteenth-century Europe, which urged mankind to seek knowledge, virtue and happiness by subjecting the world to rational enquiry and judging its contents, including its man-made institutions, empirically and not according to metaphysics, dogma, superstition or unexamined tradition. In France the Enlightenment frame of mind and the pressures for practical reform that flowed from it were perceived as subversive of the religious, economic and political order well before the outbreak of violent revolution in 1789: to a Catholic church whose authority was threatened by arguments in favour of restoring toleration for the Huguenots, for example, or to private monopolists and other vested interests threatened by the trend towards freer trade and commerce, it was clear that the future was likely to be *different* but not at all clear that it was likely to be *better* for them. Enlightenment thinking in Scotland and England, at first greatly concerned with economics, was cooler, more methodical and less obviously subversive than in France. Jeremy Bentham, the central figure of the so-called Philosophical Radicals, spent decades advocating reform of the legal system and yet, for him as for others, one thing led to another. Driven by the logic of his own convictions – and especially the conviction that human equality is built into his 'principle of utility' (or 'greatest happiness principle') because rationally 'one man's interest weigh[s] neither more nor less than another's' [70] – Bentham turned his energies increasingly to the promotion of democratic government, against monarchy and hereditary aristocracy (which he described as the 'mixt despotism' of England's constitution [71]) and for a broad electoral franchise, including, in principle, votes for women. [72]

If the spirit of nineteenth-century Britain owed much to the Enlightenment, the quality of certainty in the spirit owed much to the empirical attitude, and especially the empirical science, that had largely inspired the Enlightenment in the first place and continued to issue in a profusion of new technologies and practical capabilities. Francis Bacon, generally regarded as the founder of empirical science or, as Voltaire put it, 'the father of experimental philosophy',[73] was excused his reprehensible personal reputation (dismissed as Lord Chancellor and barred from public life in 1621 after admitting he had accepted bribes from litigants because it was recognized that he had developed a systematic means of understanding and *improving upon* the physical world to the benefit of mankind. Hence while the Whig historian, essayist and politician Thomas Babington Macaulay, writing in 1837, felt compelled to regard Bacon's character with 'mingled contempt and admiration', he characterized Bacon's legacy in monumentally optimistic terms:

> Ask a follower of Bacon what the new philosophy, as it was called in the time of Charles the Second, has effected for mankind, and his answer is ready; "It has lengthened life; it has mitigated pain; it has extinguished diseases; it has increased the fertility of the soil; it has given new securities to the mariner; it has furnished new arms to the warrior; it has spanned great rivers and estuaries with bridges of form unknown to our fathers; it has guided the thunderbolt innocuously from heaven to earth; it has lighted up the night with the splendour of the day; it has extended the range of the human vision; it has multiplied the power of the human muscles; it has accelerated motion; it has annihilated distance; it has facilitated intercourse, correspondence, all friendly offices, all despatch of business; it has enabled man to descend to the depths of the sea, to soar into the air, to penetrate securely into the noxious recesses of the earth, to traverse the land in cars which whirl along without horses, and the ocean in ships which run ten knots an hour against the wind. These are but a part of its fruits, and of its first fruits. For it is a philosophy which never rests, which has never attained, which is never perfect. Its law is progress. A point which yesterday was invisible is its goal to-day, and will be its starting-post to-morrow."[74]

The trust in science and technology that Macaulay expresses on behalf of his age is, in George Steiner's wonderful phrase, 'a trust in the unfolding excellence of fact'.[75] Trust, that is, in a principle of Progress that has the force of law and the force of fact: undeniably and unstoppably, the physical world was being made better through the application of scientific knowledge. Other certainties abounded. Following the publication of Charles Darwin's *On the Origin of Species* in 1859, social Darwinists came to believe that man and society were being made better – and in time would be perfected – by Progress operating through the evolutionary mechanism of natural selection. For Darwin (and, as I understand, for Alfred Russel Wallace, who had independently arrived at a theory of natural selection in 1858), evolution was morally neutral: organisms could only become 'better' in the functional sense of 'better adapted to their environment' and not in any other meaningful sense. But for Herbert Spencer, most influential of the social Darwinists, natural selection was a value-laden mechanism and one that, by analogy with the evolution of individual organisms, could be shown to be at work in the evolution of society as a whole: the ideal social state, in which 'the completely adapted man' was in perfect accord with 'the completely evolved society' [76] would be better in every sense – moral, ethical, cultural, political, and so on – and not just functionally. Nor were social Darwinists alone in interpreting biological evolution according to their own optimistic vision. For Karl Marx, an exile in Britain from 1849 until his death in 1883, the publication of *On the Origin of Species* was timely because it seemed to lend scientific credibility to the notions of class conflict on which he was already working. 'Darwin's book is very important,' Marx wrote in 1861,

> and serves me as a natural-scientific basis for the class struggle in history. One has to put up with the crude English method of development [of an idea or argument], of course. [77]

In chronological terms, the age that gave rise to Britain's great spirit of certainty is distant but not unimaginably so – the outbreak of war in Europe in 1914 is probably as good a date as any to mark its end. In terms of our perceptions and sensibilities, however, the spirit itself is unimaginably distant because it seems now to belong to some mythical golden age of this world, or a parallel universe that had been mistaken for this world. Ours is an age of uncertainty for many reasons and one of them is that we no longer believe in the original promise of the Enlightenment, namely that knowledge, virtue and happiness would be achieved – were *bound* to be achieved – through the rigorous application of rationality. [78] We have lost this belief because there is too much evidence that even the best-intentioned and noblest of rationalities tend to turn into abstract formulae, pseudo-scientific systems, and ultimately new dogmas every bit as rigid and stupid and cruel as the old dogmas that the Enlightenment had vowed to sweep away.[79] It is the tendency that Charles Dickens anatomizes in *Hard Times* (first published in 1854), his satire against contemporary utilitarians who, in a nation that had so successfully mechanized the production of things, devoted themselves to mechanizing the production of knowledge, virtue and especially happiness. Whereas Bentham would have us believe that his 'principle of utility' balances pleasures and pains to ensure, automatically, the greatest happiness of the greatest number, Dickens warns that in practice it sanctions individual self-interest, injustice and outright criminality. Meanwhile rational enquiry is reduced to the marshalling of statistics and the weighing of Facts, forms of 'arithmetic' (Dickens's word) which, as applied to the mill hands of Coketown, invite industrial society to continue doing what pre-industrial society had done for centuries – treating the majority of its population as a pool of functions, not human beings. We know, as Dickens could not have known, that worse was to come, much of it associated with systems to accelerate the perfection of man and society. Spencer's system, which sought to harness natural selection as a pseudo-biological social force, helped to inspire a particularly ruthless doctrine of laissez-faire capitalism in the United States early in the twentieth century; Marx's system, which sought to harness the pseudo-historical force of dialectical materialism, provided the ideological basis for the project of political, economic and social engineering that the Soviet Union attempted throughout most of the twentieth century.[80] The Enlightenment promise is only as good as its interpreters and practitioners and they, we, are an unreliable bunch. We do our best to keep the Enlightenment spirit alive, above all because of the outcome of the West's most monstrous twentieth-century project, Nazism, which renounced rationality altogether and tried to remake the world by means of triumphal will, racial mumbo jumbo, and the industrialization of genocide. But it is a doubt-ridden and intermittent spirit we keep alive now, not an unshakeable certainty that the future will be better.

The unfolding excellence of fact, that sense of Progress operating through science and technology, must have had its doubters even during

Britain's age of certainty. Perhaps Lord Melbourne, twice Prime Minister in the 1830s, had just read Macaulay's essay on Bacon when he quipped 'I wish I was as cocksure of anything as Tom Macaulay is of everything.' [81] All the same, something resembling a faith in science and technology, or a last vestige of the belief in magic, outlived the other certainties of the age and survived into the twentieth century, shaken but not snuffed out by the technological horrors of its two world wars. In fact it reached a peak of hopefulness in the 1950s, based on the fond notion that a great redeeming good would come out of the apocalyptic bomb technology that had ended the war against Japan. The *civil* use of nuclear power, it was said, would produce electricity 'too cheap to meter' and usher in a wondrous era of prosperity and ease. Appropriately enough, this new age of certainty was proclaimed in the United States, the new centre of technological prowess and confidence. And yet, we can't help noticing, it was proclaimed in exactly the language – the same slightly delirious hyperbole – that Macaulay had used in Britain more than a century before:

> It is not too much to expect that our children will enjoy in their homes electrical energy too cheap to meter; will know of great periodic regional famines in the world only as matters of history; will travel effortlessly over the seas and under them and through the air with a minimum of danger and at great speed, and will experience a lifespan far longer than ours, as disease yields and man comes to understand what causes him to age. This is the forecast of an age of peace. [82]

The wondrous era was wondrously oversold. At a rational level, we have been let down because the economics of building, operating and decommissioning nuclear power plants did not, after all, translate into unlimited energy on demand. At a visceral level, the industry's history of near-catastrophes and full-blown catastrophes, especially at the Three Mile Island plant in Pennsylvania in 1979, at Chernobyl in the Ukraine in 1986, and in 2011 at Fukushima in northeast Japan, has stirred an ancient terror of the night: nuclear power is bad magic and we should not be messing with it. Civil nuclear energy was probably the last industrial-scale technology in which we believed uncritically and the failure of its promise may finally have killed off our one-time trust, our virtual faith, in the unfolding of science-based Progress from good to better, and from better to still better, on and on forever. The penny has dropped. Progress never was a law of nature, only a man-made fiction that attaches mystical value to what is often a mysterious, but not a mystical, branch of human endeavour. As fiction it is what we will it to be, or what we allow ourselves to be persuaded or manipulated into believing it to be, whether the radiantly inexhaustible Progress of Macaulay's utopian future or the darkly fantastical Progress of Orwell's dystopian future:

> The fabulous statistics continued to pour out of the telescreen. As compared with last year there was more food, more clothes, more houses, more furniture, more cooking-pots, more fuel, more ships, more helicopters, more books, more babies – more of everything except disease, crime, and insanity. Year by year and minute by minute, everybody and everything was whizzing rapidly upwards. [83]

All these passive expectations of the real

Two golden ages of certainty then, Japan's and Britain's, superficially similar in some respects and profoundly dissimilar in others. Japan's is well within living memory but was short, the quarter-century from 1964 to 1989. Britain's is distant but was long, a whole century ending in about 1914 – even longer if we include the last gasp of our trust in scientific Progress in the 1950s. In Japan certainty (not to be confused with comfort or happiness) was inherent in the hierarchical order (not to be confused with a class order) of society, which allotted a place to almost everyone, however senior or junior, and enveloped each of them with the expectations and behaviours appropriate to their place. To put it another way, in Japan's golden age (and still today, I imagine) the certainty of *belonging* depended not on social status but on having a prescribed role, even if a very menial role, in a company or some other collective endeavour. In Britain the class-based order of society provided certainty, too, but it was only the certainty of belonging for the deciders and doers, who were distinguished by their status. The decided-for and done-to, especially the invisible people, had their roles – their functions – but they had no status and therefore they did not fully belong. The spirit of the age of nineteenth-century Britain was a threat to the old order because the spirit was dynamic while the order was static. Progress in all its forms would take hold of the old order and propel it bodily into a new and better world to which everyone, whatever their role or status, could hope to belong and one day would belong. That was the threat and that was the promise.

As several of the key dates in my little history of certainty are publication dates, notably 1837 (Macaulay's essay on Bacon), 1854 (*Hard Times*) and 1859 (*Origin of Species*), no one can accuse me of inconsistency if I suggest that a key date in our age of uncertainty is also associated with the publication of an important book. The book is Jean-Paul Sartre's *L'être et le néant*, which we know in English as *Being and Nothingness*; the date, improbably, is 1943, the fourth year of the Nazi occupation of much of France. It is a very mixed bag of a book. Leaving aside the seemingly wilful obscurity of some of Sartre's language, there are two major difficulties in my opinion. Firstly, Sartre shares in the Enlightenment enthusiasm for demolishing old dogmas but, in his own way, he also shares in the tendency to produce new ones. One of his dogmas, for example, is that there is no such thing as the unconscious in the Freudian sense of workings of the mind of which we may be partly or wholly unaware. Denying the existence of the unconscious avoids a conflict with Sartre's central tenet that our states of mind, attitudes and even emotions are all modes of consciousness which we freely choose. But the denial is hard to reconcile with the evidence – routinely encountered in everyday life, let alone in the psychoanalyst's consulting room – that there *are* workings of the mind we are unaware of, and these are explained more simply and more convincingly, I think, by the assumed existence of an unconscious than by Sartre's assertion that they are really modes of consciousness which we 'understand [*comprendre*]' but do not 'know [*connaître*]'. [84] The second major difficulty is that *Being and Nothingness* raises huge expectations which it then dashes because it is all diagnosis and no remedy – no remedy, in particular, for human relations. According to Sartre, every human relation comes down to the despair of allowing ourselves to be 'indefinitely tossed' between two 'fundamental attitudes', which in their most extreme forms express themselves as sadism and masochism. [85] His only hint of hope appears in a mysterious footnote in which he alludes to 'a radical conversion' and seems to promise 'an ethics of deliverance and salvation', not in *Being and Nothingness* but in a sequel that he never wrote, or never wrote in terms compatible with his diagnosis of the human condition. [86] As diagnosis, however, and despite its tendency to dogmatism, *Being and Nothingness* offers some brilliant insights that have a bearing both on our contemporary uncertainties and, I believe, on the supposed certainties of the past.

For Sartre, the most characteristic of our modes of conscious existence is – or would be if we were not always avoiding or evading it – *anguish*. Anguish is the mode in which we confront the reality that our freedom, synonymous with our consciousness, consists in a nothingness, which Sartre also calls a 'lack', between who we 'are' now and our future possibilities. We are never wholly identified or united with ourselves (our consciousness is always '*at a distance from itself* as a presence to itself', Sartre says [87]) because, unlike an inanimate object, we have no given properties or essence to be identified or united with (the very idea is a contradiction in terms, for our consciousness would not be consciousness if it ceased to be 'at a distance' from itself). [88] We await ourselves in the future and in our nothingness we project ourselves towards that future by choosing between our possibilities, which means endlessly choosing to act, to think and to feel in one way and not in another. We are 'condemned to be free', condemned, that is, to make ourselves up as we go along, moment by moment, day by day, year by year. [89]

Anguish would be an unbearable mode of existence if our consciousness were indeed the perpetual consciousness of an unlimited responsibility for making ourselves. For most of us most of the time, however, there is no such consciousness because the circumstances of our daily lives do not bring us face to face with our responsibility. The immediate demands of the world enable us to avoid anguish, as Sartre illustrates with examples that are arresting in their banality. We can never view a humble alarm clock in quite the same way again after he has done with it:

> Now at each instant we are thrust into the world and engaged there. .... The alarm which rings in the

> morning refers to the possibility of my going to work, which is *my* possibility. But to apprehend the summons of the alarm as a summons is to get up. Therefore the very act of getting up is reassuring, for it eludes the question, "Is work *my* possibility?" Consequently it does not put me in a position to apprehend the possibility of quietism, of refusing to work, and finally the possibility of refusing the world and the possibility of death. In short, to the extent that I apprehend the meaning of the ringing, I am already up at its summons; this apprehension guarantees me against the anguished intuition that it is I who confer on the alarm clock its exigency – I and I alone. [90]

And what is true of the routines and preoccupations of our daily lives is true also of our values. They too seem to come from the world of the immediate:

> Ordinarily, ... my attitude with respect to values is eminently reassuring. In fact I am engaged in a world of values. .... The immediate is the world with its urgency; and in this world where I engage myself, my acts cause values to spring up like partridges. .... Values are sown on my path as thousands of little real demands, like the signs which order us to keep off the grass. [91]

'Our being is immediately "in situation",' Sartre explains, 'that is, it arises in enterprises and knows itself first in so far as it is reflected in those enterprises', which is when we discover ourselves 'in a world peopled with demands, in the heart of projects "in the course of realization".' These enterprises are comfortingly familiar:

> I write. I am going to smoke. I have an appointment this evening with Pierre. I must not forget to reply to Simon. I do not have the right to conceal the truth any longer from Claude. All these trivial passive expectations of the real, all these commonplace,

> everyday values, derive their meaning from an original projection of myself which stands as my choice of myself in the world. But to be exact, this projection of myself toward an original possibility, which causes the existence of values, appeals, expectations, and in general a world, appears to me only beyond the world as the meaning and the abstract, logical signification of my enterprises. For the rest, there exist concretely alarm clocks, signboards, tax forms, policemen, so many guard rails against anguish. [92]

So how can anguish affect us, for it is a mere abstraction and in any case we appear to be comprehensively guaranteed against it? Sartre's answer is, in a sense, that we only find anguish if we choose to go looking for it and to do that we have to be on the level of 'reflective' consciousness, in which our consciousness deliberately turns its attention on itself as an object of study. To take Sartre's example of working on a book, in 'reflective' consciousness we discover the nothingness that separates us from our future possibilities because nothing compels us to write the book and we might equally choose not to write it as to write it ('I discover that the permanent possibility of abandoning the book is the very condition of the possibility of writing it and the very meaning of my freedom' [93]). This discovery is not just one of the ways we are 'anguished' in connection with one particular activity: it is a glimpse into the abyss that threatens to open beneath our feet *whenever* we choose to be on 'the plane of reflection' and not exclusively on 'the plane of action'. Yes, there are alarm clocks and signboards and all the other guard rails against anguish. 'But as soon as the enterprise is held at a distance from me,' Sartre continues,

> as soon as I am referred to myself because I must await myself in the future, then I discover myself suddenly as the one who gives its meaning to the alarm clock, the one who by a signboard forbids himself to walk on a flower bed or on the lawn, the one from whom the boss's order borrows its urgency, the one who decides the interest of the book which he is writing, the one finally who makes the values exist

> in order to determine his action by their demands. I emerge alone and in anguish confronting the unique and original project which constitutes my being; all the barriers, all the guard rails collapse, nihilated by the consciousness of my freedom. I do not have nor can I have recourse to any value against the fact that it is I who sustain values in being. Nothing can ensure me against myself, cut off from the world and from my essence by this nothingness which I *am*. I have to realize the meaning of the world and of my essence; I make my decision concerning them – without justification and without excuse. [94]

It is little wonder that, far from choosing to go looking for anguish, we seek to escape it by attitudes and behaviours which Sartre dubs 'patterns of flight'. Escape is possible because our 'reflective' consciousness can choose one of two attitudes when confronted with anguish: either we face the nothingness of our freedom and accept that we must project ourselves into the future through our choices, or we flee our freedom and try to 'fill up' [95] the nothingness by adopting roles and playing parts, conforming to conventional expectations, and behaving in other ways that are not our own free choices. The first attitude, good faith, delivers us to anguish. The second, bad faith, evades anguish through self-deception, 'a lie to oneself'. [96]

Sartre identifies many varieties of bad faith, most famously in his description of the café waiter who plays at *being* a waiter (and, less famously, the grocer who does not dream because his customers expect a grocer to be wholly a grocer and not a dreamer [97]). One of these varieties is 'the spirit of seriousness'. While 'seriousness' sounds as if it should denote a positive attitude, in Sartre's terminology it denotes our attempt to evade anguish by regarding values not as contingent upon the possibilities that we choose in our own inner nothingness but as *facts* or *objects* that pre-exist in the world around us. Whereas in anguish 'I apprehend myself at once as totally free and as not being able to derive the meaning of the world except as coming from myself', in the serious attitude I apprehend 'the meaning which my freedom has given *to* the world … as coming *from* the world and constituting my obligations.' [98] In good faith man actively awaits himself in the future and makes his own free choices; in bad faith he 'makes himself such that he is *waited for* by all the tasks placed along his way. Objects are mute demands, and he is nothing in himself but the passive obedience to these demands.' [99] To live in good faith, Sartre says, we must 'repudiate' the spirit of seriousness and accept that we make the meaning of the world through the values we cause to exist. An absurd notion, we protest. If we make the meaning of the world, there can be no coherence or consistency in the world because we may bring one value into existence by one choice of our possibilities and then a completely different or contradictory value by another choice. Values become wheels that we each reinvent from moment to moment as we project ourselves towards our individual futures; by implication, anything that appears to be an organized and shared body of values, including our religious and secular ideals, principles, morality itself, can only be the product of coincidence, wheels that happen to have been reinvented by two or more individuals at the same moment. And to believe otherwise, to locate right and wrong, justice and injustice, the desirable and the undesirable in, for instance, a political programme prescribed for us by others – as Sartre himself evidently did when he chose to become a Marxist sometime in the 1950s – is to be guilty of self-deception. The world is turned upside down: behaving consistently according to received and widely shared values, which conventionally we think of as moral behaviour, becomes bad faith, while behaving inconsistently and perhaps unlawfully according to values we have decided for ourselves, conventionally immoral behaviour, becomes good faith.

This is absurd, but just calling it that does not get us very far because Sartre's whole point (at least until he became a Marxist) was that the very fact human reality *is* absurd gives us all the more reason to be suspicious of the trivial passive expectations of the real and the reassuringly familiar values that seem to underpin our world. If we are willing to suspend our disbelief for a while and see our world through Sartre's eyes, his diagnosis of the human condition becomes, more precisely and more urgently, a warning against existential complacency and an injunction to scrutinize and challenge the values that ordinarily we take for granted. I am not suggesting that Sartre's way of looking at the world is uniquely revealing, only that it is revealing and merits closer evaluation. How well does it work as a description? Does it help us to understand our own attitudes, behaviour and values more effectively or more convincingly than other descriptions do? What we need is a test. Or three tests.

The proof of the pudding

Test one: **sarariiman** *and* **okāsan**

Let's start in golden-age Japan with the lives (or life-programmes) of the good 'company man', the *sarariiman* , and of the good wife and mother, the *okāsan*. From a Western perspective, the patterns of their lives are recognizable and yet somehow alien, which is why our first reaction is to try and explain them away or pigeonhole them as 'different'. Racially and culturally Japan is exceptionally homogeneous, we are told, a high-context culture in which, as encapsulated in the proverb 'Hear one, understand ten', [100] much communication is implicit and even non-verbal because assumptions, values and expectations are so widely shared that explicit communication is unnecessary. Perhaps for ancient reasons connected with the development of wet rice cultivation (which demands the sharing of water and other collective endeavours), it is a society that encourages group effort and consensus and discourages individual initiative and non-conformity. A great borrower from other cultures, Japan has assimilated its borrowings in a sort of stop-go-stop process, often modifying them but sometimes preserving or fossilizing them long after conditions have changed in their country of origin: maybe this explains why a Confucian notion of hierarchy that originated in China more than two thousand years ago survives as the dominant ordering principle of modern Japanese society. Given all these historical and cultural factors, we ask rhetorically, how could the typical *sarariiman* and the typical *okāsan* be other than they are? They are wholly predictable products of their society. But, we are quick to add, it is a society very different from ours and, while we may admire the *sarariiman* and the *okāsan* for their discipline and fortitude, we would never want to *be* them – 'them' as in 'them and us', that is, because we are 'us' and we are quite content to be 'us'.

In the world according to Sartre, on the other hand, we have no recourse to 'them and us' in the familiar sense because cultural differences alone, even the most undeniably real cultural differences, do not explain why a person behaves in one way rather than another. The *sarariiman* and the *okāsan*, Sartre would say, *could* be other than they are because they are not just cultural stereotypes bound to behave stereotypically but individual consciousnesses each with a capacity to determine their own future by choosing between their own individual possibilities. They had to be born into some society and some set of circumstances and, as chance would have it, they have been born into the society and circumstances of Japan, but there is nothing inevitable about the choices they make once they find themselves there. On the contrary, the first meaningful question to ask is whether the *sarariiman* is a *sarariiman* because that is what he freely chooses from among all the possibilities before him, or because he evades anguish by conforming passively to the behaviours, attitudes and values expected of a *sarariiman*. If the first answer, he is in good faith; if the second, he is deceiving himself in bad faith. Likewise, is the *okāsan* in good faith as a dutiful wife and mother, or would good faith require her to make other choices – abandoning her family, perhaps, or going on a shoplifting spree? From recognizing that the *sarariiman* and the *okāsan* are not faceless and alien stereotypes but individuals who happen to be Japanese, it is not such a great step to recognizing that there but for accidents of geography and birth go you or I. Another small step then takes us from asking what they make of themselves in their particular circumstances to asking what *we* make of ourselves in *our* particular circumstances and whether, by Sartre's definition, we do it in good faith or in bad faith. Hence my own verdict on this first test of Sartre's way of looking at the world is that it does tell us things that otherwise we might not discover, because by demolishing 'them-and-us' barriers, in this case a supposed barrier of culture, it throws us back on ourselves and jolts us into questioning our own behaviours, attitudes and values when we least expect to have to do so. [101]

Test two: Macaulay

The next guinea pig is my spokesman for the Victorian trust in the unfolding excellence of science and technology and, more broadly, for all those who have ever believed in Progress with a big 'P'. Surely no one seriously subscribes to Progress today but many regret it, I would say, because we feel we have lost so much certainty by its passing. If truth be told, we envy Macaulay for his unshakeable belief in the idea that Progress is taking us somewhere, and that where it is taking us will always be better than where we have been. We envy Macaulay because he personifies the spirit of certainty that existed in Britain's golden age of certainty.

But do we have any grounds for envying him? In Sartre's terms, after all, what Macaulay personifies is not the spirit of certainty but the spirit of *seriousness*, the attitude that apprehends meaning and value as flowing from the world to us, whereas in reality they flow from us to the world. To believe that Progress is a principle or law of nature turns it into a passive expectation of the real, albeit a very grand and not a trivial expectation, which, because it appears to come loaded with value, encourages us to confuse judgements of value (this is better than that with mere measures of fact (this is newer, bigger, faster, more efficient, more profitable than that. Conversely, Sartre offers a device – a warning device – to help us distinguish value from fact and one which has applications on the collective level as well as the individual level. Although we knock down fewer historic buildings in the name of Progress than we did in Macaulay's day, and our eyes were supposedly opened by the failure of civil nuclear power to live up to its promises, I suspect that we will always be susceptible to arguments of the you-can't-stand-in-the-way-of-Progress kind. In the debate on genetically modified (GM crops, for instance, it is tempting to think that the value of GM technology is the sum of its demonstrable benefits – significantly improved yields and resistance to drought, disease and pests – and that these are so compelling only diehard Luddites could oppose its unimpeded commercialization. Yet Sartre might say that this temptation is a temptation to lapse into the spirit of seriousness, and then caution us *en masse* exactly as he would caution an individual in danger of falling into seriousness: with a reminder that value is something we have to judge for ourselves on a case-by-case basis, not something that is embedded in and inseparable from fact. Thus reminded, would we decide that progress – and if we have to use the word at all, let's cut it down to size and spell it with a small 'p' – is served better, qualitatively better, by continuing to put obstacles in the way of GM agriculture as it is currently envisaged? And would we do so because, as judgements of value and not of fact, we had agreed that it is unacceptable to take risks (especially the risk of accidental cross-fertilization with the integrity and diversity of non-GM crops, and wrong to permit the agrochemical industry to reduce farmers (in the developed world as well as in the developing world to the status of licensees dependent on a single supplier for their seed and for the pesticides engineered into GM technology? There will be many more such issues in the twenty-first century, particularly in relation to climate change and the environment, and it may be that Sartre's notion of the spirit of seriousness, seemingly misnamed and seemingly only of metaphysical interest, will be of practical use in dealing with them.

Test three: Edgecombe

Edgecombe, driver to Captain Kinross/Mountbatten, is a minor character in the action of *In Which We Serve* and yet, we feel, a good character – steadfast, a loyal member of the ship's company, and probably very proud to be serving his country. But he is also my imaginary representative of the 'big masses' who symbolically rejected the old social and political order by voting Winston Churchill out of office in 1945. Up until that point, I have implied, Edgecombe had accepted the old order as though in a trance or under a spell, by which I mean that he had no conception things could be different, or no conception that he had any choice in the matter. Things were as they were. This reckoning makes Edgecombe quietly heroic for renouncing the old order in 1945 but, from a lenient (and non-ideological point of view, absolves him from blame for colluding in the injustices it had inflicted on himself and others before 1945.

Sartre's reckoning would, I think, be much less lenient: definitely before 1945, and possibly in and after 1945, Edgecombe was in bad faith. By performing functions (especially in his capacity as personal servant to his commanding officer and conforming with expectations (respect your class superiors, keep to your place, be seen and not heard dictated by the world around him, he had spent his adult life avoiding and evading the recognition that he *did* have a choice in the matter. The fact that he had been born into a poor working-class family and left school at fourteen, say, would be no excuse: as for the *sarariiman* half a century later and half a world away, accidental circumstances of birth and social environment were the raw materials Edgecombe had to work with, not an explanation in themselves for anything he might or might not choose to do. True, given his particular circumstances, becoming a surgeon or a bishop or Prime Minister were probably not among the possibilities before him, but he could have chosen not to be a sailor or, having become one (or been made one through conscription [102], not to remain a sailor. What was to stop him from hurling his alarm clock through a porthole one morning and refusing to rise from his bunk? The threat of punishment for dereliction of duty, we might say, court-martial and, in an extreme case, execution. So be it. If death was one of Edgecombe's possibilities, and one that he freely chose, he would die – but he would die in good faith. And was he not in good faith when, very much alive, he cast his ballot on 5 July 1945? That would depend on the choice he was making as he did so. If his vote to end the old social and political order was a vote to end his own decided-for and done-to mode of existence in the world, a vote for anguish, in Sartre's terms, then in good faith Edgecombe had chosen to face the nothingness of his individual freedom. If, however, he looked to the new, more egalitarian order to envelop him in its hope and ideals and prescribe how he should live, then in bad faith all he had done was to vote for a more palatable array of expectations, tasks and values by which to go on living in passive obedience.

It is easy to parody Sartre. Had Edgecombe voted Labour at 12:00 noon, for example, he might have voted Conservative at 11:59, torn up his ballot paper at 12:01, or made any one of a great number of free choices at any moment in between. But this, it seems to me, is another instance in which we have something to gain by seeing the world through Sartre's eyes: suspend our disbelief in the absurdity of what he is saying and instantly we find ourselves called to account not just for what we have done and do with our own lives, but for *why* we have done and do it. Unlike Sartre, we may maintain that psychologically we cannot be held responsible for absolutely everything we do because some of our motives and intentions will be affected by unconscious workings of the mind. Even so, we should hesitate to dismiss Sartre`s insistence that we are 'condemned to be free' because, exaggerated or melodramatic as it sounds, it invites us to ask ourselves at every turn whether our lives really are so filled up with external obligations, preoccupations and routines that we have no opportunity – or no need – to examine and determine our own choices.

Scaled up to the social level, Sartre's formulation of good and bad faith may even shed light on the political-philosophical conundrum implicit in what, according to David Kynaston and other revisionist historians, actually happened in 1945.[103] A lot of people, myself included, perceive Labour's election victory as a collective act of self-emancipation by the 'big masses'. But what if their vote for decent housing, family allowances and pensions was just that – incidentally a vote to be recognized as more than mere functions and as properly part of the world, but primarily a vote for the material benefits promised by a new lot of deciders and doers, the Labour Party, ideologically committed not only to improving living standards but also to telling people what was best for them? In other words, in 1945 did the 'big masses' in fact squander the opportunity for a collective act of self-emancipation and vote instead for a collective act of bad faith? And was it a case of collective bad faith or collective *good* faith when, in 1979, a large part of the electorate broke with its by then established habit of voting Labour and brought to power a Conservative administration, led by Margaret Thatcher, which promised material and other benefits (especially the legal right for tenants of local-authority housing to buy the properties they rented) but whose ideological message was that it is not the job of government to tell people how to run their own lives?

****

Existentialism is out of fashion. Sartre himself is not a very appealing figure and, if true, the charge that he plagiarized significant elements of *Being and Nothingness* from *L'invitée*, a novel-in-progress by Simone de Beauvoir, makes him even less appealing.[104] Nor is he a paragon of good faith: with whatever reservations or reforming zeal he may have embraced Marxism in the 1950s, to subscribe to any prescriptive ideology at all was, by his own lights, a gross act of bad faith. In my opinion, however, it is our loss if we neglect *Being and Nothingness* because it is unfashionable or because we are repelled by the personality of its author. Despite his lapses into gobbledygook, much of Sartre's language is very accessible and his imagery – signboards and tax forms as 'guard rails against anguish', obligations that are ‘mute demands’, values that ‘spring up like partridges’ – is often so vividly outlandish that it robs the ordinary of its ordinariness and we find ourselves re-examining behaviours, attitudes and values that hitherto we have always taken for granted. It is an uncomfortable state and that, I believe, makes it a healthy state because it is not one conducive to complacency.

4. THE AMBIVALENCE OF STAR DUST

> 'Above all, act impulsively: don't let yourself get stuck between alternatives, or you're lost. You're not that strong. If the alternatives are side by side, choose the one on the left; if they're consecutive in time, choose the earlier. If neither of these applies, choose the alternative whose name begins with the earlier letter of the alphabet. These are the principles of Sinistrality, Antecedence, and Alphabetical Priority – there are others, and they're arbitrary, but useful.'
>
> John Barth, *The End of the Road*[105]

The Doctor prescribes Sinistrality, Antecedence and Alphabetical Priority to Jacob Horner to help him cope with his tendency to run out of reasons and motives, which leaves him unable to choose between Cincinnati, Ohio, or Crestline, Ohio, or Dayton, Ohio, or Lima, Ohio, as destinations all available for the same twenty dollars. Don't get stuck between alternatives. It is easy to regard this patient's problem as a peculiarity of the age of existentialism, the age that discovered itself condemned to be free, but of course it is really the old affliction of conscious choice and free will that has tormented man ever since Adam and Eve ate the forbidden fruit of the tree of knowledge. The Ohio conundrum would have been no surprise to the seventeenth-century Protestant divine Godfrey Goodman, who wrote:

> Methinks it should stand with right reason that as sense hath sensible objects, so things themselves should present themselves to the understanding, that the mind should not busy herself to make her own objects intelligible but should only pass judgement and censure. This is the condition of dumb beasts in regard to their sense; this is the state of the angels in regard of their infusion; and this should have been the state of man, were it not that man is fallen.[106]

According to the conventional notions of Goodman's time, the dumb animals are equipped with an instinctive, sensuous perception that enables them to eat, sleep, reproduce themselves and otherwise deal with their world as it presents itself to them. The 'infusion' of the angels is a purely intellectual perception, which enables them to imbibe the divine essence as it presents itself in an emanation from God. Despite the fundamentally different qualities of their perception, beasts and angels are alike in that they respond to things, whether sensible objects or divine essence, *without further ado.* Only the mind of man insists on further ado, busying itself to make its objects intelligible, because only man is compelled to find his own reasons for responding to things in one way rather than another. Goodman's lament is for a world that might have been, a world in which man would not be in his fallen state and a destination would present itself to Jacob Horner's twenty dollars without any need for reasons or motives. [107]

The old affliction and where it came from

The more or less certain facts are these. The universe came into being at the Big Bang 13.7 billion years ago. [108] Our galaxy, the Milky Way, was probably one of the first to form, about 13.6 billion years ago. [109] Our sun, the earth and all the other solid bodies in our solar system formed more than 4.5 billion years ago. [110] The first life forms, possibly simple membranes of fatty acids that enveloped strings of self-replicating genetic molecules, evolved more than 3.5 billion years ago – that is to say, the transition from chemical evolution to Darwinian evolution seems to have happened within the first billion years of earth's existence. [111] Let's cut a long story short. *Ardipithecus ramidus*, currently the oldest undisputed link to the common ancestor of humans and chimpanzees, lived about 4.4 million years ago; the tool-making *Homo habilis*, generally regarded as the first 'true' man, may have appeared more than two million years ago; but *Homo sapiens sapiens*, the sub-species of anatomically modern humans to which we all belong, probably dates to within the last two hundred thousand years. [112] All life on earth shares a common origin not just with the first rudimentary assemblies of organic molecules but also with the inanimate matter that makes up the earth itself, for virtually every one of the earth's naturally occurring chemical elements was created in distant stars that had burnt out long before our solar system was born. We are all, literally, made of star dust. It is mystery enough that star dust should ever have given rise to life at all, but the mystery of mysteries is that life should have gone on to acquire a conscious awareness of its own existence.

If we assume, I hope uncontroversially, that in terms of human evolution the development of complex cognition and consciousness correlates with changes in brain size and structure, it seems reasonable to suppose that consciousness as we recognize it is a phenomenon of *Homo sapiens* (cranial capacity 1,200-1,400 cubic centimetres, compared with 500-800 cubic centimetres for *Homo habilis*).[113] In other words, by evolutionary timescales consciousness is a very recent development, a novelty. As to how and why consciousness developed, however, there seems little more to be said with any confidence because we are in the realms of conjecture and imaginative speculation. But if we are willing to accept that imaginative speculation has the potential to arrive at imaginative truth, and that imaginative truth is a meaningful form of truth, then there is more to be said – and it has been said, in mythological and metaphorical accounts of the coming of consciousness. While there must be many such accounts, or consciousness-creation myths, in many different cultures, I shall stick to two in particular: Plato's and the Bible's.

According to the *Timaeus*, man is endowed with an immortal soul but his body and parts of his soul are mortal. These components were put together in the cosmic workshop. The master craftsman, the creator himself, mixed man's immortal soul in the same bowl that he had used to make the soul of the universe. Then he handed over to a team of lesser gods, who fabricated the body by bonding together portions of fire, earth, water and air borrowed from the world. At this point it has to be said that the production process resembles one of those spot-the-difference cartoon puzzles. There is the creator at his bowl. Is he making the soul of the universe or the soul of man? Can't tell. Look again. Ah, he's mixing leftovers, and not in the same proportions, 'not quite so pure, but in a second and third degree'.[114] And there are the junior gods. They're fixing the body of man together in just the same way as the creator had fixed them together. Wrong. The creator used an indissoluble bonding agent to make the lesser gods, but they go for 'a multitude of rivets too small to be seen' to make man. [115] Rivets! Contrary to appearances, this is not slipshod workmanship but fine calculation. As the creator tells the gods, there ought to be something in mortal creatures 'that can be named immortal, something called divine, to guide those of them who are ready to follow you and the right.' [116] The creator alone is qualified to supply this something, the immortal principle of soul. If he uses ingredients of the maximum purity and does the whole job himself, however, the creatures will be equal to the gods he has already made, which is not his intention. On the other hand, these gods are just right for finishing the job because it is 'natural' for them to make living, mortal things. 'Bring them to birth,' the creator instructs the gods, 'give them food and growth, and when they perish receive them again.' Hence the rivets: permanent bonding would be redundant in a product destined for recycling.

All this fine calculation is of little comfort to the product, man, for it makes him part of the inventory of the world of change, his body subject to becoming, corruption and decay, riven by turmoil and conflict. Worst of all, it leaves man free to act as he chooses assisted only by a guide, his soul, that cannot be relied upon to lead him to the right choices (virtuous choices, tending to the good) because its functioning is impaired by the presence of the mortal elements in its own constitution. [117] Man is burdened, nonetheless, with responsibility for the choices that he makes and for their consequences, which Plato expresses as changes in the soul's position in space. In the *Laws*, the Athenian tells us that the creator has worked out the positions to match each soul's changes of character, but 'left it to the individual's acts of will to determine the *direction* of these changes [because] the way we react to particular circumstances is almost invariably determined by our desires and our psychological state.' Since this is the same Athenian who has declared that change in the character of the soul, as in all things except something evil, is 'extremely dangerous' (my page 15 above), we grasp at once that our free will is itself fraught with danger – a curse, not a blessing. 'So all things that contain soul change,' the Athenian continues,

> the cause of their change lying within themselves, and as they change they move according to the ordinance and law of destiny. Small changes in unimportant aspects of character entail small horizontal changes of

> position in space, while a substantial decline into injustice sets the soul on the path to the depths of the so-called "under"world, which men call "Hades" and similar names, and which haunts and terrifies them both during their lives and when they have been sundered from their bodies. [118]

Nor, according to the myth of Er in Plato's *Republic*, does our responsibility for our own choices end when we die, because sooner or later after death our soul transmigrates into a new body and the cycle of our acts of will and their consequences starts all over again. Er, a warrior killed in battle, has already been placed on his funeral pyre but he returns to life, for the divine Judges have chosen him as a messenger to men. He tells of what he has seen in the other world, including the process by which souls that are about to transmigrate come before Lachesis (one of the three Fates) and choose, in an order determined by lot, their next incarnations from among types of life 'of every conceivable kind, animal and human'. '"Souls of a day",' they are told, '"here you must begin another round of mortal life. … Goodness knows no master; a man shall have more or less of her according to the value he sets on her. The fault lies not with God, but with the soul that makes the choice".' [119] Despite this warning, the soul with the first lot impulsively chooses the greatest life of tyranny he can find, and only then realizes that he is destined to eat his own children and suffer other horrors; in a mythological anticipation of existential bad faith, the soul cannot bring himself to accept responsibility for his choice and instead blames 'fate and heaven and anything but himself.' [120] The full dread of our condition is not immediately obvious from the *Timaeus*, however, because when the creator distributes the soul-mix of man (as opposed to woman) he insists that each individual soul shall start off on an equal footing:

> And when he had compounded the whole, he divided it up into as many souls as there are stars, and allotted each soul to a star. And mounting them on their stars, as if on chariots, he showed them the nature of the universe and told them the laws of their destiny. To ensure fair treatment for each at his hands, the first incarnation would be one and the same for all and

> each would be sown in its appropriate instrument of time and be born as the most god-fearing of living things; and human-kind being of two sexes, the better of the two was that which in future would be called man. [121]

This is the 'necessary incarnation' of man, the allocation of his soul to a body. But even as the lesser gods roll him off the final assembly line, it becomes all too clear that he is not well equipped to lead the good life expected of him because he is not well equipped to master the desires and contradictory feelings that come with the mortal elements of his soul:

> into [man's] body, subject to the flow of growth and decay, they fastened the orbits of the immortal soul. Plunged into this strong stream, the orbits were unable to control it, nor were they controlled by it, and because of the consequent violent conflict the motions of the whole creature were irregular, fortuitous and irrational. [122]

In Plato's consciousness-creation myth, the creator intentionally imparts knowledge to the souls mounted on their stars by explaining the nature of the universe and the laws of their destiny. Each and every soul is let into secrets that otherwise would be confined to the gods. But this is a terrible knowledge – and one that can never be unlearned – because not only does it tell man that his body is subject to loss, pain and discord, it makes man and his soul responsible for everything they choose to do, and for the consequences of everything they choose to do. In the biblical consciousness-creation myth, by contrast, God has sought to withhold all such knowledge from Adam and Eve by forbidding them, under pain of death, from eating of that one tree in the garden. Putting the two myths together confronts us with a deep-seated ambivalence in ourselves. The word from Plato's creator is that there is no escaping the knowledge of our predicament: knowing our destiny and knowing that we know it – consciousness – is the unavoidable condition of our humanity. The God of Genesis, however, says no, the prohibition against knowing is for our own good: witness the calamities that follow if we disobey, starting with the involuntary opening of our eyes, symbolic of an *unintended* irruption of consciousness that we will regret forever after. Pulled between the two contradictory voices, we have two contradictory responses to our being in the world: try to know it, however desperate the knowing may be; or leave the knowing to somebody or something else.

So far as we can tell or imagine, for most of human history we tended, collectively and individually, to leave the knowing of ourselves to somebody or something else. We entrusted it primarily to the gods, God, prophets, holy men, heroes, ancestors, elders, scripture, myth, tradition, custom, precedent – all these and other names for the received (or revealed) and *unchanging* lore of the past. Our being in the world and the meaning of our lives had been determined for us, once and for all, and there was nothing more we could or needed to discover for ourselves. The significance of the Enlightenment is that it wanted to sweep away this lore of the past, exposing its supposed sanctity and authority as superstition and dogma, and encouraging us to look for our meanings, and reality itself, not in a static past but in a dynamic future unfolding in a rational progression of change from good to better. Macaulay's essay on Bacon of 1837 is not just a celebration of the new scientific philosophy which, never resting, takes possibilities undreamt of yesterday as the starting point for tomorrow's achievements: it speaks for an entirely new world reaching towards what might be called, to borrow a phrase, 'the flying goal of the whole of things'.[123] Yet less than thirty years earlier the Reverend Edward Coplestone, a fellow of Oriel College, Oxford, had spoken out for the old static world when, in response to charges that the Oxford curriculum did not recognize the importance of science and failed to instil a spirit of free enquiry in its students, he declared 'The scheme of Revelation we think is closed, and we expect no new light on earth to break in upon us.'[124] And in 1790 Edmund Burke had expressed – or seemed to express – a powerful attachment to the old world when he pronounced that 'A spirit of innovation is generally the result of a selfish temper and confined views. People will not look forward to posterity, who never look backward to their ancestors.'[125] If we go further back, to the late sixteenth century, we find ourselves in Edmund Spenser's allegorical Garden of Adonis, 'first seminarie / Of all things, that are borne to live and die, / According to their kindes'.[126] The great enemy of everything in the Garden is time, which, as for generations of earlier poets, churchmen and philosophers, is another word for change or mutability. The whole world is in the sway of the goddess Mutability and yet, where it would seem that despair must triumph and make man 'loath this state of life so tickle [unstable]', Spenser consoles us with the thought that even time and change are contained within a greater, divine stability:

> Then gin I thinke on that which Nature sayd,
> Of that same time when no more *Change* shall be,
> But stedfast rest of all things firmely stayd
> Upon the pillours of Eternity,
> That is contrayr to *Mutabilitie*:
> For, all that moveth, doth in *Change* delight:
> But thence-forth all shall rest eternally
> With Him that is the God of Sabbaoth hight:
> O that great Sabbaoth God, graunt me that Sabaoths sight. [127]

The key biblical text has to be the Book of Ecclesiastes, which denies the very existence of change or innovation:

> The thing that hath been, it *is that* which shall be; and that which is done *is* that which shall be done: and *there is* no new *thing* under the sun. [128]

From Plato's *Laws* we have the Athenian's warning that the menace of change lurks everywhere, especially in the playground:

> If you control the way children play, and the same children always play the same games under the same rules and in the same conditions, and get pleasure from the same toys, you'll find that the conventions of adult life too are left in peace without alteration. But in fact games are always being changed and constantly modified and new ones invented, and the younger generation never enthuses over the same thing for two days running. [129]

But even the unknown author or authors of Ecclesiastes (probably writing around 250-200 BC) and Plato (writing in about 320 BC) are relatively late spokesmen for a world thousands, and more likely tens of thousands, of years older. What was the unchanging lore of this much older world? Although we are back in the realms of speculation, there are grounds on which to speculate. On the one hand, there is the physical evidence. In the case of Upper Palaeolithic Europe at least as far back as the late Solutrean and Magdalenian cultures (about 18,000 to 10,000 BP [Before Present]), magical hunting and fertility rites can be interpreted from the wealth of rock paintings in France, Spain and elsewhere. [130] More contentiously, it may be possible to infer ritual or symbolic significance from the seemingly intentional burials practised by early modern humans (*Homo sapiens sapiens*) and Neanderthals in the Middle Palaeolithic (roughly 200,000 to 40,000 BP); if so, it would greatly extend the speculative timescale because some of these burials, discovered at cave sites in the Near East, are thought to be about fifty thousand years old and others may be closer to one hundred thousand years old. [131] On the other hand, if we are willing to conceive of the distant past in terms of an imaginative rather than a rigorously ordered truth, we can take myths and metaphors known to us from written sources – or sometimes preserved orally – and from them try to extrapolate backwards to the beliefs and ways of seeing the world of ages that, while long predating the first writing systems, are otherwise indeterminate chronologically.

The historian of religion Mircea Eliade, who spent much of his life studying the myths and metaphors of a great variety of cultures, came to the conclusion that modern man and premodern man ('premodern' denoting not a point on a timeline but a state of mind or world view, which may persist into 'modern' ages) are distinguished from each other by their very different conceptions of history and of reality itself. Modern man, especially when associated with 'certain post-Hegelian philosophical currents' (by which Eliade principally means Marxism, historicism and existentialism), is historical man: he '*is* insofar as he *makes himself, within history*.' [132] Premodern man is ahistorical man: he ascribes no meaning to history – in fact he constantly seeks to 'suspend' or 'abolish' history's linear flow of events, which he regards as profane and unreal. As Eliade puts it, 'interest in the "irreversible" and the "new" in history is a recent discovery in the life of humanity. On the contrary, archaic humanity … defended itself, to the utmost of its powers, against all the novelty and irreversibility which history entails.' [133] The notion of *making himself* is equally meaningless to premodern man, because for him meaning, value and reality attach only to activities that have an exemplary model in a mythical past, a model created by gods, heroes or ancestors. Consequently, premodern man's life is 'the ceaseless repetition of gestures initiated by others' and this pattern of repetition, Eliade argues, reveals 'an original ontology':

> The crude product of nature, the object fashioned by the industry of man, acquire their reality, their identity, only to the extent of their participation in a transcendent reality. The gesture acquires meaning, reality, solely to the extent to which it repeats a primordial act. [134]

Activities which have no exemplary models are profane, but

> every act which has a definite meaning – hunting, fishing, agriculture; games, conflicts, sexuality – in some way participates in the sacred. ... Thus we may say that every responsible activity in pursuit of a definite end is, for the archaic world, a ritual. [135]

Repetition of a ritual, whether in dance or sacrifice or healing ceremony, transports archaic man into the mythical epoch in which the ritual was originally revealed. Hence to the extent an act or object acquires reality through ritual repetition, 'and acquires it through that alone,' Eliade concludes, 'there is an implicit abolition of profane time, of duration, of "history".' [136]

Some of Eliade's asides are as fascinating as his main argument. He suggests, for instance, that 'primitive' ontology has a 'Platonic structure' (in the sense that the exemplary models which confer reality upon archaic man's acts and objects are analogous to, *and precursors of*, Plato's ideal forms); in which case, he goes on, 'Plato could be regarded as the outstanding philosopher of "primitive mentality", that is, as the thinker who succeeded in giving philosophic currency and validity to the modes of life and behavior of archaic humanity.' [137] Elsewhere Eliade asserts that the need 'primitive' peoples feel to regenerate themselves through the expulsion of evil and other rituals is proof that '[even] their memory is capable ... of revealing the irreversibility of events, that is, of recording history. Thus, among these primitive peoples too, the existence of man in the cosmos is regarded as a fall.' [138] Eliade speaks of this 'fall into history' both as a failure of archaic man to annul or transcend time and, a sentiment that would not seem out of place in Sartre's *Being and Nothingness*, as evidence of his freedom to make another attempt to succeed. [139] Overall, however, I think Eliade's greatest achievement is to have reconstructed an archaic ontology, as he calls it, that rings true and that indicates a very ancient origin for the aversion to innovation and change expressed by Plato, the Book of Ecclesiastes, Spenser, Burke, Coplestone, and many other voices.

Paradoxically and yet somehow fittingly, the richest imaginative evidence on which to speculate about the distant past comes from a few surviving cultures that have no written languages of their own. These include the Aborigines of Australia and the Bushmen (or the San, as some people prefer to call them [140]) of southern Africa, whose oral traditions may stretch back twenty thousand years or more into the prehistory of the southern hemisphere. And the most valuable thing that these oral traditions have preserved, it seems to me, is the quality of 'archaic' man's reality – not just an unchanging reality but a *greater* reality, so intense that in its telling we almost experience it ourselves with phenomenological directness. We are indebted to the anthropologist Megan Biesele for the following account, told her by an old, blind Bushman healer named K"xau, of what to expect when visiting the abode of Kauha, the great God, above the threads of the sky:

> My friend, when you go to visit God, you sit this way [in an attitude of respect, with arms folded across the knees]. People sit this way when they go to God, the great, great God, the master. ... When you go there, women are singing, they are singing for a dance. ... They dance the giraffe dance. ... What you do there, where God is, is to dance like this. ... And the women sing like this [K"xau sings]. They sing and they sing. ... When God sits on his chair, he watches all around. And when people come from somewhere else and see him, they tremble with fear. They tremble themselves to death over him! He's a terrible thing! Friend, that's what people say. ... A horse is there, and God rides him! God's horse! Yes, friend, he rides that horse. He sits up on a saddle and rides. He has a gun,

> the kind of gun that goes "!Khwi!". He rides his horse and goes places. His boots – they come all the way to his knees. … Big ones! And they are made of metal. … God wears metal boots. And they`re as high as his knees. … When you go there, friend, you make yourself small like this. Friend, when you go there, you don`t go standing up straight. You make yourself small so that you are a mamba. … That`s how you go to him. Because if you do that, he`ll let you live. If you go to him like a regular person, you`ll die. … You won`t come back. … You come in small to God`s place. You do what you have to do there. Then you return to where everyone is, and you hide your face. You hide your face so you won`t see anything. You come and come and come and finally you enter your body again. All the people [K"xau`s people, the !Kung] who have stayed behind waiting for you – they fear you. Friend, they are afraid of you. You enter, enter, enter the earth, and then you return to enter … the skin of your body. … And you say "he-e-e-e!" [K"xau makes the trembling moan of those who have 'died' in trance and returned]. That is the sound of your return to your body. … Friend, this is what it does, this *n/um* [medicine, healing power] that I do, this *n/um* here that I dance. [141]

Evolution`s gift to metaphor

In their fundamental outlook our ancestors, distant and not so distant, inhabited a static world governed by the unchanging lore of *their* ancestors, their gods and their rituals – a world we might still inhabit ourselves were it not, as Goodman had lamented, that man is fallen. And we are well and truly fallen, into the moving shadows of the world of change, into the irreversible flow of history and, above all, into the knowledge that we are responsible for the choices we make in life and for their consequences. These three varieties of Fall are all metaphorical aspects of one factual reality, the evolution of human consciousness. Over the millennia, we have turned fact into metaphor as a way of trying to explain consciousness to ourselves and find an accommodation with it, an attempt that has produced a lot of very rich verbal imagery. Some of the richest circles round and round the same nagging problem: if, as Plato's Fall warns us, we can never know anything for certain in this world, what basis do we have for making our choices, let alone taking responsibility for them? It is the problem of uncertain knowing.

The biblical metaphor for uncertain knowing turns on the difference between the representation or image of something and the thing itself (which immediately recalls Plato's distinction between likenesses and perfect forms). In the Authorized Version, the famous lines of Paul's First Epistle to the Corinthians read:

> 8 Charity never faileth: but whether *there be* prophecies, they shall fail; whether *there be* tongues, they shall cease; whether *there be* knowledge, it shall vanish away.
>
> 9 For we know in part, and we prophesy in part.
>
> 10 But when that which is perfect is come, then that which is in part shall be done away.
>
> 11 When I was a child, I spake as a child, I understood as a child, I thought as a child: but when I became a man, I put away childish things.
>
> 12 For now we see through a glass, darkly; but then face to face: now I know in part; but then shall I know even as also I am known.

The connotations of the English word 'glass' have changed since the seventeenth century but there is no doubt that St Paul's image is of a looking glass or mirror. His meaning is unambiguous in the Second Wycliffite Version, dating from about 1395, which reads:

> 12 And we seen now bi a myrour in derknesse, but thanne face to face; now I knowe of parti, but thanne I schal knowe, as I am knowun. [142]

'Then', in heaven, we shall know God and His works with perfect, unimpeded vision. But 'now', here on earth, what we know we can know only as an obscure reflection in a mirror, not directly, and that in part, not whole. Never whole. In this life we cannot hope for more than an approximate and *incomplete* knowledge of anything. It drives us to distraction, for how are we expected to exercise our free will, choose this rather than that, when we have no certain way of knowing whether this is better than that? It is all a matter of interpretation, and not only do our interpretations often differ from those of other people, our own interpretations may change from day to day and even from moment to moment. St Paul's mirror condemns us to a lifetime of unrelieved doubt.

Unrelieved doubt suffuses Franz Kafka's novel *The Castle*. One of the story's surreal motifs is the coming and going of letters and messages between the Castle up on the hill and the village down below. They appear to be of crucial importance as the means of attempted communication between K., the central character, and Klamm, the mysterious Castle official who exerts power over every aspect of K.'s life. But at the same time it seems that, if the letters ever reach the Castle at all, they are likely to lie disregarded among the piles of documents already gathering dust under some clerk's desk. What value, if any, attaches to them? There comes a point where K., worn down by his failure to communicate meaningfully with Klamm (still less to meet him face to face, which K. claims to be his aim), rounds on the messenger, Barnabas, and on Barnabas's sisters, Amalia and Olga. 'You've all been playing with me,' K. complains to Olga, accusing the sisters of indifference. Olga retorts that they have been at pains to avoid giving an impression either of overestimating or of underestimating the importance of K.'s missives, for fear he would misunderstand their motives. She ends her convoluted explanation as follows:

> And to hold the mean, without exaggeration on either side, in other words to estimate the just value of those letters, is impossible, they themselves change in value

> perpetually, the reflections they give rise to are endless, and chance determines where one stops reflecting, and so even our estimate of them is a matter of chance. [143]

Das Schloss, the German-language original of *The Castle*, was published in 1926, the year before Heisenberg first formulated his quantum uncertainty relations and before the Como conference (my page 11) at which Bohr spoke of the practical difficulty of describing experiments in which, by the nature of complementary phenomena, the act of observing an object changes its behaviour. In a quantum laboratory, the information about a subatomic particle knowable at any one time is defined by the experimental arrangements that the observer chooses to make – or, in the sense that the observer might equally well choose a different arrangement, chances to make. In Kafka's fictional world, the value of a message is defined by the estimation that the messenger, the recipient and (presumably) the sender choose or chance to put upon it. In short, what Kafka's world and the laboratory have in common is that *chance determines where one stops reflecting or arranging*. It is as if Kafka had picked up on something that was in the air and, imaginatively anticipating Heisenberg and Bohr, got in first with his metaphor for the impossibility of disentangling our knowledge of the world from our subjective and arbitrary grasp of it. [144]

In a decade of metaphorical proliferation, Kafka himself was beaten to it by the Japanese writer Ryūnosuke Akutagawa, whose short story *Yabu no naka* (*In a Grove*) first appeared in 1922. It is built around a few seemingly straightforward and objectively knowable facts about a crime: a samurai and his wife, travelling together, have been lured into a grove of bamboo and cedar by the brigand Tajōmaru; the wife has been raped; the samurai is dead. We are presented with seven different testimonies by seven different witnesses, including Tajōmaru, the wife, and the dead samurai speaking through a medium. We never learn what happened in the grove. Least of all do we learn how the samurai died, for Tajōmaru claims that he killed him in a duel (in which, Tajōmaru concedes, the samurai put up a good fight) demanded by the dishonoured wife, the wife claims that she killed her husband (still helplessly tied to a tree according to her) as part of an intended suicide pact, and the samurai claims that he killed himself in scornful rage at his wife's behaviour (offering to leave with Tajōmaru and inciting him to murder) following the rape. As one essayist has put it, 'All that is common to these mutually contradictory accounts is each character's self-centred wish to justify himself or herself. There is no way for us to know which version is true or even closest to the truth....' [145] Under the title *Rashōmon*, Akutagawa's story was filmed by Akira Kurosawa in 1950, barely two years after the end of the Tokyo war crimes trial, at which an international tribunal of eleven judges had heard the testimonies of more than four hundred witnesses and produced, in effect, six different results – an official verdict of guilt against all the 'Class A' defendants and five qualifying or dissenting opinions issued separately by individual judges. Of the twenty-eight 'Class A' defendants (former Japanese political and military leaders charged with 'crimes against peace'), seven were sentenced to death and sixteen to life imprisonment. The most remarkable of the separate opinions was that submitted by Radhabinod Pal of India, one of only three Asian justices on the tribunal, which by word count was probably longer than the official judgement itself and robustly dissented from it. While Pal did not deny the reality of the atrocities committed by Japanese forces, he did deny the judicial basis on which the defendants had been held responsible for such war crimes. Denouncing the 'so-called trial held according to the definition of crime now given by the victors' as an exercise in 'formalized vengeance', he also implicitly questioned why the atomic bombings of Hiroshima and Nagasaki were not the subject of a war crimes tribunal: 'if any indiscriminate destruction of civilian life and property is still illegitimate in warfare,' Pal wrote, 'then, in the Pacific war, [the] decision to use the atom bomb is the only near approach to the directives of the German Emperor during the first world war and of the Nazi leaders during the second world war.' [146]

Uncertain knowing: light enough to see by, and never enough

Akutagawa's tangled and murky grove is a powerful metaphor for uncertain knowing: this is the nature of perception and misperception, it says, and yet without suggesting how we could or should accommodate ourselves to it. It has no response, no remedy to offer.

St Paul's metaphor, by contrast, does suggest a response and a remedy: *try harder.* Precisely because the images in the glass are so indistinct and fragmented, we must try all the harder to understand them. Every one of the images means something, and they mean something because they are images of God's works and purposes. While we may be condemned to a lifetime of doubt, it need not be unrelieved doubt if we believe that the uncertainties of this world are, like time and change, safely contained within some great plan of God's. Our perfect vision will have to wait until the next life but, as John Donne, Dean of St Paul's Cathedral, preached in his sermon on Easter Day in 1628, even in this world we have mirrors enough and light enough by which to know that God exists. The mirrors are all around us and the light is the light of our own reason:

> For our sight of God here, our theatre, the place where we sit and see him, is the whole world, the whole house and frame of nature, and our medium, our glass, is the book of creatures, and our light, by which we see him, is the light of natural reason. ……
>
> There is not so poor a creature but may be the glass to see God in. The greatest flat glass that can be made cannot represent anything greater than it is. If every gnat that flies were an archangel, all that could but tell me that there is a God; and the poorest worm that creeps tells me that. If I should ask the basilisk, how camest thou by those killing eyes? he would tell me, thy God made me so; and if I should ask the slow-worm, how camest thou to be without eyes? he would tell me, thy God made me so. The cedar is no better a glass to see God in than the hyssop upon the wall; all things that are, are equally removed from being nothing; and whatsoever hath any being is by that very being a glass in which to see God, who is the root and the fountain of all being. [147]

In John Milton's prose tract *Of Education*, first published in 1644, the contemplation of creation becomes the model for a strenuous educational regime. The end of learning, Milton insists, is

> to repair the ruins of our first parents by regaining to know God aright, and out of that knowledge to love him, to imitate him, to be like him, as we may the nearest, by possessing our souls of true virtue, which, being united to the heavenly grace of faith, makes up the highest perfection. But because our understanding cannot in this body found itself but on sensible things, nor arrive so clearly to the knowledge of God and things invisible as by orderly conning over the visible and inferior creature, the same method is necessarily to be followed in all discreet teaching. [148]

Written during the first phase of England's civil war, that 'dangerous fit of the commonwealth',[149] Milton's programme of educational reforms would produce a better world, or rather, a better class of gentlemen to govern the world. Lawyers, for example, would ground their purposes on 'the prudent and heavenly contemplation of justice and equity' and not, as their usual education encouraged, on the 'promising and pleasing thoughts of litigious terms, fat contentions, and flowing fees', while politicians would be 'steadfast pillars of the state' and not 'such poor shaken uncertain reeds, of such a tottering conscience as many of our great councillors have lately shown themselves'. [150] But the radical aim of Milton's programme is, as he says, to 'repair the ruins of our first parents' – *to undo the Fall* – by reverting to the state of knowledge that Adam and Eve had possessed until they ate the forbidden fruit. The state that Milton envisages is not one of abject and passive obedience to God; more subtly and more ambiguously, we would still have free will but a constrained, yes/no-answer sort of free will (which, as Goodman had put it, would allow us to 'pass judgement and censure' without busying our minds to make things 'intelligible' to ourselves). After all, there had been no problem when God brought the beasts of the field to Adam to see what he would call them, for Adam had chosen his names for the beasts in the 'pure light of natural knowledge' (Francis Bacon's expression for a state of knowledge in which Milton likewise believed [151]). The problem only began when

Adam and Eve were (Bacon again) 'allured with appetite of light and liberty of knowledge' and tempted by 'an aspiring desire to attain to that part of moral knowledge which defineth of good and evil, whereby to dispute God's commandments and not to depend upon the revelation of his will'.[152] It was the temptation of 'moral' knowledge, knowledge appropriate only to God, that had given rise to the Fall. Hence a return to 'natural' knowledge, the knowledge appropriate to man, would both enable us to regain to know God aright and regain to know ourselves aright.

All this contemplation of creation in the mirror, all this orderly conning to restore man's relation with God and make a better world, would have been a lifetime vocation even for the most pious of Milton's scholar-gentlemen.[153] So what hope is there for the rest of us? We lack both the religious faith and the rigour of the Puritan conscience, and most of us are fully occupied with the concerns of our own lives. The whole business of regaining to know anything aright is far too much like hard work, and besides the idea that there is some state in which our free will operates within 'natural' bounds bears no relation to our everyday experience. Before the Fall Adam was called upon, once, to assign names to a bestiary of animals. But we, from day to day and moment to moment, are called upon to make all sorts of choices, one decision over another, one thing over another, one action over another. And while there are no constraints on the demands made on our free will, there *are* constraints on the knowledge, the knowing, on which we have to base our choices. Lacking the faith and discipline of Donne or Bacon or Milton, we lack the wherewithal and even the inclination to try harder. The mirrors are as dim as ever. We are defeated. Because we will never know enough to choose with absolute certainty between all the alternatives before us, our capacity for free will is worse than useless, a curse, and we want none of it.

If it is our failing to want to be rid of free will, it is, according to Fyodor Dostoyevsky's Grand Inquisitor, Jesus's failing to have overlooked or forgotten this irredeemable weakness in the humanity He would redeem. Jesus has come down to earth, in Seville, the day after almost one hundred heretics have been burnt in a magnificent *auto-da-fé*. Arrested after miraculously raising a child from the dead, the son of God now faces his accuser, the Grand Inquisitor, who explains with impeccable reasoning why He will have to be put to death all over again. And one of the reasons is that He will not recognize, as the church is only too ready to recognize, the true nature of the bread that humanity craves – the familiar earthly kind and not the baffling bread of heaven that Jesus offers. 'I tell you,' the Grand Inquisitor says to Jesus,

> man has no more agonizing anxiety than to find someone to whom he can hand over with all speed the gift of freedom with which the unhappy creature is born. But only he can gain possession of men's freedom who is able to set their conscience at ease. With the bread you were given an incontestable banner: give him bread and man will worship you, for there is nothing more incontestable than bread; but if at the same time someone besides yourself should gain possession of his conscience – oh, then he will even throw away your bread and follow him who has ensnared his conscience. You were right about that. For the mystery of human life is not only in living, but in knowing why one lives. Without a clear idea of what to live for man will not consent to live and will rather destroy himself than remain on the earth, though he were surrounded by loaves of bread. That is so, but what became of it? Instead of gaining possession of men's freedom, you gave them greater freedom than ever! Or did you forget that a tranquil mind and even death is dearer to man than the free choice in the knowledge of good and evil? There is nothing more alluring to man than this freedom of conscience, but there is nothing more tormenting, either. And instead of firm foundations for appeasing man's conscience once and for all, you chose everything that was exceptional, enigmatic, and vague, you chose everything that was beyond the strength of men, acting, consequently, as though you did not love them at all – you who came to give your life for them! Instead of taking possession of men's freedom you multiplied it and burdened the spiritual kingdom of man with its sufferings for ever. You wanted man's free love so that he should follow you freely, fascinated and

> captivated by you. Instead of the strict ancient law, man had in future to decide for himself with a free heart what is good and what is evil, having only your image before him for guidance. But did it never occur to you that he would at last reject and call in question even your image and your truth, if he were weighed down by so fearful a burden as freedom of choice?[154]

According to Milton, the end of education is to reverse the Fall. According to Kafka, the end of every human activity is not so much to reverse the Fall as to *postpone* it, to pretend that our knowledge of the difference between good and evil still awaits us in the future:

> Since the Fall we have been essentially equal in our capacity to know Good and Evil; and yet it is precisely here that we seek to outdo our fellows. But it is only on the far side of this knowledge that the real differences begin. That the opposite should appear to be the case is due to the following: No one can be content with knowledge alone, but must strive to act in accordance with it. But he is not endowed with the strength to do this, hence he must destroy himself, even at the risk of not acquiring the necessary strength that way either, but nothing else remains for him save this last attempt. (This is also the meaning of the threat of death associated with the ban on eating from the Tree of Knowledge; perhaps this is also the original meaning of natural death.) Now this is an attempt he is afraid to make; he would rather annul the knowledge of Good and Evil (the term 'the Fall' has its origin in this fear); but what has once happened cannot be annulled, it can only be blurred. It is for this purpose that the justifications arise. The whole world is full of them, indeed the whole visible world is perhaps no more nor less than the self-justification of man in his wish to find a moment of peace. An attempt to distort the fact that knowledge is already given, to make knowledge a goal still to be reached.[155]

There is a profound truth in Kafka's observation that knowledge is inseparable from action. We pretend that knowledge is a goal still to be achieved and, as if the images in the mirror were not blurred and uncertain enough, we blur them ourselves, because we would have to act on our knowledge. Whether or not we make a donation to a particular charity, for example, comes down to a decision whether or not to allow our knowledge of a particular suffering, cruelty or injustice to turn into action. Do we, as the Salvation Army appeal bluntly invites us, 'Give a damn' or do we, as an equally expressive Japanese phrase has it, 'make a face that does not know'? [156] I am not suggesting, of course, that we should donate to every good cause we are aware of: for practical reasons we cannot and we just have to hope that others will support the causes we do not. My point – and it is principally a reproach to myself – is that for every occasion when we choose to respond to a good cause, there are dozens of occasions when we choose to cross the street, turn the page or switch off the radio before the appeal can get to us. And we do that not (or not necessarily) because we are heartless or stingy or prone to chronic 'compassion fatigue' but because we sense, acutely, that too much awareness of suffering, cruelty and injustice will overwhelm us. Do something. Do something. We feel personally threatened in the little bubble of our familiar realities and preoccupations and so what many of us do, I suspect, is to forestall action by blotting out the knowledge that would demand action. Something analogous happens at the collective level, for there are occasions when the whole world, or the world represented by the United Nations and other international institutions, clings to its moment of peace even in the full knowledge of egregious man-made horrors. The international community is confronted with evidence of genocide, ethnic cleansing and other extreme abuses of human rights on an almost daily basis. Moreover, grounds for acting on such evidence are provided by the doctrine of humanitarian intervention, according to which some abuses are so exceptionally bad that the need to stop them, if necessary by applying force against the state that perpetrates or permits them, should override the normally sacrosanct principles of national sovereignty and territorial integrity. But what makes an abuse so bad that it justifies armed intervention from outside? [157] In 1999 the North Atlantic Treaty Organization went to war for the first time in its history to protect the ethnic Albanian population in Kosovo, former Yugoslavia, but there was no comparable intervention at the height of the ethnic-political violence in Darfur, western Sudan, where an estimated three hundred thousand people have died since 2003.[158] In what way is the mass murder of a population in Africa less exceptionally bad than the mass murder of a population in Europe? By choosing to intervene in some situations and not others the international community invites accusations of arbitrary behaviour and hypocrisy, which matters because it plays into the hands of those who reject humanitarian intervention and maintain that national sovereignty and territorial integrity must remain paramount under all circumstances, without exception. And that matters because a consistency of inaction is no improvement on an inconsistency of action.

Uncertain knowing: two ideas of history

What follows is a first-hand account of uncertain knowing which captures one of the strangest manifestations of the condition: the tendency to experience the world through, and sometimes confuse it with, a personal or parallel configuration of reality. 'I grew up with two ideas of history,' writes V.S. Naipaul of his childhood in the Indian community in Trinidad, 'almost two ideas of time.'

> There was history with dates. That kind of history affected people and places abroad, and my range was wide: ancient Rome … ; nineteenth-century England; the nationalist movement in India.
>
> But Chaguanas, where I was born, in an Indian-style house my grandfather had built, had no dates. If I read in a book that Gandhi had made his first call for civil disobedience in India in 1919, that date seemed recent. But 1919, in Chaguanas, in the life of the Indian community, was almost unimaginable. It was a time beyond recall, mythical. About our family, the migration of our ancestors from India, I knew only what I knew or what I was told. Beyond (and sometimes even within) people's memories was

> undated time, historical darkness. Out of that darkness (extending to place as well as to time) we had all come. The India where Gandhi and Nehru and the others operated was historical and real. The India from which we had come was impossibly remote, almost as imaginary as the land of the *Ramayana*, our Hindu epic. I lived easily with that darkness, that lack of knowledge. I never thought to inquire further. [159]

In 1962, after a year in India, Naipaul reluctantly visited his grandfather's village in Uttar Pradesh. 'I wasn't prepared for the disturbance I felt,' he recalls, 'turning off from the India where I had been a traveller, and driving in a government jeep along a straight, dusty road to another, very private world. Two ideas of history came together during that short drive, two ways of thinking about myself.'

> And there I discovered that to my grandfather this village – the pond, the big trees he would have remembered, the brick dwellings with their enclosed courtyards (unlike the adobe and thatch of Trinidad Indian villages), the fields in the flat land, the immense sky, the white shrines – his village was the real place. Trinidad was the interlude, the illusion. [160]

It is easy to read the story of Naipaul's grandfather at arm's length, almost as an ethnographic study of 'archaic man' defending himself against change and the meaninglessness of 'profane' time. The truth, however, is more complicated: it is that we all carry our own world, an individual and sometimes unfathomable 'real place', within us. In its most extreme configurations it may be a place of psychosis or other mental derangements, but such labels do not apply, I think, to the sort of 'real place' represented by the grandfather's Uttar Pradesh village. Although for him that village denied the existence of the geographical and historical place, Trinidad, where he was physically present, and we might call that illusion or even delusion, I doubt we would call it madness. Because his sense of reality had remained in India, he had never brought Trinidad and Uttar Pradesh together; and yet, on the evidence of his grandson's memoir, he does not seem to have been troubled by any need to bring the two together. He lived two realities, simultaneously and without contradiction. But some 'real places' cannot be lived simultaneously with the reality of the here and now, or not without contradictions and pernicious effects, as I can vouch from personal experience. To the extent that my 'real place' could be located on a map at all, it would be Tonga, a scattered group of Pacific islands I have never visited and probably never will, so obscure that many people will have no idea where it is and no interest in knowing – not a bad metaphor for the refuge of the mind from which I have sallied, and to which I have retreated, ever since childhood. The obvious images, of palm-fringed silver sands, emerald lagoons and dusky Polynesian maidens in grass skirts, have always appealed in an inconsequential, daydreaming fashion. But in my mind there is also a consequential image of Tonga, of its pink, gilt-edged, island-shaped postage stamps, which were quite unlike anything else in my album. It is a pernicious association, for it seems that long ago something in me reduced all the lushness, life and exotic possibility of a South Pacific paradise into a few beautiful but inert shapes of coloured paper that I could classify and file away under 'T' for Tonga, between 'T' for Togo and 'T' for Trinidad and Tobago. And it has to be significant that in adult life as in juvenile stamp-collecting the reality of my Tonga, my 'real place', has often asserted itself in exactly this process of turning living content, exotic and otherwise, into lifeless form and system.

Sometimes it appears not to matter if inner reality and outer reality never meet. Sometimes it does matter, demonstrably. But Naipaul's account of his own visit to India suggests a third possibility, and a new permutation of uncertain knowing: sometimes we cannot tell whether it is better to bring the two realities together *or to keep them apart*. Naipaul had already written about his grandfather's village in one short chapter ('The Village of the Dubes') of *An Area of Darkness*. That earlier book chronicles Naipaul's quest, messy, at times overwrought and ultimately inconclusive, to open up the semi-mythical India of his childhood ('the India of my fantasy', 'an area of the imagination', and the 'area of darkness' of the title [161]) to the historical India of his visit. From the raw discomfiture that Naipaul describes, we are left feeling that a quest such as his may be a confusion of purpose, that two ideas of history and two ways of thinking about oneself cannot and should not come together. Like Plato's forms and their moving shadows, perhaps they are not just two different realities but two different orders of reality. And in Naipaul's case, which would be which? Historical India the form and Naipaul's India of the imagination the shadow? Or vice versa?

The secret of brute matter

There is a consciousness-creation myth in *Being and Nothingness*, too. It is not explicitly stated but arises incidentally from Sartre's attempt to describe and explain the relations between two fundamentally different dimensions of being: being-for-itself (*l'être-pour-soi*) or, more concisely, the for-itself (*le pour-soi*); and being-in-itself (*l'être-en-soi*) or the in-itself (*l'en-soi*). In plain language, being-for-itself/the for-itself are synonyms for man or, more specifically, human consciousness, about which we have already said a great deal. Being-in-itself/the in-itself, by contrast, are synonyms for inanimate objects and other non-conscious things – the primeval matter of Sartre's creation myth.

In his introduction, Sartre describes being-in-itself (which generally he abbreviates to 'the in-itself' but here, confusingly, abbreviates simply to 'being') as having three characteristics: 'being is in itself'; 'being is what it is'; and 'being is'.[162] To say that 'being is in itself' is to say that, unlike the for-itself, consciousness, which is always 'at a distance from itself' (page 47 above), the in-itself is perfectly identified with itself, 'an immanence which can not realize itself, an affirmation which can not affirm itself, an activity which can not act, because it is glued to itself [*parce qu'il s'est empâté de soi-même*].' By 'being is what it is' Sartre means (among other meanings) that the in-itself is inertly, lumpishly and statically present in the world. 'The in-itself has nothing secret; it is *solid* [*massif*],' he says and then, in terms reminiscent of Plato, continues:

> Transition, becoming, anything which permits us to say that [the in-itself] is not yet what it will be and that it is already what it is not – all that is forbidden on principle. … It knows no otherness; it never posits itself as *other-than-another-being*. It can support no

> connection with the other. It is itself indefinitely and it exhausts itself in being. [163]

Lastly, 'being is' expresses the *contingency* of the in-itself, which 'can neither be derived from the possible nor reduced to the necessary' – in other words, which happens to exist but might well not have existed because no necessity says it should exist, while 'the possible' is associated exclusively with the for-itself (and, as we have seen, the free choices the for-itself makes as it projects itself into its own future). The in-itself is *just there* without any reason for its being or connection with other things, meaningless, '*de trop* [superfluous] for eternity'.

Sartre conjures up the characteristics of the in-itself most forcefully – and most surreally – in his novel *Nausea*, which predates *Being and Nothingness* by five years. The novel takes its title from the nauseous disgust that comes upon its narrator-diarist, Antoine Roquentin, as he progressively discovers the brute existence of things. One of his discoveries is that things cannot be captured or contained by generalizing them, as we habitually try to do, into functions or categories (such as 'useful' and 'not useful') and that, stripped of their labels, things fragment into an infinity of unconnected, ungraspable and obstinately *particular* existences. [164] 'Things have broken free from their names,' Roquentin writes, recalling the red plush ('thousands of little red paws in the air, all stiff, little dead paws') of a tram-seat. 'They are there, grotesque, stubborn, gigantic, and it seems ridiculous to call them seats or say anything at all about them.' [165] Sitting on a bench in the park, he is fascinated and horrified by the root of a chestnut tree, which he finds he cannot pin down by repeating '"It is a root" … [because] you could not pass from its function as a root, as a suction-pump, *to that*, to that hard, compact sea-lion skin, to that oily, horny, stubborn look.' [166] Suddenly he notices that the top of the tree has started to sway and he is relieved because movements, as he says to himself, '"never quite exist, they are transitions, intermediaries between two existences, unaccented beats"' and at last he is going to 'surprise existences in the process of being born.' But his hopes are immediately dashed, for the idea of transition is one of man's inventions:

> All those tiny agitations cut themselves off, set themselves up on their own. They overflowed the branches and boughs everywhere. They whirled

> about those dry hands, enveloping them in tiny cyclones. Admittedly a movement was something different from a tree. But it was still an absolute. A thing. My eyes never met anything but repletion. There were swarms of existences at the ends of the branches, existences which constantly renewed themselves and were never born. The existing wind came and settled on the tree like a big fly; and the tree shivered. But the shiver was not a nascent quality, a transition from the potential to the act; it was a thing; a thing-shiver [*une chose-frisson*] flowed into the tree, took possession of it, shook it, and suddenly abandoned it, going further on to spin around by itself. Everything was full, everything was active, there was no unaccented beat, everything, even the most imperceptible movement, was made of existence. [167]

Filled with and glued to itself, the in-itself seems indeed to have nothing secret about it. But the point of Sartre's implied creation myth is that, anthropomorphically speaking, the in-itself *does* have a secret: it wants to 'found itself' and 'remove contingency from its being' [168] – in short, to justify its own existence. And to do that it has to 'recover' [169] itself as a for-itself, consciousness, because consciousness is uniquely 'at a distance' both from itself and from the brute existence of things and therefore uniquely capable of being aware of things and of providing reasons for their existence. A lump of inert matter perfectly identified with itself is not in a mode to be aware of anything, still less to find reasons for its own existence. 'It is only by making itself for-itself,' Sartre says, that the in-itself 'can aspire to be the cause of itself.' [170] It is only in relation to consciousness that, for example, meaningless fragments of wood and metal and fabric can 'become' a tram-seat and, for as long as the label will stick, have the unity, function and meaning of a tram-seat. [171] Sartre is not claiming that things would have no being or reality in the absence of consciousness – on the contrary, he asserts the 'ontological primacy of the in-itself over the for-itself' [172] – but he is claiming that it is through consciousness alone that things can remove the contingency of their unconnected, self-contained and 'superfluous' existences.

There is nothing very logical about Sartre's account of the origin of consciousness because, even if the in-itself does want reasons for its existence, there is no reason *why* it should want them. Its desire for reasons is as arbitrary and contingent as the contingency from which it seeks to escape. Sartre evades the issue by a verbal sleight of hand, it seems to me,[173] but in any case a bit of illogicality is hardly a problem if we regard his creation story as mythical. Quite the reverse, we find ourselves warming to this in-itself with its muddle-headed ambitions, which surely get it into far more trouble than it has bargained for. We can tell that trouble is on the way because Sartre's imagery, in common with the biblical imagery, is of rending and loss. He refers to 'a rupture in the identity-of-being' of the in-itself, which tries to rid itself of contingency by 'degenerating' into a for-itself, 'losing itself as in-itself in order to found itself as consciousness'.[174] Sartre himself almost waxes biblical when he speaks of this as a 'fall of the in-itself toward the self, the fall by which the for-itself is constituted'.[175] As for the trouble that ensues, we are familiar by now with the unconditional, 'anguished' freedom to which individual consciousnesses are condemned. Yet with consciousness comes something else that has consequences beyond the realm of our individual realities: a capacity to conceive of things and the world in general as other than they are, or *as they are not*. This capacity for negation comes from consciousness (itself synonymous with nothingness, remember) via man's imagination and his fundamental attitude of asking questions, for a question is a sort of expectation, which may be disappointed by the answer 'no' as well as satisfied by a 'yes'. Moreover, Sartre argues, it is a mistake to assume that we can only address questions to other human beings, because the same capacity enables us to question non-conscious beings and to discover what they are not (including, crucially, that they are not us and we are not them – not a tram-seat, not a tree, not any *thing*[176]). 'If my watch stops,' says Sartre, 'I can question the watchmaker about the cause of the stopping, but it is the various mechanisms of the watch that the watchmaker will in turn question.'[177] Examining the mechanisms, the watchmaker may confirm that the watch is *not working* or 'broken'. But because a 'broken' watch only has meaning in relation to the human expectation of a working watch, we have to say that this 'brokenness' has been brought to the watch – and to the world – through the attitude of questioning, without which the watch would still just be an arrangement of components each filled and identified with itself. Although in this sense it enters the world *through* consciousness, 'brokenness' nevertheless has a negative reality that is independent of consciousness's awareness and knowledge of it because, like 'destruction', 'brokenness' is 'an *objective fact* and not a thought'.[178] It is on the subject of 'destruction', I feel, Sartre suggests most persuasively that the very nature of the world has been radically and irrevocably changed by the coming of negation. 'In order for destruction to exist,' Sartre says, 'there must be first a relation of man to being … and within the limits of this relation, it is necessary that man apprehend one being as destructible.' No destruction can be 'accomplished' without such a relation:

> A geological plication, a storm do not destroy – or at least they do not destroy *directly*; they merely modify the distribution of masses of beings. There is no *less* after the storm than before. There is *something else*. Even this expression is improper, for to posit otherness there must be a witness who can retain the past in some manner and compare it to the present in the form of *no longer*. In the absence of this witness, there is being before as after the storm – that is all. [179]

It is conventional to blame man for war, genocide, environmental plundering and his innumerable other acts of direct destruction. But Sartre adds a stranger and, in a metaphysical or mythological sense, more fundamental charge to the indictment: even if man had never *acted* destructively himself, he would still have introduced destruction into the world by apprehending the *meaning* 'destruction', which otherwise would have remained unapprehended. Earthquakes, volcanic eruptions, floods, hurricanes – in the absence of human consciousness, the most violent of natural events would not be 'destruction' but merely a redistribution of matter and a rearrangement of being. [180]

So far, so bad. It gets worse, as we can't help noticing that there is a curious symmetry in Sartre's consciousness-creation myth. Whereas the in-itself, driven by its urge to cast off contingency, moves in the direction of consciousness, for its part consciousness seems compelled to go in the opposite direction – *back towards the brute existence of things*. In *Being and Nothingness* there are many instances of consciousness's contrary motion and their common denominator is that they are also instances of bad faith: not, or not only, the 'spirit of seriousness' (my pages 50-51 above) but the even cruder bad faith of attempting to revert to thingness. Take Sartre's celebrated café waiter, who displays this variety of bad faith in his mechanical, game-like behaviour serving the customers:

> His movement is quick and forward, a little too precise, a little too rapid. He comes toward the patrons with a step a little too quick. He bends forward a little too eagerly; his voice, his eyes express an interest a little too solicitous for the order of the customer. Finally there he returns, trying to imitate in his walk the inflexible stiffness of some kind of automaton while carrying his tray with the recklessness of a tight-rope-walker by putting it in a perpetually unstable, perpetually broken equilibrium which he perpetually reestablishes by a light movement of the arm and hand. … He applies himself to chaining his movements as if they were mechanisms, the one regulating the other; his gestures and even his voice seem to be mechanisms; he gives himself the quickness and pitiless rapidity of things.[181]

There is no mystery about the man's behaviour: what he is trying to realize is 'a being-in-itself of the café waiter' and a denial of the reality that, through his own free choices, he alone confers value and urgency upon his work as a waiter. Likewise the soldier at attention:

> [He] makes himself into a soldier-thing with a direct regard which does not see at all, which is no longer meant to see, since it is the rule and not the interest of the moment which determines the point he must fix his eyes on (the sight "fixed at ten paces"). There are indeed many precautions to imprison a man in what he is, as if we lived in perpetual fear that he might escape from it, that he might break away and suddenly elude his condition.[182]

Or take the young woman on a date. Well aware that her companion has a sexual intent, which she both welcomes and does not welcome, she first 'disarms' *his* words and actions by turning them into things with objective qualities, so that he appears to her 'sincere and respectful as the table is round or square'. She is perplexed when he takes her hand, for this action now obliges her to choose between accepting the sexual nature of his approach or rejecting it: in bad faith she evades the choice by leaving her hand where it is, 'inert between the warm hands of her companion – neither consenting nor resisting – a thing'. [183]

In the beginning was inanimate matter. But inanimate matter, in an urge to justify its own existence, ruptured the perfect identity of itself with itself and fell into consciousness. Consciousness, finding that *it* was not identified with itself or with anything else in the world, was overwhelmed by intolerable anguish and, in bad faith, sought to renounce its perfect freedom by falling back into inanimateness. Now we see it: Sartre's story does not just invite comparison with the biblical Fall, it *rewrites* the Fall. Perhaps it is a matter of taste whether we prefer his retelling to the original of Genesis. Personally I do and I think that of these two consciousness-creation myths Sartre's offers the more plausible explanation for the ambivalence of consciousness. Genesis has the advantage of brevity – eighty taut verses to Sartre's rambling six hundred pages – and, for English-speakers, the incomparably beautiful language of the King James Version. Yet it is cluttered with the baggage of Christian dogma. 'Original sin' is a myth within a myth, a doctrinal myth within the biblical myth: man is not *inherently* 'wicked', he *makes* himself 'wicked' by what he chooses to do or not do. And because Christian dogma gets the diagnosis wrong, it gets the remedy wrong, too. The remedy, it says, is to acknowledge our guilt by association with the primal sin of Adam and Eve, and to repent and mend our ways. But because the primal sin is represented as an act disobedience, mending our ways tends to mean avoiding further disobedience and does not confront the real issue. The real issue is that consciousness, once acquired, cannot be unacquired or, as Kafka put it (page 79), 'what has once happened cannot be annulled, it can only be blurred'. God has expelled Adam and Eve from the Garden but He has not expelled consciousness from their minds, so Christian dogma, most obviously in its Old Testament manifestation, does the next best thing of trying to reimpose obedience by decree: do this, do that, don't do the other. We have to make allowance for the fact that the Ten Commandments derive from old tribal injunctions concerned principally with enforcing respect for authority (invested in one God, not many gods), ritual (including refraining from work every seventh day in imitation of the creator's day of rest) and property (hierarchically ranked in importance, with wives above servants and livestock but below real estate: 'Thou shalt not covet thy neighbour's house, thou shalt not covet thy neighbour's wife …' [184]). Nevertheless, however much we make allowance for its historical and cultural origins, this remains a dogma that expects unquestioning submission or, as Sartre might say, that strews tasks and obligations along our way, all mute demands requiring our passive obedience.

In its milder New Testament guise, Christian dogma is less clear-cut. Whereas Old Testament commandments depend for their effectiveness on enforcement by diktat, the Gospels seem to appeal to individual conscience and invite a voluntary response from within. 'Thou shalt not' has given way to parables and persuasion by example: as the Grand Inquisitor accuses Jesus, 'Instead of the strict ancient law, man had in future to decide for himself with a free heart what is good and what is evil' (page 79). Is it just my imagination, or has the New Testament broken with the Old so radically that it credits man with a capacity to evaluate and understand for himself what is 'good' and what is 'bad'? If so, it implicitly acknowledges the existence of man's consciousness, for there can be no such capacity and no individual conscience without consciousness. It is as if the New Testament is signalling that it wants a new accommodation with consciousness, no longer simply to suppress it as the unforgivable consequence of an act of disobedience. Even though Bacon, Milton and others interpret this as meaning only that we should revert to the conditional and constrained free will of our prelapsarian state of 'natural knowledge', it looks a very promising signal. Moreover, New Testament precepts have moved far beyond narrow tribal concerns: in place of prohibitions on graven images and the coveting of oxen, we find tolerance, compassion, peaceableness – among our most cherished ideals now but, the Old Testament suggests, principles that would have been regarded as weak and dangerous at the time of Moses. In Sartre's terms, as we know, to subscribe to religious and ethical precepts of any quality, weak or ideal, is to be guilty of the 'spirit of seriousness' because they come from a body of values not of our own making. And yet surely I am not alone in thinking that New Testament values are exactly the sort of values we would all hope to arrive at independently, and in good faith, through our own free choices and actions. To hope thus, of course, is itself to be guilty of bad faith, for it implies that the values we choose can have a consistent, moral tendency, whereas to be in existential good faith we must make them up spontaneously from moment to moment. But at this point we start to look for ways of bending Sartre's rules: how could even he object to values that are undeniably 'good', regardless of the historical and religious context from which they have come? We can't resist the temptation to exempt New Testament values from the charge of the 'spirit of seriousness'. Although heretical in Sartre's terms, this is promising.

Or is it? Etymologically, 'gospel' means 'good news' and Christianity's good news is the promise of salvation – salvation, that is, from our own wicked thoughts and deeds. But having seemed to credit us with a capacity for discriminating 'good' from 'bad' and therefore, we might expect, with a capacity for saving ourselves by freely choosing between the two, the Gospels take all that back and insist that salvation can only come *to* us, not *from* us. We cannot hope to save ourselves, only to *be saved* by faith, and faith not in the content of the Gospel message but in the authority of the messenger (the son of God, no less, with miraculous powers to prove it), a Redeemer who has allowed Himself to be ritually sacrificed on our behalf. The Grand Inquisitor's accusation only tells half the story because, while Jesus is content that we follow Him freely, He is not content that we freely follow any other Redeemer, or no Redeemer: 'if ye believe not that I am *he*,' Jesus warns, 'ye shall die in your sins.' [185] Even if we exempt the New Testament's values from the charge of the 'spirit of seriousness', no amount of rule-bending will exempt this insistence on the need for Jesus, and only Jesus, as a Redeemer, for ultimately it demands that we surrender the meaningfulness of our own choices and – another heretical thought, this time in Christian terms – submit to the Good Shepherd *in bad faith*. Christian dogma had seemed willing to let us keep the apple, only to snatch it away when we were not looking. We are back where we started. The remedy is still wrong.

As I complained some time ago, Sartre has no remedy at all for the human condition in general or human relations in particular, and he is no stranger to dogma himself. But not only does his diagnosis correctly identify the real issue, which is that consciousness cannot be undone, his explanation of how consciousness first came about, namely that brute matter wanted reasons for its existence, also rings true. While Christian dogma has a lot to say about the regrets that have assailed man since the irruption of his consciousness, banishment from Eden and the rude shock of having to live in the sweat of his face, it has nothing convincing to say about the origin of consciousness. It blames disobedience because it has no other way to account for the *curiosity* of Adam and Eve, and that is because the dogma itself originated in an ancient world that had no curiosity, no need or inclination to ask the reasons for things. It was a world in which all realities had already been revealed, fully and eternally, by deities, heroes, ancestors, patriarchs and priests; revealed, not explained, because it was a world before conscious enquiry or, in its most pristine state, before consciousness itself. Sartre's origin of consciousness is as mythical as the Bible's but the metaphor at the heart of his myth, matter seeking to justify its own existence, is closer to the truth than that lame old metaphor of disobedience. Closer to the truth, I mean, that consciousness is inseparable from an urge to stand back and try to make sense of the world – to explain it for ourselves, not have it revealed to us. This is why I think Sartre has the more plausible explanation for our ambivalent attitude towards consciousness, which, he says, we both regret (as expressed in our 'patterns of flight' from anguish: my page 50) and at the same time recognize as defining human reality (perpetually 'at a distance' from everything and therefore capable of questioning everything and conceiving of what is *not*). Moreover, in at least one crucial respect Sartre's dogma is an improvement on Christian dogma: by recasting 'sin' (of which we are guilty, automatically and collectively, by ancestral association) as 'bad faith' (of which we are guilty, individually, only if we *choose* not to live in good faith), Sartre has disposed of the red herring of man's supposed 'wickedness' and brought us face to face with the truth that properly we should be judged, and should judge ourselves, by the choices we make and not by some fictitious, doctrinal defect of our nature.

Being and Nothingness brings on a motley crew of people for us to judge by their choices, among them the mechanical waiter, the soldier-thing and the young woman who turns her hand into a thing. These three, let's agree, are all guilty of the same variety of bad faith: the attempt to revert to thingness. The waiter and the woman seem harmless enough, slightly ridiculous, an embarrassment to themselves but not an obvious danger to anyone else. The soldier-thing, by contrast, his unseeing gaze fixed at ten paces, suggests the potential for something darker – killer-thing, or cannon-fodder-thing. This variety of bad faith, then, has a menacing aspect to it, an aspect that Sartre explores in much greater depth in the essay on anti-Semitism that he wrote in the second half of 1944. [186]

The starting point for the essay seems to have been Sartre's observation that, two months after the liberation of Paris (August 1944), French newspapers were full of stories of returning prisoners of war and non-Jewish deportees but made no mention of the return of Jews who had survived or of the mass murder of those who had not survived (the scale of which was already becoming clearer as the Russians, advancing from the east, came across Nazi concentration camps in Poland [187]). As in *Being and Nothingness*, Sartre's method is to focus on the attitudes and behaviours of an individual in bad faith. The individual now is the anti-Semite, a man (always a man in Sartre's descriptions) who 'attributes all or part of his own misfortunes and those of his country to the presence of Jewish elements in the community'. [188] He has become an anti-Semite in the particular conditions, the 'situation', of his social class (typically 'the lower middle class of the towns' according to Sartre's analysis [189]) and occupation (he and his kind are 'functionaries, office workers, small businessmen, who possess nothing'). Nonetheless, as we would expect, Sartre holds the anti-Semite fully responsible for all the choices he has made within the constraints of his 'situation': anti-Semitism is 'a free and total choice of oneself,' Sartre writes, 'a comprehensive attitude that one adopts not only toward Jews but toward men in general, toward history and society; it is at one and the same time a passion and a conception of the world.' [190] The anti-Semite chooses to live in a state of passion, more specifically a state of hate, but why? Because hate is 'a faith [*une foi*[191]]' that precludes argument and makes him impervious to reason and experience. And why does imperviousness attract the anti-Semite? Because if he lived by reason, argument and experience, he would have to confront his fear of the true, 'that thing of indefinite approximation [*cet objet d'indéfinie approximation*]': it would be as if his existence were 'perpetually in suspension [*perpétuellement en sursis*]', whereas he wants to exist without suspension, without ambiguity and without ambivalence, 'all at once and right away [*tout à la fois et tout de suite*]'.[192]

He has chosen hate and he has also chosen to be terrifying:

> He is not afraid of himself, but he sees in the eyes of others a disquieting image – his own – and he makes his words and gestures conform to it. Having this external model, he is under no necessity to look for his personality within himself. He has chosen to find his being entirely outside himself, never to look within, to be nothing save the fear he inspires in others.[193]

The anti-Semite 'considers himself an average man, modestly average, and in the last analysis a mediocre person.' This mediocrity, too, is something he has chosen, because it makes him part of 'an elite of the mediocre' and relieves him of his fear of 'any kind of solitude, that of the genius as well as that of the murderer: he is the man of the mob; no matter how short he is, he still takes the precaution of stooping for fear of standing out from the herd and of finding himself face to face with himself.'[194] Besides, intelligence is abstract and 'Jewish' and therefore to be disdained. He possesses nothing and yet he possesses one thing the Jew does not, 'true' Frenchness, a mystical union through blood and soil and language with the 'true Frenchman [who], rooted in his province, in his country, carried along by a tradition of twenty centuries, having the advantage of ancestral wisdom, guided by proved customs, *does not need* intelligence. The basis of his virtue is the assimilation of the qualities which the work of a hundred generations has lent to [the] objects which surround him, *i.e.,* property.'[195] Whether embodied in land, tradition or the alexandrine couplets of Jean Racine, Frenchness to the anti-Semite is no abstraction but an object that he can grasp and derive his meaning from, for the principle underlying anti-Semitism is that 'concrete possession of a particular object magically conveys its meaning.' [196]

Above all, the anti-Semite has chosen *certainty* and he has done that by choosing to be 'massive and impenetrable', more inanimate than inanimate matter itself. He has no urge to find reasons for his own existence because that is massively and impenetrably explained by the counter-existence of the Jews. There is nothing secret about him, nothing suspended, ambiguous or ambivalent. He is a thing, an anti-Semite-thing:

> We can now understand him. He is a man who is afraid. Not of the Jews, of course, but of himself, of his [consciousness], his freedom, of his instincts, of his responsibilities, of solitude, of change, of society and the world; of everything except the Jews. .... He chooses finally that [the Good] be ready made, not in question, out of reach; he dare not look at it for fear of being forced to contest it and seek another form of it. The Jew is only a pretext: elsewhere it will be the Negro, the yellow race. The Jew's existence simply allows the antisemite to nip his anxieties in the bud by persuading himself that his place has always been cut out in the world, that it was waiting for him and that by virtue of tradition he has the right to occupy it. Antisemitism, in a word, is fear of [the human condition]. The antisemite is the man who wants to be pitiless stone, furious torrent, devastating lightning: in short, everything but a man. [197]

As Sartre himself points out, the anti-Semite is not unique in picking on a particular people, the Jews in his case, as 'a pretext' for his own flight from himself. By implication, Sartre might have written of any one of a number of other peoples, 'pretexts' for other bigotries and other flights. But the fact is that he chose to write primarily of the Jews, to do so with an explicit warning that what the anti-Semite 'desires and prepares is the *death* of the Jew' [198] and at a time when the first concrete evidence of the Nazi programme (facilitated in France by the Vichy authorities) to achieve the wholesale death of the Jew was just coming to light. We are bound, therefore, to subject Sartre's essay to the severest test imaginable: what, if anything, does it tell us about the Holocaust?

Having asked the question, my first instinct is to decline to answer it myself, for the Holocaust feels to me almost a taboo subject. This is evasive and I will attempt a brief answer. It is a personal answer based on a personal interpretation of Sartre's essay; while I have no wish to give offence to anyone, the responsibility if I do unwittingly give offence will be mine alone.

The events of the Holocaust are documented in mountains of fact, but no mountains of fact will explain the *meaning* of the Holocaust. Sartre gets us nearer to the meaning, or at least a meaning. His essay has been criticized on many grounds that I am not qualified to judge, including its allegedly 'willful and programmatic' ignorance of Judaism.[199] My own objection to Sartre's essay is the same as one of my objections to *Being and Nothingness* – that it makes no allowance for the workings of the unconscious mind because Sartre is committed to his dogma that all human choices are by definition conscious choices. To insist that the anti-Semite has chosen to live in a state of hate, chosen to be terrifying, chosen to be mediocre, and so on, is all very well as a rhetorical device but it is simply not believable as literal, psychological truth. To allow that anti-Semites, and bigots of every other kind, are driven in part by unconscious motives and impulses is not to exonerate them from responsibility for their actions, only to recognize the reality that not all of their attitudes and actions result from conscious choices. On this basis, there are more convincing explanations than Sartre's for the mentality of those who were to prove capable of perpetrating and colluding in the Holocaust. One such had already been in print for four years before Sartre's essay first appeared: Erich Fromm`s *Escape from Freedom* (published in the United States in 1941, in Britain in 1942 under the title *The Fear of Freedom*). A sociological and psychoanalytic study of what Fromm calls 'the totalitarian flight from freedom',[200] it explores the complexity of the relationship between individual and group behaviour and suggests that the sadistic appeal of anti-Semitism, for example, has to be understood largely in terms of unconscious processes.[201] Nevertheless, while it may be psychologically less believable, Sartre's portrayal of anti-Semitism as a consciously chosen flight from the human condition finds its own way to the heart of the matter: anti-Semitism and, by extension, the Holocaust itself, represent an attempt to return the world to a state of thingness. We are familiar with the thingness of the Holocaust's victims, tattooed into numbers, disassembled into piles of shoes and clothing and family photographs, processed into carcases, rendered into ash. But Sartre not only confronts us with the thingness of the perpetrators and collaborators responsible for what was done to the victims, he confronts us with a very stark and uncomfortable question: what choices would *we* have made under the conditions, the 'situation', that prevailed throughout Nazi-occupied Europe? We like to think, of course, that we would have behaved in good faith, in every sense of the phrase. But in all honesty, are we so sure that we would not have reverted to the thingness of looking the other way, even as our Jewish neighbours were loaded onto the trucks?

According to Genesis, man's fault, his 'sin', is to have picked the apple of consciousness in the first place; it is the origin of all his regrets and, as we would say, his ambivalent feelings towards consciousness itself. According to Sartre, man's fault, his 'bad faith', is that he is endlessly trying to escape his regrets (his 'anguish') and resolve his ambivalence by gluing the apple back onto the tree. One meaning of the Holocaust may be that the latter fault, the attempt to renounce consciousness, is the more dangerous of the two.

5. THE FEAR OF EXTINCTION

> In our activity alone do we find the sustaining illusion of an independent existence as against the whole scheme of things of which we form a helpless part.
>
> Joseph Conrad, *Nostromo* [202]

The sustaining illusion

Why does Nostromo, the character at the heart of Conrad's story, steal the boat-load of silver that has been entrusted to him in the confusion of Costaguana's revolution? What has happened to the magnificent man whose only care had been to live a life of admired publicity, a man made incorruptible by the very enormity of his vanity? What destroys the genuineness of all his qualities and reduces him to the wretchedness of a thief enslaved to his unlawful treasure, humiliated by the enforced stealth of his actions, haunted by superstitious fears and the guilt of his failure to summon a priest for a dying woman?

The solving of the mystery begins, I think, with an observation made by Martin Decoud, one of Nostromo's two unwelcome passengers in the silver lighter. As Decoud's complacent scepticism deserts him in the darkness of the Placid Gulf, he still has some measure of Nostromo:

> There remained only one thing he was certain of, and that was the overweening vanity of his companion. It was direct, uncomplicated, naïve, and effectual. … He had discovered a complete singleness of motive behind the varied manifestations of a consistent character. This was why the man remained so astonishingly simple in the jealous greatness of his conceit. And now there was a complication. It was evident that he resented having been given a task in which there were so many chances of failure. 'I

> wonder,' thought Decoud, 'how he would behave if I were not here.' [203]

This is a Nostromo no one has ever seen before and even Decoud is troubled:

> The murmuring loquacity of the Capataz disturbed Decoud like a hint of weakness. ... The usual characteristic quietness of the man was gone. It was not equal to the situation as he conceived it. Something deeper, something unsuspected by everyone, had come to the surface. [204]

Decoud wonders how Nostromo would behave if he were alone: events tell us how Nostromo does behave once he *is* alone after landing Decoud, together with the cargo of silver, on an uninhabited island off the coast. Until his deathbed confession to Mrs Gould, he says nothing to gainsay the general assumption that the silver has gone down with the sunken lighter. And in a crazed reasoning of his vanity Nostromo conceives that, as he is the only man in the world who could have paid the double price (the lost soul of Signora Teresa, the woman for whom he had refused to call a priest, and the unexplained but certain death of Decoud) demanded by the situation, he has entered into a 'bargain' with the accursed treasure, which he will now appropriate to 'grow rich very slowly'.[205] But what of that 'complication' and of the unsuspected element in Nostromo's character that has come to the surface?

Nostromo is not afraid for his life; we have no reason to doubt Decoud's assessment that the man, as opposed to his reputation, would rather die than 'deface the perfect form of his egoism'. [206] Yet Decoud is subtly wrong when he supposes that Nostromo resents being given a task with so many chances of failure. What he resents is being given such a task as a matter of course, by people who have no appreciation of its deadly seriousness. 'Those gentlefolk,' he complains, recalling (or imagining? the blandishments with which he had been persuaded to take Decoud with him in the lighter, 'do not seem to have sense enough to understand what they are giving one to do.' [207] When Decoud suggests that Charles Gould, proprietor of the silver mine, and the other gentlefolk surely did not mean Nostromo to take such a desperate view of the affair, Nostromo snarls back 'What was it, then?

A joke?'[208] The bitter substance of the joke for Nostromo is not the danger of the task itself, but the casual indifference of those who have entrusted it to him. It is all the same to them whether the silver is saved or lost, whether their faithful Capataz de Cargadores lives or dies. If he returns, well and good, he will be available for a new task. If not, his defeated patrons and masters will be too busy with other concerns even to spare him a thought. The simplest and most complete explanation of his predicament comes to Nostromo later:

> The Capataz de Cargadores, on a revulsion of subjectiveness, exasperated almost to insanity, beheld all his world without faith and courage. He had been betrayed! .... The word had fixed itself tenaciously in his intelligence. His imagination had seized upon the clear and simple notion of betrayal to account for the dazed feeling of enlightenment as to being done for, of having inadvertently gone out of existence on an issue in which his personality had not been taken into account. A man betrayed is a man destroyed.[209]

Just as Nostromo has a peculiar (Decoud's word) view of the enterprise of saving the silver, so he has a peculiar definition of betrayal. For him it means any lapse in the certainty that at every moment of every day someone, man or woman, of good birth or common, has the Capataz in their approving thoughts. Nostromo needs an audience for all his larger gestures, and the audience that counts, the audience of his customary life of publicity, is onshore: Decoud's ironic manner has always made Nostromo vaguely uneasy, while the second passenger, Señor Hirsch, is nothing but a panic-stricken stowaway. We grasp now that the 'complication' in the desperate venture out in the Placid Gulf is Nostromo's realization that he has lost his audience. It is as though an actor delivered his best lines and then stepped into the wings to savour his triumph, only to return and find the theatre empty.

We grasp too that the unsuspected element in Nostromo's character is the paradoxical fragility of his vanity, which is a consequence of his need for an audience. On the one hand, he is possessed so strongly by a sense of the indestructible existence of his own reputation that he rejects suicide, because the shame and disgrace of suicide would likewise go on forever. On the other hand, possessed so weakly by a sense of existing on his own account, Nostromo the man is hostage to the uninterrupted attention and approbation of his audience. He *only* exists in the opinion of others and therefore his life is, in the narrator's words, one 'whose very essence, value, reality, consisted in its reflection from the admiring eyes of men.' [210] To deprive Nostromo of his audience is to precipitate 'the downfall of all the realities that made his force' and confront him with the 'confused and intimate impressions of universal dissolution',[211] and that is why Conrad says of his faithful devotion that there is 'something despairing as well as desperate in its impulses':[212] the faithful devotion helps to ensure Nostromo a permanent audience, without which he may as well be a thief as a magnificent Capataz de Cargadores, or may *inadvertently go out of existence altogether.* [213]

The sustaining illusion, if illusion it be, takes many different shapes. This can be illustrated from other literatures, other lives and even family histories, which brings me back to V.S. Naipaul. Naipaul wrote his novel *A House for Mr Biswas* with the thought, as he puts it, of 'reconstructing the life of someone like my father'.[214] Born in Trinidad, his father had been spared from work in the sugar fields and sent to school because his widowed mother wanted him to become a pundit. In the event, he became a reporter for the *Trinidad Guardian*, where he did well, taught and encouraged by the paper's managing editor and his own guru, Gault MacGowan. 'No other editor,' Naipaul writes,

> gave my father any sense of the worth of his calling. It was the idea of the vocation that exalted my father in the MacGowan days. It was in the day's story, and its reception by a sympathetic editor, that the day's struggle and the day's triumph lay. He wrote about Chaguanas, but the daily exercise of an admired craft would, in his own mind, have raised him above the constrictions of Chaguanas: he would have grown to feel protected by the word, and the quality of his calling. [215]

In effect, the son's novel grew out of the ledger in which his father had pasted cuttings of his early writings for the *Trinidad Guardian*, 'relics of his heroic and hopeful time with MacGowan'. [216]

Nine years after *A House for Mr Biswas* was published, Naipaul was sent a cutting he had not seen in the old ledger. It told a terrible story: in 1933 his father had been forced to sacrifice a goat to appease local farmers of Hindu origin who, offended by his reporting of their ritual practices, had threatened him with a supernatural death. 'It was the story,' says Naipaul, 'of a great humiliation.'

> It had occurred just when my father was winning through to a kind of independence, and had got started in his vocation. The independence was to go within months. The vocation – in a colonial Trinidad, without MacGowan [who left in 1934 for unrelated reasons] – was to become meaningless; the vacancy was to be with my father for the rest of his life. [217]

Naipaul's father became disturbed, lost his regular work, and was 'idle and dependent' [218] for four years. Although he was reemployed by the *Trinidad Guardian* in 1938, it was only as the result of pleading and the job was no longer a vocation but a source of daily humiliation. He died in 1953. Having learnt at last of the origins of his father's illness, Naipaul asked his elderly mother what form it had taken. 'He looked in the mirror one day,' she replied, 'and couldn't see himself. And he began to scream.' [219]

Naipaul's narrative ends by recording the extraordinary fact that his father had somehow passed on to him the same horror of going out of existence, bound up with a desperate sense of vocation, 'a panic about failing to be what I should be':

> [W]hat is astonishing to me is that, with the vocation, he so accurately transmitted to me – without saying anything about it – his hysteria from the time when I didn't know him: his fear of extinction. That was his subsidiary gift to me. That fear became mine as well. It was linked with the idea of the vocation: the fear could be combated only by the exercise of the vocation. [220]

The strange legacy that Naipaul inherited from his father goes a long way, I think, towards explaining the overwrought quality of *An Area of*

Darkness, which repeatedly speaks of a fear of creeping extinction (in London, for example, Naipaul finds himself 'confined to a smaller world than I had ever known. I became my flat, my desk, my name'; in Bombay, 'denied part of my reality … faceless' [221]) and ends, back in London, with a dark meditation upon illusion and despair, prompted by a dream:

> An oblong of stiff new cloth lay before me, and I had the knowledge that if only out of this I could cut a smaller oblong of specific measurements, a specific section of this cloth, then the cloth would begin to unravel of itself, and the unravelling would spread from the cloth to the table to the house to all matter, *until the whole trick was undone*. Those were the words that were with me as I flattened the cloth and studied it for the clues which I knew existed, which I desired above everything else to find, but which I knew I never would.
>
> The world is illusion, the Hindus say. We talk of despair, but true despair lies too deep for formulation. It was only now … that I saw how close in the past year I had been to the total Indian negation, how much it had become the basis of thought and feeling. And already, with this awareness, in a world where illusion could only be a concept and not something felt in the bones, it was slipping away from me. I felt it as something true which I could never adequately express and never seize again. [222]

This seems to me a deeply ambivalent dream, in which the dreamer looks for a distinct individual existence of his own (*a specific section* of the cloth) and yet expects a dissolution (*unravelling*) of all things, which must include his individual existence. It is a dream many of us have dreamt, each in our own particular ways.

Another life, another ambivalence. Donna Williams was born in Australia in 1963. She is autistic. The account she has written of her childhood and adolescence, *Nobody Nowhere*, describes many of the known traits of autism but, because it is largely written from the inside and not with textbook detachment, it has an immediacy that can be shocking. Here, for instance, she remembers an incident at the special school she attended at the age of three:

> I never liked to sit on chairs. I had restless legs I couldn't keep still and they always made it impossible to sit still in a chair. I liked to feel the ground underneath me. The more of me that was on it, the better. But one day I got up on to the seat next to a big girl named Elizabeth. She was making a person out of a cardboard cone and paper. I was intrigued by her hair, which was pulled back into a long plait. I ran my hand down her plait. She looked around at me and I was frightened by the way that her face was joined to her hair. I had wanted to touch her hair, not her. [223]

Elsewhere she recalls:

> I still remember the smell of my grandmother. She wore chains around her neck. She was soft and wrinkly, wore knitted things that I could put my fingers through, had a husky laughing voice and smelled of camphor. … For me, the people I liked *were* their things, and those things (or things like them) were my protection from the things I didn't like – other people. [224]

These passages reveal the fascination with inanimate things that is one hallmark of autism. Equally typical is Donna Williams's fear of being touched, and her compulsion to arrange and rearrange objects into ordered states and knowledge into systems. This compulsion – which, in an uncanny echo of the Doctor's advice to Jacob Horner (my page 59), had her name stray cats and kittens in alphabetical order after streets listed in a directory – was, she writes, part of 'exploring the concept of consistency'. [225] Consistency and, for want of it, *preparedness* are at the heart of the conflict that Donna Williams identifies right at the start of her book.

‘This is a story of two battles,’ she begins, ‘a battle to keep out “the world” and a battle to join it.’ I think we can safely regard ‘the world’ as a synonym for those ‘other people’, perceived as intruders who threaten ‘the invasion of touch and words and expectation to participate.’ [226] One of her principal means of protecting herself against ‘the world’ was to close out emotion (especially love or affection), which, because it involved ‘coping with “whole people” [and] their motivations and expectations’, [227] she experienced as something that always threatened to catch her unprepared. Being caught unprepared by anything seems to have been her overriding fear. ‘The constant change of most things never seemed to give me any chance to prepare myself for them,’ she recalls, and hence her demand for consistency and continuity, the ‘reassurance that things will stay the same long enough to grasp an undeniable guaranteed place within the complex situation around me.’ [228] If there had to be change, at least she should have a chance to prepare for it. But if other people or the situations she found herself in denied her the chance to prepare, she would do her best to ‘slow everything down’. [229] Failing that, she would close out emotion and all the other threats and bring down her barrier on ‘the world’. [230] The combined effect of all her keeping-out devices was to confine Donna Williams within a quite separate realm, ‘my own world’ or ‘my world under glass’.

The most tangible, adult evidence of her battle to join and belong to ‘the world’ is the writing of *Nobody Nowhere* itself, which very movingly documents her gradual success in making an independent life for herself. However, the evidence is already there in her childhood experiences. She recounts, for example, how at the age of about twelve she used to pee on the purple carpet in her prison-like room in the attic, which was one way of delimiting her private world (‘“my world” with a “me” in it’) and yet which also helped to locate ‘my world’ within ‘the world’ (‘The more I covered that carpet, the more of a “me” in the world there was’). [231] As Donna Williams herself says in her ‘outline of language in “my world”’ (by which she means repeated and repetitive gestures, not verbal language), ‘making one’s surroundings symbolically part of “one’s world” [through deliberate soiling] … is the beginning of accepting a world outside the confines of one’s own body. From a body to a room. From a room to a house. From a house to a street. From a street to a world.’ [232] Her ‘outline’ suggests, too, that often the battle to join ‘the world’ was a battle between two fears in particular – the fear of invasion by ‘other people’ and something like a fear of extinction, which only the attention of ‘other people’ could allay because only that could assure her of her own existence:

> *Hurting oneself and also knowingly doing embarrassing things to cause a shock reaction in others*
> To test whether one is actually real. As no other person is experienced directly because all feeling gets held at some sort of mental checkpoint before being given to self by self, it is easy to wonder whether one in fact exists. [233]

One last piece of evidence from her childhood:

> *Rocking from one foot to another*
> ……………………………………….
> I always saw a foreboding darkness between myself and ‘the world’. The fact that getting through this imaginary darkness to the other side would take quite a leap may have been captured by the preparatory rocking from front foot to back foot so indicative of someone about to take a running leap: ‘Ready, on your mark, get set, jump through the darkness to the other side …’ [234]

In short, *Nobody Nowhere* is a story not just of two battles but of two worlds, and of the discontinuous leap required to get from one to the other. Out of the supposedly exceptional conditions of her autism, it seems to me, Donna Williams offers a powerfully simple image for an experience of the world that is far more common than we might care to recognize.

This body, not that; me, not you

Richard Hooker hit the nail on the head long ago. What would become of *man himself*, he had asked (my page 5), if the celestial spheres – and by extension all other embodiments of the law of nature – should 'by irregular volubility turn themselves any way as it might happen'? What ultimately concerns us is not the certainty of natural phenomena, but the certainty of our own existence. As part of the inventory of Plato's world of change, we belong to that inferior order of reality that comes into existence in and vanishes from a particular place. If we blink into being, arbitrarily, randomly, in one place at one time, what is to stop us from blinking out of being, just as arbitrarily and randomly, at some other place and time? The black void that threatens us is not, as we might think, death. [235] Our fear of death exacerbates the true problem but also disguises it: what we dread, and this may happen before death and is far worse than death, is that we will flit away because our sense of our own existence has flitted away.

The problem must be traced right back to our 'necessary incarnation' in a body, this object of sensation, this disposable container knocked together by the minor gods in the creator's workshop. If we had no body, if somehow we subsisted in the ether without being assigned to one particular container rather than another, there would be no danger of losing our sense of existing in place and time. Since we would not be located in any one place or time, we could have no such sense to lose. Instead, in a perfect realm above and beyond this world would float the *idea* of ourself, everywhere and nowhere, indestructible for all eternity. However, it is not to be. We do have a body, a particular body unique to ourself; this body, not that. Our 'necessary incarnation', we recall, results from the creator's method of distributing the mix for our immortal soul:

> And when he had compounded the whole, he divided it up into as many souls as there are stars, and allotted each soul to a star. [236]

According to Plotinus (who lived in the third century AD but remained an important influence on Christian and other theologies, and on Western philosophy into the nineteenth century), the significance of this passage from the *Timaeus* lies in the fact that Plato here 'distinguishes those [human souls] of the second mixing-bowl, describes them as "parts", and goes on to say that, having in this way become partial, they must of necessity experience birth.' [237] Plotinus spells out, in imagery that is even richer and more varied than Plato's, the consequences of the *partialness* of the human star-soul and of its necessary descent into body.

Plotinus's metaphysics is based upon a threefold hierarchy of principles: the One (or the Good [238]); *Nous*; and, at the bottom, Soul. The One is recognizably Plato's Form of the Good, which is the source not only of the value and intelligibility (to the mind of man or, more precisely, the mind of the suitably qualified philosopher) of all the other Platonic forms 'but also of their existence and reality', and yet which is itself 'beyond reality, and superior to it in dignity and power.' [239] Although Plotinus insists that the One is only to be described in terms of negatives ('we can and do state what it is not, while we are silent as to what it is' [240]), it would be a mistake to think it a negative principle: on the contrary, in one of its aspects it is a fundamentally positive and generative principle. [241] And the first product of its generativeness is *Nous*, most commonly translated as 'Intellect' or 'Intellectual-Principle', which is engendered because in a 'self-quest' the One has seeing and 'this very seeing is the Intellectual-Principle'. [242] (Bertrand Russell suggests that the way to understand this obscure notion is through Plotinus's own simile of the sun and the sun's rays: if the One is the sun, *Nous* is the light by which the sun/One sees itself. [243]) *Nous* seems to function as a metaphysical device for reconciling the manyness of the forms with the absolute indivisibility of the One, which *Nous* achieves by thinking or contemplating the distinctness of each of the forms within, so to speak, the greater unity of the One. [244]

And so to Soul. Soul is engendered from *Nous* in a process analogous to that by which *Nous* is engendered from the One and, in the same way that *Nous* is 'not merely one [... but] one and many', Plotinus says, 'there must be both many souls and one, the one being the source of the differing many just as from one genus there rise various species, better and worse, some of the more intellectual order, others less effectively so'. [245] Most importantly for us, the many souls include our individual human souls. A common characteristic of all three of Plotinus's metaphysical principles is that they operate in two directions at once – inwards and outwards or, in the case of *Nous* and Soul, upwards and downwards. For Soul, upwards means towards *Nous* and, together with *Nous*, upwards again towards ultimate union with the One. Soul's downward-facing activities, by contrast, are associated with its acquisition of a procreative 'appetite' and a desire to replicate the order that it has seen above in *Nous*:[246] Soul expresses this 'appetite' through Nature and the making of the stars, planets and all the other bodies of the visible universe, as Plotinus explains in a passage that might have come from Genesis:

> [S]oul is the author of all living things, … it has breathed the life into them all, whatever is nourished by earth and sea, all the creatures of the air, the divine stars in the sky; it is the maker of the sun; itself formed and ordered this vast heaven and conducts all that rhythmic motion … [247]

The same Janus-like characteristic is evident in individual human souls. They too have an urge to 'return to their source' in the realm of *Nous* and, so long as they remain absorbed in the one Soul (which at its highest level is virtually assimilated to *Nous*), they are 'immune from care and trouble.' But, Plotinus continues, 'there comes a stage at which they descend from the universal to become partial and self-centred; in a weary desire of standing apart they find their way, each to a place of its very own.' [248] The individual souls voluntarily break away from the oneness of Soul and 'descend'. Why? We have arrived at Plotinus's Fall – the fall of Soul into body, which is another story full of ambiguity and ambivalence. The individual souls break away because it is good and necessary that they should do so, that the principle of Soul should flow down to the lowest level possible. However, most souls also break away because they have a weak and wilful craving for the lower realm, which is a base motive, not a good one. [249] An individual soul which remains in a state of apartness for too long is a 'deserter from the All', and that has momentous consequences for it:

> its differentiation has severed it; its vision is no longer set in the Intellectual [i.e., *Nous* or realm of *Nous*]; it is a partial thing, isolated, weakened, full of

> care, intent upon the fragment; severed from the whole, it nestles in one form of being; for this, it abandons all else, entering into and caring for only the one, for a thing buffeted about by a worldful of things: thus it has drifted away from the universal ….
>
> With this comes what is known as the casting of the wings, the enchaining in body: the soul has lost that innocency of conducting the higher which it knew when it stood with the All-Soul, that earlier state to which all its interest would bid it hasten back.
>
> It has fallen: it is at the chain: debarred from expressing itself now through its intellectual phase, it operates through sense, it is a captive; this is the burial, the encavernment, of the Soul. [250]

It seems to me that what Plotinus describes (and other sources in other cultures describe [251]) as the cataclysmic and abrupt severing of the part from the whole is what developmental psychologists would describe, less emotively and more in terms of a gradual process, as the emergence of individual consciousness from the undifferentiated awarenesses of the infant mind. For Plotinus, the severing is something to bemoan because it results in *partialness*, isolation, and intentness upon the fragment instead of the whole; for the developmental psychologist, by contrast, it is something to welcome because – under the right conditions – it results in *individuality*, assertiveness, and the sense of 'I-ness' or 'me-ness' that defines our self-identity. And where for Plotinus the body is a prison cell from which we will never escape, for the developmental psychologist the body is a protective but responsive nurturing vessel which, far from incarcerating us, enables us to explore the world in safety and later launch ourselves out into it. One developmental view of the body-consciousness relationship is psychoanalytic in origin, for it was Sigmund Freud who declared that the *ego* (the lifeless term most English translations use for Freud's 'the I [*das Ich*]' [252]) is 'first and foremost a bodily *ego*; it is not merely a surface entity, but is itself the projection of a surface.' According to a footnote he is said to have authorized, what Freud means is that the *ego* is 'ultimately derived from bodily sensations, chiefly from those springing from the surface of the body. It may thus be regarded as a mental projection of the surface of the body, besides … representing the superficies of the mental apparatus.' The surface of the body has a very special significance:

> A person's own body, and above all its surface, is a place from which both external and internal perceptions may spring. It is *seen* like any other object, but to the *touch* it yields two kinds of sensations, one of which may be equivalent to an internal perception. …. Pain, too, seems to play a part … and the way in which we gain new knowledge of our organs during painful illnesses is perhaps a model of the way by which in general we arrive at the idea of our body. [253]

Crucially, Freud speculates, it is through bodily sensations that in infancy we first discover the difference between 'inside' and 'outside' and he suggests time and again that this discovery, together with what he calls the 'disengagement of the *ego* from the general mass of sensations', is the fundamental basis of our adult ability to live as an 'I-ness' in the midst of the 'there-ness' of the world outside:

> An infant at the breast does not as yet distinguish his *ego* from the external world as the source of the sensations flowing in upon him. He gradually learns to do so, in response to various promptings. He must be very strongly impressed by the fact that some sources of excitation, which he will later recognize as his own bodily organs, can provide him with sensations at any moment, whereas other sources evade him from time to time – among them what he desires most of all, his mother`s breast – and only reappear as a result of his screaming for help. In this way there is for the first time set over against the *ego* an 'object', in the form of something which exists 'outside' and which is only forced to appear by a special action………

> In this [and other ways], then, the *ego* detaches itself from the external world. Or, to put it more correctly, originally the *ego* includes everything, later it separates off an external world from itself. Our present *ego*-feeling is, therefore, only a shrunken residue of a much more inclusive – indeed, an all-embracing – feeling which corresponded to a more intimate bond between the *ego* and the world about it.[254]

Genesis confronts the emergence of consciousness through its metaphor of the opening of the eyes, while Plato explores the consequences of our capacity for making conscious choices through his metaphor of the soul's changes of position in space. Although Freud, too, frequently speaks in metaphors, he comes up with a theory of the 'disengagement' of individual consciousness from the 'general mass of sensations' in which all our lives begin. But no theory, however plausible, can explain away the undertones of loss and foreboding so characteristic of consciousness-creation myths, because they capture a paradox that even Freud cannot resolve. The paradox is that the more successfully we 'disengage' our 'I-ness', the more we find ourselves, as Plotinus would say, *standing apart* each in a place (a body) of our very own. The more we stand apart, the more we are buffeted about by a worldful of things and the more we are forced to make choices. The consequences of the things that happen to us and the choices we make divide and branch, and then divide and branch again, and again. Before we know it, that has been our life: events and circumstances, choices and non-choices in a tangle of trajectories, often arbitrary, random and ill-judged and yet irreversible. And through it all we struggle to hold on to our 'I-ness' and to the belief that the tangle is meaningful because, for better or worse, it expresses the uniqueness and dignity of our 'I-ness'. Nostromo in his fragile vanity, Naipaul driven to write as his way of combating an inherited fear of extinction, Donna Williams in her battles to join the world *and* keep it out[255] – these are imagined and real people who know that they stand apart and who, in their various ways and more or less successfully, try to preserve their sense of their own existence and the meaningfulness of that sense.

Sartre, as we might expect, has a lot to say about the body. He tends to describe it not as a living organism but as a bloodless entity in which and by which we make contact with the outside world and, more specifically, experience our relations with other people. In the perceptions of others, according to Sartre, our body is an object or thing to be seen and dealt with, just as in our perception the bodies of others are objects that we see and deal with. He conveys this idea with imaginative ingenuity in a section of *Being and Nothingness* that he calls 'The Look'. He pictures himself in a dark wood at night, ill at ease:

> What I apprehend immediately when I hear the branches crackling behind me is not that *there is someone there*; it is that I am vulnerable, that I have a body which can be hurt, that I occupy a place and that I can not in any case escape from the space in which I am without defence – in short, that I *am seen.* [256]

Then Sartre imagines that, moved by jealousy, curiosity or prurience, he is peeping through a keyhole. Suddenly he hears footsteps behind him: he has been seen, and in the shame of being discovered he becomes an 'object-for-the-Other', an object, in other words, for the person who has discovered him: 'It is shame or [in other circumstances] pride which reveals to me the Other's look *and myself at the end of that look.*' [257]

If only we had no body, if only we could subsist in the ether, we would never find ourselves at the end of any look, never struggle to hold on to a sense of our own existence, and never have to acknowledge responsibility for our choices because we would have no choices to make. But what on earth – or rather, not on earth – would it be like to *be* in such a disembodied, unseen, untroubled and unaccountable state? I think there is an answer of sorts in *Nausea*, Sartre's metaphysical story about a man who, unbeknown to himself at first, longs to cast off the partialness and *particularness* of his bodily presence in the world and dissolve once and for all into a perfect, translucent ether.

Plato meets the jazz age

The discoveries that Roquentin, the central character of *Nausea*, makes about the brute existence of things are all the more unsettling because they occur in locations of banal, civic normality – in the park, in the town square, in the museum and, this being a very French civic normality, in the café. Whenever he goes to one café in particular, Roquentin asks the waitress to put on the same gramophone record, the jazz song *Some of These Days*. It begins with just the instrumentalists, who are then joined by the vocalist (in fiction as in fact, probably Sophie Tucker [258]) with the refrain 'Some of these days / You'll miss me honey'. Roquentin is all anticipation as the music starts to play:

> The refrain will be coming soon: that's the part I like best and the abrupt way in which it flings itself forward, like a cliff against the sea. For the moment it's the jazz ... playing; there's no melody, only notes, a host of little jolts. They know no rest, an unchanging order gives birth to them and destroys them, without ever giving them time to recover, to exist for themselves. They run, they hurry, they strike me with a sharp blow in passing and are obliterated. I should quite like to hold them back, but I know that if I managed to stop one, nothing would remain between my fingers but a vulgar, doleful sound. I must accept their death; I must even *will* it; I know few harsher or stronger impressions. [259]

The refrain is only a few seconds away:

> It seems inevitable, the necessity of this music is so strong: nothing can interrupt it, nothing which comes from this time in which the world is slumped; it will stop of its own accord, on orders. If I love that beautiful voice, it is above all because of that: it is neither for its fullness nor its sadness, but because it is the event which so many notes have prepared so far in advance, dying so that it might be born. [260]

In the moment of silence before the singer comes in, Roquentin finds that *something has happened*: his nausea has disappeared. 'I am *in* the music,' he records in his diary, and 'I feel my body like a precision tool at rest.' [261] The clue to what has happened is in the 'necessity' of the music, and in the manner of death of its notes. As Roquentin writes later, 'melodies alone can proudly carry their own death within them like an internal necessity; only they don't exist.' [262] And later still he expresses a sort of exasperation towards the 'little diamond pain' that spins around above the record and dazzles him:

> *It* does not exist. It is even irritating in its non-existence; if I were to get up, if I were to snatch that record from the turn-table which is holding it and if I were to break it in two, I wouldn't reach *it*. It is beyond – always beyond something, beyond a voice, beyond a violin note. Through layers and layers of existence, it unveils itself, slim and firm, and when you try to seize it you meet nothing but existents, you run up against existents devoid of meaning. It is behind them: I can't even hear it, I hear sounds, vibrations in the air which unveil it. It does not exist, since it has nothing superfluous: it is all the rest which is superfluous in relation to it. It *is*. [263]

The last of Roquentin's discoveries, his final epiphany, reveals the nature of his affliction and of the longing, the 'unnameable Idea', [264] that has plagued him all his life:

> And I too have wanted to *be*. Indeed I have never wanted anything else; that's what lay at the bottom of my life: behind all these attempts which seemed unconnected, I find the same desire: to drive existence out of me, to empty the moments of their fat, to wring them, to dry them, to purify myself, to harden myself, to produce in short the sharp, precise sound of a saxophone note. That could even serve as a fable: there was a poor fellow who had got into the wrong world. He existed, like other people, in the world of municipal parks, of *bistros*, of ports and he

> wanted to convince himself that he was living somewhere else, behind the canvas of paintings, with the doges of Tintoretto, with Gozzoli's worthy Florentines, behind the pages of books, with Fabrice del Dongo and Julien Sorel, behind gramophone records, with the long dry laments of jazz music. And then, after making a complete fool of himself, he understood, he opened his eyes, he saw that there had been a mistake: he was in a *bistro*, in fact, in front of a glass of warm beer. [265]

Roquentin is trapped in the wrong world. He wants to *be* with nothing superfluous, in a world where 'circles and melodies kept their pure and rigid lines'.[266] This is sheer Plato. For Roquentin's circles and melodies, read Plato's eternally perfect forms; and for Roquentin's world of municipal parks and *bistros*, read Plato's world of change with its moving shadows, those shoddy likenesses of reality. Although it seems that for Roquentin, as for Plato, the superior dimension of reality is associated with changelessness (it is an *unchanging* order that causes the jazz notes to be born and die), Roquentin's greatest complaint against the everyday world is not that things change but that they exist at all, contingently, without reason or justification. According to Plato, ultimate reality is above and beyond change; according to Roquentin, ultimate reality is behind and beyond contingency – or, we might say, in the ether, everywhere and nowhere. [267] And yet the fact is that Roquentin himself exists contingently and is as superfluous, *de trop*, as the bandstand, the fountain and everything and everyone else in the park:

> We were a heap of existents inconvenienced, embarrassed by ourselves, we hadn't the slightest reason for being there, any of us, each existent, embarrassed, vaguely ill at ease, felt superfluous in relation to the others. *Superfluous*: that was the only connexion I could establish between those trees, those gates, those pebbles. … *Superfluous*, the chestnut tree, over there, opposite me, a little to the left. … And *I* – weak, languid, obscene, digesting, tossing about dismal thoughts – *I too was superfluous*. [268]

Now we understand Roquentin's fascination with melodies that proudly carry their own death within them like an internal necessity, so unlike every existent which is 'born without reason, prolongs itself out of weakness and dies by chance.'[269] He considers suicide 'to destroy at least one of these superfluous existences', but realizes that killing himself would make no difference because even his bones would still be superfluous. Alive or dead, he is superfluous for all time.[270] We understand Roquentin's fascination with firmness and sharpness: he finds it 'almost painful to become so hard, so bright' while listening to the jazz because ordinarily he thinks of his body and his whole presence in the world as grotesquely slack and repulsive – 'is it my fault,' he asks, 'if I am superfluous, if the sincerest and driest of my sufferings trails along heavily, with too much flesh and its skin too loose, like the sea-elephant, with bulging eyes which are wet and touching yet so ugly?[271] This tone of bewildered self-disgust characterizes Roquentin's perception of himself. 'I hadn't any right to exist,' he has admitted in the museum, standing before the portrait of Pacôme the merchant, a civic worthy. 'I had appeared by chance, I existed like a stone, a plant, a microbe. My life grew in a haphazard way and in all directions. Sometimes it sent me vague signals; at other times I could feel nothing but an inconsequential buzzing.'[272]

Roquentin does not want to *exist*, he wants to *be*, which means escaping his contingency. But why is he captive to or, Sartre's word, 'haunted' with contingency in the first place? The explanation is in the consciousness-creation myth of *Being and Nothingness*: in its attempt to justify its own existence, brute matter (the in-itself) has fallen into consciousness (the for-itself) but it has brought contingency along with it and that 'remains at the heart of the for-itself as its original contingency'. Sartre has a new name for this 'perpetually evanescent contingency of the in-itself which, without ever allowing itself to be apprehended, haunts the for-itself and reattaches it to being-in-itself – this contingency is what we shall call the *facticity* of the for-itself.'[273] If it were not for facticity, as Sartre observes in a reference to Plato's myth of Er, 'consciousness could choose its attachments to the world in the same way as the souls in Plato's *Republic* choose their condition.'[274] Unlike Plato's souls, however, we cannot choose our attachments to the world because our facticity asserts itself in the body we happen to be born into, the place and time of birth, our social environment, and all the other circumstances and accidents of our 'situation', the raw and particular materials of our lives. While we are free to make or unmake ourselves out of those raw materials, we are not free to make or unmake the attachments originally determined for us by our facticity.

In order to *be*, Roquentin would have to remove the facticity and justify his own existence by 'founding' himself. How? As we know from *Being and Nothingness*, the in-itself and the for-itself are the two fundamental dimensions of being. Contingency largely defines the in-itself ('can neither be derived from the possible nor reduced to the necessary': my page 85 above), which would not matter if Roquentin wanted to revert to thingness, the dimension of the in-itself, in the familiar pattern of a flight from anguish. But given that his true ambition is to rid himself of contingency and facticity, Roquentin would be jumping out of the frying pan into the fire if he did revert to thingness. The for-itself, meanwhile, holds out no better prospect of escape: not only is it defined as a consciousness of anguish, but also as a consciousness of facticity. As Roquentin expresses it, the very meaning of the existence of consciousness 'is that it is a consciousness of being superfluous' [275] or, as his creator expresses it in *Being and Nothingness*, facticity 'simply resides in the for-itself as a memory of being, as its unjustifiable *presence in the world*.' [276] Neither thingness nor consciousness offer Roquentin any hope of removing his facticity, so how can he transform his existence into being?

He cannot do it, because to 'found' himself he would have to combine the solidness of a thing perfectly identified with itself *and* the 'lack' or translucency of a consciousness 'at a distance' and therefore capable of providing reasons for the existence of everything, including itself. He would be glued to himself and at a distance from himself, inanimate being and animate nothingness, at one and the same time. Roquentin personifies the project of consciousness, which, in the jargon of *Being and Nothingness*, 'is *in fact* a project of … attaining to the dignity of the in-itself-for-itself or in-itself-as-self-cause'. [277] It is a project that demands an 'impossible synthesis' of the 'incompatible characteristics' of the in-itself and the for-itself:

> Human reality is a perpetual surpassing toward a coincidence with itself which is never given. … [The] perpetually absent being which haunts the for-itself is itself fixed in the in-itself. It is the impossible

> synthesis of the for-itself and the in-itself; it would be its own foundation not as nothingness but as being and would preserve within it the necessary translucency of consciousness along with the coincidence with itself of being-in-itself.[278]

Only a supernatural being would be capable of this impossible synthesis, which is why Sartre goes on to say that 'the best way to conceive of the fundamental project of human reality is to say that man is the being whose project is to be God.'[279] Sartre's consciousness-creation myth has, we discover, an unexpected twist. What Roquentin wants to be – what, according to Sartre, we all want to be – is not a thing, not even a circle or a melody, but *God.* The 'passion' of man, Sartre concludes, 'is the reverse of that of Christ, for man loses himself as man in order that God may be born. But the idea of God is contradictory and we lose ourselves in vain. Man is a useless passion [*l'homme est une passion inutile*].'[280]

6. SOME POINT OF THE PENDULUM'S SWING

> I mean *Negative Capability*, that is when man is capable of being in uncertainties, Mysteries, doubts, without any irritable reaching after fact & reason ....
>
> But there are people who are attracted by the durability of stone. They want to be massive and impenetrable, they do not want to change ... They want to exist all at once and right away.

Why the many are so many

As a state of being in the world, Negative Capability is the polar opposite of massiveness and impenetrableness. Massiveness and impenetrableness demand certainty, especially the certainty of a world that is orderly, consistent, unambiguous and, as we conceive it, reasonable. One definition of Negative Capability, therefore, might be that it stands for the willing suspension of all such demands, an ability to accommodate disorderliness, inconsistency and discontinuity, ambiguity, unreasonableness – a capability, as Keats puts it, for *being in uncertainties*. To return where I began, it seems to me that very few people have this capability. In the case of presidents, prime ministers, central bankers, generals, doctors, air traffic controllers, business executives and many, many others whose job it is to make clear and effective decisions, that is probably just as well for all of us. But we have no reason to feel threatened by the few who do have the ability to be in uncertainties, for typically they are poets, playwrights, novelists, sculptors, potters, painters and musicians with no responsibility for the safety of our skies and no powers to set interest rates or take the country to war. And they are the few within the few, the ones who will still be read and exhibited and performed a hundred years from now, still recognized for their openness to all experience and their capacity, as Keats would say, for 'remaining content with half knowledge'.[281]

One of these few is Seamus Heaney. The final poem in his collection *The Spirit Level* is both a quiet example of openness and half knowledge at work in his language and, I think, a quiet plea for openness and half knowledge in the world at large:

> And some time make the time to drive out west
> Into County Clare, along the Flaggy Shore,
> In September or October, when the wind
> And the light are working off each other
> So that the ocean on one side is wild
> With foam and glitter, and inland among stones
> The surface of a slate-grey lake is lit
> By the earthed lightning of a flock of swans,
> Their feathers roughed and ruffling, white on white,
> Their fully grown headstrong-looking heads
> Tucked or cresting or busy underwater.
> Useless to think you'll park and capture it
> More thoroughly. You are neither here nor there,
> A hurry through which known and strange things pass
> As big soft buffetings come at the car sideways
> And catch the heart off guard and blow it open. [282]

Another of the few is the Estonian composer Arvo Pärt, whose austere, hypnotic music tends to be built on the simplest of structures. His *Cantus in memoriam Benjamin Britten* of 1977, for example, written for string orchestra and a single bell, is based entirely on the descending scale of A minor played simultaneously at three different speeds.[283] Although his music is often described as 'minimalist', 'sacred' seems more appropriate, partly in the liturgical sense (Pärt's choral works are predominantly settings of religious texts) but more broadly in the sense that all of it sounds in the presence of something which, so to speak, it never looks in the face, still less resolves. It is as if the music is suspended indeterminately between its own fragile structure and the mystery from which it averts its gaze. Pärt is famously a man of few words but from the interviews he does give we gather that his music is at a distance from itself because *he* is at a distance from the music when, and even after, he writes it. This is evident from his replies to one interviewer, Immo Mihkelson, who asks about the role and responsibility of the interpreter (shorthand for the conductor, orchestra and choir) in performing Pärt's music: [284]

> **Mihkelson:** What, in your own opinion, is the most important component of your music? That which your music would lose the most if it were ignored?
>
> **Pärt:** When we speak with an architect about a building we cannot get a complete picture only from inside, being inside a single room. We must see it from many perspectives. From outside, from above, from the front, from the back. This distance must first occur to the interpreter towards the whole work's form and content. Strange as it may sound, this distance must also occur to the composer as well. It is one thing when a work is written and another when it is heard for the first time. This is like an airplane ride from one end of the earth to the other. After landing, you are not quite all in place yet, some part of you doesn't quite join up until later.

What Pärt describes is plainly a painstaking, organic process: 'Many thousands of configurations are necessary for the formation of one phrase, before it can become a free-standing carrier of information,' he explains, and 'Quite often the work is born after many performances, when the correct contours become apparent.' It is a birth process:

> **Pärt:** This is the most difficult and interesting moment at a premiere. Everything must now be born – just as a person is born. The thing becomes quite serious. You can't lose a single minute as the newborn's life is in the balance. Every wrong movement can bring unexpected and unwanted results. [285]

Pärt characterizes his relationship with his audiences as 'very odd', something that 'cannot be explained' and a source of embarrassment to him because he feels that 'perhaps I somehow betray their expectations.' If the interviewer is nonplussed by Pärt's almost painful modesty and humility, he hides it well and asks the big question he has been working up to, which is, as he might have put it, 'Have you some message for your audience? What does it all mean?' Pärt's reply, equally oblique, makes it clear that he has no message for his audience:

> **Mihkelson:** People want to develop a contact with something. … it often seems that music is like a door or a gate, like a road to somewhere. People want to travel that road, even if they don't know what exactly awaits them. They have this sense that, once into listening to the music, when the door opens, they will find something extraordinary.
>
> **Pärt:** Perhaps together with the audience, we are at the same distance from something larger. Perhaps that is what I wanted to write down, this something which people seek when coming to a concert.

For Pärt himself, a devout Russian Orthodox Christian, the 'something larger' may well be God. But there is no suggestion that he assumes or expects anyone else will perceive it in the same way. 'There are as many different ways of perception as there are listeners,' he says, 'and all of them are justified.'

Those capable of being in uncertainties, I have suggested, are typically creative artists of one sort or another. Typically but not uniquely, and I wish to suggest also that one of the greatest exponents of Negative Capability was the physicist Niels Bohr. Not only did Bohr accommodate disorderliness, inconsistency, discontinuity and ambiguity in the description of quantum phenomena, by renouncing causality ('the classical ideal': my page 23 above) in a sense he renounced the whole demand for reasonableness or intelligibility in the world – the very demand that Einstein could never bring himself to renounce. The difference in attitude between the two men is encapsulated in the story of the EPR thought-experiment (pages 12-14). Einstein and his co-authors set out to prove conclusively, as they thought, that an acausal, quantum-mechanical description of their experiment would be *incomplete*; Bohr countered that only a quantum-mechanical description – the Copenhagen interpretation, in other words – was capable of recognizing that their experiment in fact involved two *complementary* properties (momentum and position) for each of the two particles and that the choice of which property to measure would in effect determine the reality of that property within the conditions of the experiment.[286] The most striking feature of the EPR story is the sequel which neither Einstein nor Bohr lived to witness: the laboratory tests in and since the late 1970s (page 21) which verify that, more than forty years before the requisite technology existed, Bohr had implicitly and correctly predicted that an actual EPR experiment would demonstrate acausal action at a distance – the final nail in the coffin of Einstein's 'reasonable definition' of reality. While a variety of '-ism' labels (perhaps including logical positivism: my note 16) could be attached to Bohr's attitude, the risk is that '-isms' obscure the raw significance of his ability to see and accept that 'completeness' and 'reasonableness' are requirements of the human mind, but not necessarily of the matter and energy that make up the rest of the universe. Paradoxically, Bohr is saying, there are circumstances in which we understand the world better by not understanding it 'completely'. And though I cannot claim Bohr as a living exponent of Negative Capability, I think it is meaningful to claim that the legacy of his capacity for being in uncertainties lives on through the almost universal acceptance of the Copenhagen interpretation, the education of generation after generation of professional physicists, and the influence of reputable popular science (as opposed to pseudo-scientific mumbo jumbo).

As to why the vast majority of ordinary mortals are not capable of being in uncertainties, I have two possible explanations to offer. The first is evolutionary-developmental, or physiological-psychological to the extent that it assumes a correlation between the development of individual consciousness (the psychological part of the explanation) and the physiology of the brain bequeathed to us by evolution. It is difficult to imagine that the first strings of self-replicating genetic molecules, which may have appeared within the first billion years of the earth's existence (page 60), would have been much concerned with the orderliness, consistency or reasonableness of the world they inhabited. Such concerns only start to become imaginable of life forms that evolved well over three billion years later, especially the larger-brained mammals and, most specifically and probably within the last two hundred thousand years, *Homo sapiens sapiens*, the sub-species of anatomically modern humans to which we belong. In other words, does the original source of our preoccupation with orderliness and intelligibility lie in the structure of our brain, and particularly the huge neocortex (in evolutionary terms, the newest part of the cerebral cortex) that distinguishes it from other mammalian brains? A single human neocortex is probably made up of at least 2×10^{10} (twenty billion) electrically-excitable cells or neurons, and on average each neuron is connected with other neurons via about seven thousand junctions or synapses; it is estimated that one cubic centimetre of cerebral cortex contains about 10^{12} (one trillion) synapses, all linked to each other and to neurons elsewhere by nerve fibres (located in the white matter below the grey matter of the cortex) which, laid end to end, would stretch between 150,000 and 180,000 kilometres.[287] The sheer redundancy in this supply of linkages – so many that from the age of twenty onwards we can afford to lose about 85,000 cortical neurons per day (almost one per second) and still have enough left to mitigate the effects of normal ageing-related cognitive impairment – suggests a sort of megalomania or overkill in the brain's capacity for connecting. Is it far-fetched, therefore, to suppose that the cellular, and ultimately molecular, structure of the brain not only enables perception, reasoning, memory and all the other inner workings of our minds but also sets us up to *look for* connections everywhere in the outer world we inhabit, whether that means finding true connections there or fabricating false ones?

The structure of our brain may be the prime evolutionary source of our preoccupation with orderliness and intelligibility but it cannot be the whole story because it takes little or no account of the part played by consciousness. There is not a lot to say about the development of consciousness in general, except that in evolutionary terms it probably relates to changes in the size and organization of the *Homo sapiens* brain and that in physiological terms there must be some relationship, however poorly charted, between what we experience as consciousness and the firing of those trillions of synapses. Our understanding of the development of individual or 'I'-consciousness, however, is relatively well founded. According to Freud's speculations (my pages 111-113), the first hazy awarenesses of the world come to the infant mind through the discovery of 'inside' and 'outside' – the discovery, that is, that some bodily sensations may occur at any time from within while others occur only intermittently (or in response to screaming, for example) and not from within. On this model, which seems very plausible, the gradual differentiation of 'inside' and 'outside' into a sense of 'I-ness' vis-à-vis the 'there-ness' of the world is the fundamental basis of individuality, self-assertiveness and many of the other character traits that our culture in particular values so highly. But it also gives rise to new discoveries and new and disturbing sensations that come with them.

Firstly we discover uncertain knowing, the state in which we rarely, if ever, have an unambiguous and complete grasp of what goes on in the world, including events that would appear to be objectively knowable, or of our experiences. This is because mostly they are matters of perception and interpretation and even our own perceptions and interpretations, let alone those of other people, are apt to change from moment to moment, day to day, year to year. Uncertain knowing is prefigured in Plato's Fall (pages 14-16), which warns that everything in the world of change is an object of sensation and opinion, coming to be and ceasing to be but never fully real, and in St Paul's mirror (pages 71-72), which warns that the most we can hope for in this life is an approximate and partial knowledge of things. Down the centuries uncertain knowing has been explored in all manner of devotional and secular meditations, including Donne's Easter Day sermon (page 75) and Naipaul's reflections on his grandfather's experience of reality (pages 81-82). Plato and St Paul have been restated by Heisenberg in the quantum uncertainty relations with their message that, even in principle, we can never know the present in all its detail at the subatomic level (page 10). And Plato and St Paul have been played out in the interpretation of historical events, including the atrocities committed by Japanese forces during the Pacific War (page 74). Uncertain knowing is not just a metaphorical conceit: it is the stuff of physical laws and history as well.

Our second discovery is that we are separate from everything and everybody else in the world, and that what makes us separate is essentially random or accidental: we happen to be born at a particular time, in a particular place, and into all sorts of particular circumstances that are not of our own choosing and yet are the raw materials of our whole lives. Long before Sartre gave the name 'facticity' (my page 118) to this condition, Plato and Plotinus had recognized that it all stems from the way in which we first come into the world – assigned to one particular container, a body, as depicted in Plato's 'necessary incarnation' of man (pages 64, 108) and, much more graphically, in Plotinus's severing of the part from the whole and its enchainment in body (pages 110-111).[288] Our third discovery, closely related to the second, is of the fragility of our own sense of existence: the more we become aware that we are separate and particular (or, as Plotinus would say, that each of us is a *partial* thing intent upon the fragment and not the whole), the more we may doubt the viability of our separateness and particularness. We may even fear, like Nostromo (my pages 101-102),[289] that we will casually disappear unless we have the admiration, approbation or at least the constant attention of other people to provide a reflected assurance of our being. Or, like Donna Williams (106-107), we may struggle both with the fragility of our sense of being in the world and the fragility of our will to be in it at all.

Painfully aware of the shifting and incomplete nature of our understanding, and of our separateness, particularity and fragility, we are outraged by Keats's call for us to *be in uncertainties*. We have more than enough uncertainties, mysteries and doubts to worry about already without being told to tolerate and, insult upon injury, welcome any new ones. On the contrary, most of us will take every opportunity to avoid being in uncertainties, especially by making connections – conscious or unconscious, true or fabricated – that have the effect of explaining away, masking, suppressing, or otherwise denying mysteries and doubts. In short, we connect our way out of uncertainties because we perceive them as threats to our sense of 'I-ness', but it is possible that this psychological explanation has a physiological basis in the architecture of the brain, which may predispose us to look for connections in all our dealings with the 'there-ness' of the world.

So much for my first attempt to explain why so many people seem incapable of being in uncertainties. My second attempt starts with one indisputable fact of natural science but thereafter makes no pretence of being anything other than metaphysical speculation. The indisputable fact is that, quite literally, we are all made of the dust of distant stars that had burnt out and scattered their chemical elements into interstellar space long before our sun and the earth were formed. The metaphysical speculation centres on Sartre's consciousness-creation myth (pages 84-86), according to which consciousness has come about because inanimate matter seeks a justification for its own brute existence: in anthropomorphic terms, inanimate matter cannot bear its contingency, its condition of *just being there* without any necessary reason or meaning or connection with other things, and it is only by 'falling into' consciousness that it can hope to achieve the distance from itself that will enable it to find reasons and meanings and connections.[290] If we accord it metaphysical or metaphorical validity, Sartre's account of the emergence of consciousness suggests an alternative explanation of our tendency to deny uncertainties, mysteries and doubts wherever we encounter them – the tendency that Keats dismissed as irritable reaching after fact and reason, and Freud identified more dispassionately as an 'intellectual function' that demands unity, connection and intelligibility from every perception and thought (*Totem and Taboo*, quoted on my page 2). According to my first, physiological-psychological explanation, we cannot tolerate uncertainties because they threaten our sense of 'I-ness'; according to this alternative explanation, it is the brute matter in us that cannot tolerate uncertainties because they threaten its whole ambition of escaping the contingency of its star-dust origins, an ambition which demands the conscious, unambiguous and uninterrupted certainty that there is a justification for its own existence.

The alternative explanation offers alternative, albeit no less metaphysical or metaphorical, interpretations of important human impulses, including impulses that ordinarily we categorize as religious, philosophical, or scientific. Heraclitus and Hooker (pages 5-6), for example, may seem anxious to reassure themselves of the supernatural or divine orderliness of the cosmos when they forbid the sun to wander from its customary course. But could it be that what they both betray is not religious (or magical-religious) doubt, but the anguish of inanimate matter alarmed at the very thought that there would be no point in trying to justify its own existence in a cosmos that itself had no orderly justification? Likewise, is it the anguish of inanimate matter that has Milton (page 76), in common with Donne and many others of their time (and the creationists of our time), look for evidence of God's purposes – more orderliness, more justification – in the smallest and humblest works of nature? And does the same anguish drive Plato (page 16), Leibniz (16-18) and Einstein (18-20) all to insist on connecting the world as we perceive, describe and measure it with an eternal order of perfect forms or objective 'physical reality'? On the level of collective human endeavour, the alternative explanation may also have something to say about the paradoxical legacy of the Enlightenment and its great projects for changing and improving society. The paradox is that the eighteenth-century spirit of open, rational enquiry, which was largely inspired by the development of empirical science, tended to degenerate in the nineteenth and twentieth centuries into rigid dogma and pseudo-science, which, indirectly if not directly, inadvertently if not always by design or intention, then turned into dogmatic and pseudo-scientific *systems* to improve society by re-engineering it, and even by re-engineering human nature. Such systems range from Bentham's formulae for the mass-production of happiness by numbers (pages 40, 43), through Spencer's blueprints for the weeding-out of anyone not 'completely adapted' in accordance with social-Darwinian principles (page 42), all the way up to the programmes of tyranny and mass murder sanctioned by Joseph Stalin in the course of his realization of Marxist dogma, and by the Nazis in the course of their project to renounce Enlightenment rationality altogether and rebuild the world by will alone. Perhaps Godfrey Goodman (pages 59-60) would have said that the Enlightenment was doomed from the start, a misguided confederacy of minds busying themselves to make their objects intelligible and, as a result, asking more questions and creating more uncertainties than they could ever resolve. In terms of Sartre's metaphysics, however, the Enlightenment paradox could be explained by analogy with the cyclical pattern of inanimate matter's escape into consciousness and consciousness's panic-stricken retreat into inanimateness – explained, in other words, as the contrary motion of many individual consciousnesses all taking fright at the same time. What shaped the Enlightenment and its subsequent history, Sartre might say, was that the changers and improvers were unable to sustain the openness and uncertainty of rational enquiry, and therefore lurched back towards the massiveness of thing-like dogma, pseudo-science and brute force.

Not in the nature of things

> Man … makes himself such that he is *waited for* by all the tasks placed along his way. Objects are mute demands, and he is nothing in himself but the passive obedience to these demands.
>
> Sartre, *Being and Nothingness* [291]

Whatever the origins of our aversion to being in uncertainties, we are, as they say, where we are and the more pressing question is what to do about it. How should we live, given that most of us do find it very difficult to accommodate the disorderliness, inconsistency, ambiguity and, as we perceive it, unreasonableness of the world? Perhaps we can get closer to an idea of how we should live if we start by recognizing how we should *not* live, and that means recognizing the ways in which, sometimes consciously and sometimes not, we evade uncertainties.

Let's begin with the conventional evasions, which are mostly bound up with making a living and 'getting on' in life. They are easier to spot, I have suggested, in a society living through a golden age, defined not so much as an age of prosperity (although a general increase in prosperity is one of its important conditions) but as an age of collective certainty. By this definition, Britain's golden age (pages 40-42) came to an end in about 1914, so distant to our perceptions and sensibilities that we struggle to get a feel for it. But Japan's golden age (page 31) ended only in 1989 and, with a bit of imagination, is more accessible. Japan's first postwar generations were born into a quarter-century of rapid economic and industrial growth, a time of discipline and extremely hard work and yet a golden age of certainties: the continuity of lifetime employment in one company; the sure prospect of promotion by seniority and a steadily rising income; the sense of purpose and belonging that went with a place, however exalted or menial, in some collective endeavour; and, above all, the certainty of a life arranged programmatically in accordance with the expectations of a rigidly hierarchical social order. The very fact that Japan is now stuck in a grey age of recession and insecurity, and therefore resembles the sort of mature industrialized country we are more familiar with, imparts a quality of universal nostalgia to the golden age it once enjoyed. Regardless of cultural differences, to a greater or lesser extent we all conform to conventional expectations (which come to us through family, teachers, mentors, bosses, peers, friends, neighbours and many others) and allow our lives to unfold, more or less programmatically, in accordance with those expectations. The nostalgia of Japan's golden age reflects back to us our own wish that some great collective hustle and bustle would banish the uncertainties of our lives by wrapping us about with its unquestioned and unquestioning purposes. Denied our wish for a wholesale evasion of uncertainty, we resort to piecemeal evasions – to Sartre's alarm clocks, signboards, tax forms and policemen (my page 49). Taken to its logical conclusion, Sartre's objection to the alarm clock is that it does not allow us to apprehend the possibility of withdrawing from the world and starving ourselves to death: by apprehending the ringing of the clock as a summons, he says, we preclude all possibilities except the possibility of getting up and going to work. I am not suggesting for one moment that we should starve ourselves to death as a matter of philosophical consistency, or that there is anything wrong with 'getting on' successfully, happily and prosperously. What I am trying to suggest is that however successful, happy and prosperous we may or may not be, we should all ask ourselves how we do apprehend the ringing of our alarm clock. *Is* it a summons? If so, is it a summons not just to get up but to put ourselves, day after day, into situations in which our uncertainties are blotted out by the familiar demands and tasks that await us, by our trivial passive expectations of the real, by the values posted along our way like the signs that tell us to keep off the grass?

The crudest and most pernicious forms of evasion are the ones that bring us progressively closer to things and thingness. At the trivial end of the scale, it is what happens whenever we behave as dutiful consumers in thrall to things and their acquisition, for then we become so many peaks and troughs in the sales trends of designer goods, flashy cars and ever smaller and cleverer gadgets. Points on a graph. Objects. We move towards the more serious end of the scale, and yet some of the evasions there too – heavy drinking, drugs, obsessive work and the like – are so commonplace and seemingly unremarkable that their significance escapes us. The very euphemisms we attach to them ('alcohol abuse', 'substance abuse', 'obsessive-compulsive disorders') prevent us from seeing these evasions for what they really are: metaphorical and sometimes literal means of slow suicide, signalling that it is better not to be at all than to be in uncertainties. And even at the most extreme and dangerous end of the scale, still we do not realize that what we are trying to do is to *make things of ourselves*, revert to thingness, in order to renounce the uncertainties of individual consciousness. In Sartre's language, it is the pattern of flight from anguish exemplified by the waiter, the soldier-thing, the young woman who turns her hand into a thing (my pages 89-90) and, above all, by the anti-Semite who turns not just his hand but the whole of himself into a thing (pages 94-96). Although written almost seventy years ago, Sartre's analysis of the anti-Semite is capable, I think, of shedding light on the individual dynamics behind more contemporary events, including events that have nothing to do with racially- or ethnically-based bigotry. I write this not long after the state visit to Britain in October 2010 of Pope Benedict XVI, which was partly overshadowed by revelations relating to the thousands of cases of sexual abuse of children committed and alleged to have been committed by Catholic priests in many countries over many decades. One of the cases to have emerged in Britain is that of a woman now in her sixties who, at the age of thirteen, was raped by the family priest in her own home. [292] The most shocking aspect of the story, in my opinion, is not that effectively the rapist was protected by his church (although inexcusable, cover-up is exactly what we would expect of any secretive institution when its reputation and authority are threatened), but that the girl's own mother, fully aware of what had happened, made no attempt to report the priest and instead told her daughter that it was 'one of God's plans', never to be talked about again. In her own words, the daughter's interpretation is that her mother behaved as she did because she was 'so fanatical and so fear-driven and so obsessed with the church that … I don't think she could bear to deal with what happened to me.' Who can know what uncertainties the girl's mother might have been evading in her fanatical devotion to the church, or the family history, psychology and other circumstances that led her to betray her daughter in such an appalling way. If we did know, however, it is just possible that her seemingly inexplicable behaviour would become more explicable (which is not to say forgivable) as the behaviour of someone so fearful of indefinite approximations that she could not tolerate *any* threat to her church, the one source of certainty that protected her, massively and impenetrably, against doubt and uncertainty. In any event, the outcome speaks for itself and, I would say, it also illustrates a broader problem with institutional religions: all too often what may seem to be a faith in the content of religious beliefs is in fact a faith in the authority of the high priests who operate and enforce them, and who, whatever else they and their institutions might want us to believe, are themselves no more than very fallible human beings.

****

Neither in his writings nor by personal example does Sartre offer any credible model of how to accommodate ourselves to uncertainty, for he had no remedies to go with his diagnosis of the human condition and failed to practise what he preached. While the diagnosis itself is flawed, particularly in its dogmatic refusal to acknowledge the existence of the unconscious, the real problem is that it seems to be a counsel of despair. If, as Sartre claims, all human relations come down to just two adversarial 'attitudes' (in their most extreme forms, sadism and masochism: my pages 46-47), what becomes of love? Compassion? Altruism? Community? Man ceases to be a social animal, or loses the capacity to live as one. And if values are wheels that each of us reinvents independently as we go along, even the individual can have no basis for behaving consistently. Sartre's gambler, for instance, walks away from the gaming table one day because he has an apprehension that it would be bad to ruin himself and cause distress to his family; yet the very next day he may be back at the table, no longer enclosed in his 'magic circle of a resolution' and faced all over again with the recognition that *nothing* prevents him from gambling. [293] To cap it all, Sartre himself evidently found the uncertainties of existential good faith so unsustainable, so unlivable, that in the 1950s he opted instead for bad faith and subscribed to the ready-made certainties of Marxist ideology.

Largely thanks to Sartre, we have a better idea of how we should *not* live, but are we any the wiser about how we might or should live?

Some point of the pendulum's swing

> It's strange how the human mind swings back and forth, from one extreme to another. Does truth lie at some point of the pendulum`s swing, at a point where it never rests, not in the dull perpendicular mean where it dangles in the end like a windless flag, but at an angle, nearer one extreme than another? If only a miracle could stop the pendulum at an angle of sixty degrees, one would believe the truth was there.
>
> Graham Greene, *The End of the Affair* [294]

Once we accept that evading uncertainty is not the way to live, there is no escaping the conclusion that the way we *should* live is, if not by welcoming uncertainty, at least by learning to accommodate it. And yet I have spent page after page arguing that most of us find it extremely difficult to accommodate uncertainty, and even suggesting that there may be an evolutionary/physiological explanation for why this is so. Impasse. Just as it would take a miracle to stop the pendulum at sixty degrees, it seems only a miracle could reconcile us to the reality that, until all its energy is gone, the pendulum never stops at any angle. But the age of miracles is over and reconciling ourselves to that reality looks an impossible task.

Less impossible, I think, if we start by reminding ourselves that uncertainty is built into the physical fabric of our world, and of the whole of the known universe. Certainties do exist. Most familiarly, the movements of billiard balls, rockets and other macro-sized bodies are certain because they obey the laws of Newtonian physics and therefore can be predicted with great precision (my pages 10, 22). Near-certainties exist that would and will be certainties given more information: the age of the universe, for example, is now known to within a one-percent margin of uncertainty (my note 108), and the margin may well be narrowed further as new data and new measurement techniques become available. We are aware, however, that some aspects of reality can never be expressed with absolute certainty. While we blame quantum physicists, and Heisenberg in particular, for bringing us this unwelcome news, we forget that classical physicists had already told us that order, which is a form of certainty, is sometimes more a matter of statistics than of anything we would recognize as order or certainty. The magnetization of oxygen molecules in a magnetic field, for instance, is a statistical phenomenon (paramagnetism) which only occurs because such large numbers of molecules are involved that on average they orient themselves parallel to the magnetic field, whereas individual molecules are constantly changing their orientation in a random fashion. Likewise, the way a vapour sinks in a sealed vessel belies the fact that individual droplets of the vapour do not sink with a steady velocity but move upwards and sideways as well downwards: what appears to be the uniform sinking of the vapour under the force of gravity is an averaging of the irregular motions (or Brownian movement) of all the individual droplets, which, though relatively big themselves, are yet small and light enough to be knocked about as they collide with the molecules of the liquid or gas in which they are contained.[295] The laws of physics show us that there are some absolute certainties, but also that there are realms of matter and energy in which there is no certainty at all, and others where certainty only exists in the sense of a *tendency towards* order or precision and not of a clearly defined *state of* order or precision. Certainties that are certainties, certainties that are not certainties, certainties that are barely distinguishable from uncertainties – all of these are natural features of our world, so who are we to pick and choose and insist that only absolute certainty will do and that anything less is an aberration, and an abomination? When we reflect that the whole universe manages to function perfectly well despite being pervaded with uncertainty even in its most fundamental, quantum reaches, we have to recognize that uncertainty only seems an aberration and an abomination because, for whatever evolutionary, psychological or other reasons, we have made it so. We start to doubt whether absolute certainty merits the sacrosanct status we invest it with, and out of our doubt may come the first inkling that a reconciliation with uncertainty, though difficult, is not impossible.

If one route to the reconciliation begins in the laws of physics, other routes begin in lives and literatures. And if the laws of physics tell us that we are confused about the necessity of certainty, lives and literatures tell us that, presumably for the same evolutionary, psychological and other reasons, we are also confused about the nature of certainty – that we assume it is synonymous with *meaning* and fail to notice that there can be certainty without meaning, and meaning without certainty.

We don't have to look far for evidence that there can be certainty without meaning. In the case of my own life, I need look no further than my chance encounter with the Japanese tourist, which, I now realize, made such an impression on me because it was really an encounter with myself. To ask what is the tallest or oldest building in a city is to expect the certainty of an unambiguous, factual answer: this one, two hundred feet tall, or that one, built in 1405. But to ask what is the *best* building with the same expectation is a confusion because there will be many answers, not one, and they will involve opinions and judgements, not unambiguous facts. And the more we confuse our questions and our expectations, the more meaningless they become, just as consulting a guide book would be all the more meaningless the more categorically the book purported to rank historic buildings in order of their bestness. I see it now, and yet it is what I myself have done for most of my life – confusing certainty with meaning, or worse, being so preoccupied with ordering the world into sterile certainties (page 83: 'T' for Tonga) that I have rarely given any thought to meaning at all.

At the collective level, the confusion of certainty and meaning is illustrated particularly well, I think, by the paradox of the Enlightenment and its legacy. The early spirit of the Enlightenment, open, rational and capable of tolerating the uncertainty of the new, seems genuinely to have concerned itself with meaning and meanings, or knowledge, virtue and happiness in eighteenth-century terms. But over time it ceased to be a spirit of openness concerned with meaning and instead became an obsession with certainty and the systems, increasingly dogmatic and pernicious in nature, through which it was imagined that certainty would be achieved. The utilitarianism of Bentham, for example, grew out of an earnest concern with human happiness but in effect it turned the realization of happiness into an engineering problem to be solved mathematically and mechanically – exactly the confusion deplored by Dickens in a passage from *Hard Times* that is too good not to quote in full:

> So many hundred Hands in this Mill; so many hundred horse Steam Power. It is known, to the force of a single pound weight, what the engine will do; but, not all the calculators of the National Debt can tell me the capacity for good or evil, for love or hatred, for patriotism or discontent, for the decomposition of virtue into vice, or the reverse, at any single moment in the soul of one of these its quiet servants, with the composed faces and the regulated actions. There is no mystery in it; there is an unfathomable mystery in the meanest of them, for ever. – Supposing we were to reserve our arithmetic for material objects, and to govern these awful unknown quantities by other means! [296]

Despite his Enlightenment credentials, Bentham's schemes for the mass-production of happiness may have owed less to the Philosophes than to 'archaic' man, Heraclitus and Hooker and the notions of certainty by which they had reduced meaning to ritual repetition and the observation of magical-religious regularities.

For evidence that there can be meaning without certainty, let's go for the crown jewels: democracy, the rule of law, civil liberties and all the related values which, most of us would say, are not only meaningful but among the greatest achievements of a civilized society. If we ever stopped to think about it, we'd realize that the real significance of our right to vote is not that it enables us to elect a government we like the sound of, but that it enables us to *get rid of* the government if it fails to deliver on its promises, whether those promises relate to civil liberties or, more likely, to unemployment, health, education, terrorism, taxation, bankers' bonuses, or fuel duty. In theory if not always in practice, our relation to our elected governments is one of conditional consent – analogous, it would be pleasing to think, to the relation of the people of the old kingdom of Aragon in Spain to their monarch, to whom they are said to have sworn the following oath of allegiance:

> We, who are worth as much as you, make you our King and Lord provided that you guard for us our privileges [*fueros*] and liberties, and if not, not. [297]

We have, it seems, both meaningfulness and certainty: the meaningfulness of our values and freedoms plus the certainty of a mechanism, the ballot box, by which we can vote out any government that fails to respect the values or tries to curtail the freedoms. Another confusion. It is more or less true, allowing for the imperfections of electoral systems, the possibility of fraud, and the sometimes unpredictable or irrational behaviour of voters,[298] that we have the certainty of the mechanism. Yet the values and freedoms that the mechanism protects are themselves anything but certain because, fraught with tensions and contradictions, they tend to be incompatible (or 'incommensurable', as Isaiah Berlin would say [299]) with each other. To take just one, topical example, where is the certainty in the debate over the appropriate balance between the rights of an individual suspected (but not convicted) of terrorist activities and the rights of everyone else to live peacefully, lawfully and without fear of random death or injury? In practical terms, it comes down to messy compromises: twenty-eight days' detention without charge of a suspect are deemed too long, but fourteen days are acceptable; house arrest cannot be justified, but overnight residence requirements, electronic tagging and travel restrictions can be justified. [300] Although democracy, the rule of law and civil liberties are profoundly meaningful, they are not and never will be certain in the sense of being mutually consistent, unambiguous, or even coherent as a body of values.

But enough of such weighty matters, for there is plenty of evidence that there can be meaning without certainty in the mundane business of 'getting on' with our own lives. Which is to say that, wittingly or unwittingly, we're all at work in Candide's garden. Voltaire intended *il faut cultiver notre jardin* [301] as a rebuff to the dogma and overwrought speculation of his age (and of Leibniz in particular), but the underlying notion of 'getting on' with life is evidently very old. The heart of the Mesopotamian text *The Epic of Gilgamesh*, parts of which may predate 2000 BC, for example, surely lies in the following passage:

> 'Gilgamesh, where are you hurrying to? You will never find that life for which you are looking. When the gods created man they allotted to him death, but life they retained in their own keeping. As for you, Gilgamesh, fill your belly with good things; day and night, night and day, dance and be merry, feast and rejoice. Let your clothes be fresh, bathe yourself in water, cherish the little child that holds your hand, and make your wife happy in your embrace; for this too is the lot of man.' [302]

The notion recurs in the Book of Ecclesiastes (250-200 BC):

> *There is* nothing better for a man, *than* that he should eat and drink, and *that* he should make his soul enjoy good in his labour....
>
> Who knoweth the spirit of man that goeth upward, and the spirit of the beast that goeth downward to the earth?
>
> Wherefore I perceive that *there is* nothing better, than that a man should rejoice in his own works; for that *is* his portion: for who shall bring him to see what shall be after him? [303]

And again, much closer to our own time, in a saying attributed – apocryphally, as it turns out – to Freud:

> Freud was once asked what he thought a normal person should be able to do well. The questioner probably expected a complicated answer. But Freud, in the curt way of his old days, is reported to have said: '*Lieben und arbeiten*' (to love and to work).[304]

It is a notion that seems to invite an unexamined life, or the jolly despair of 'eat, drink and be merry, for tomorrow we die'. In reality, though, what it invites is a recognition that our lives may be most meaningful, and perhaps happiest, when we *stop looking for certainties* – whether symbolized by the certainty of the immortality that Gilgamesh seeks, or the bestness of the world that Pangloss would prove. Above all, in my opinion, we should stop looking for the certainty supposedly contained in the plans and purposes of a personal God: no miracles to stop the pendulum; no 'then' when we shall know God's works with perfect, unimpeded vision; no 'stedfast rest of all things firmely stayd / Upon the pillours of Eternity'. But there are other temptations we have to resist as well, including the temptation to try and endow *il faut cultiver notre jardin* itself with the authority – the certainty, that is – of an '-ism' (quietism, I suppose), or turn it into an excuse for living merely in the expectations of others (in bad faith, as Sartre would judge, escaping anguish by immersing ourselves in the circumstances of our particular 'situation'). Far from inviting an unexamined life or despair, 'getting on' demands a quiet but restless vigilance, and the conviction that a life well lived is not just a life examined but one suspended in the most delicate of balances between meaning and certainty.

Despite all the reservations I have kept expressing about Sartre, it is to his literature that I have returned most frequently. The reason is that I believe, or want to believe, that buried among the despairing insights of his diagnosis of the human condition are others that suggest how we could, and should, try to live better with ourselves and with other people. There are three such insights in particular (or are they three facets of one and the same insight?). The first is that our consciousness not only distinguishes us from inanimate matter but puts us at a distance from ourselves or, as Sartre also describes it, in a relation of ‘*perpetually unstable equilibrium*’ with ourselves. [305] This is a powerful insight because it introduces the possibility of reflecting and behaving differently into situations in which we would otherwise switch, unthinkingly, into our customary evasions of uncertainty. If only we recognized that our evasions are attempts to establish a *spuriously stable* equilibrium with ourselves, we would be less inclined to treat ourselves and, by extension, other people as though they were things. For a start, we would cease to be so obsessed with the mass-produced consumer goods that turn us, and are intended to turn us, into mechanical consumer-things. And from there we might go on to recognize that it is not just being in thrall to objects that makes objects of us, but also being in thrall to group identities, traditions, conventional expectations, ideologies, institutionalized religions, and a great many other sources of what we perceive to be collective certainty. For Sarte’s anti-Semite (my page 95), Frenchness is only ‘true’ Frenchness if it is something he can possess and merge with in a process of mystical identification: his sense of national or ethnic identity permits no distance from himself, and that is how he wants it to remain because a mystical identification with Frenchness guarantees that he can always reply ‘Yes’ to the question ‘Am I the right sort of Frenchman?’, whereas any degree of distance from himself might allow in a very different question – ‘What have I made of the accident of being born in France?’, for instance – to which he had no answer. The pattern of evasion Sartre has identified is not unique to racist bigots. Unless we tolerate, or can learn to tolerate, a relation of unstable equilibrium with ourselves, we are all in danger of living our lives in such a way that we only have to ask questions – especially ‘Am I doing what I’m expected to do? Am I *normal*?’ – to which the answer is ‘Yes’ and rarely if ever ask the meaningful questions – of a job, for example, ‘*Why* am I doing what I’m doing? Is it what I’ve chosen to do? Do I even know the difference between what I choose and what I feel is expected of me?’ We would do well, it strikes me now, to keep our distance and ask the meaningful questions.

The second of Sartre’s insights is that we are ‘condemned to be free’, by which he means that we are absolutely and unconditionally responsible for all the choices we make as we head towards the future in which we await ourselves. Sartre overstates his case. He has to overstate it, because doctrinally he is locked into insisting that our states of mind, attitudes and emotions are modes of consciousness that we freely choose. While that may not be a problem for Sartre, it is a problem for anyone, myself included, who is convinced that many of the choices we make are influenced (and sometimes determined) by nature, nurture, the unconscious, and other factors which in reality are not freely chosen. This is why I prefer to reword '[We are] condemned to be free' to 'It is *as if* we are condemned to be free'. No more than a verbal trick to save Sartre's insight from his own dogma, you may say,[306] but I put it to you that the insight is worth saving, and that the idea of thinking and acting *as if* something is true is not so strange or unfamiliar. We do not object to Marcus Aurelius's exhortation to live each day *as if* it were our last [307] on the grounds that, statistically speaking (unless we are gravely ill, at war, or in some other great peril), the day in question is very unlikely to be our last and therefore we have no reason to behave any differently. Nor, to my knowledge, has anyone ever complained that the discoveries of early navigators are somehow invalid because they were made under the pre-Copernican illusion that the earth is at the centre of the universe: the fact is that Christopher Columbus got to America, Vasco da Gama to India, and countless other explorers, traders and adventurers to their destinations using instruments (including the mariner's astrolabe, later the sextant) that work *as if* the sun goes around the earth and not the earth around the sun. [308] Moreover, living *as if* condemned to be free is no soft option. On the contrary, except in the case of certifiable insanity and other clinically or legally recognized incapacities, it leaves us with no excuses at all for our actions and no pretexts for disowning them – not even the excuse or pretext that *we don't believe we are* absolutely and unconditionally responsible for the choices we make. The most extreme implication of rewording Sartre is that there ceases to be, or it is *as if* there ceases to be, any such thing as 'evil' or 'wickedness' (as opposed to criminal insanity, which does exist and would continue to exist as a distinct condition): 'evil' and 'wickedness' become not defects supposedly inherent in man but names we give to the consequences of what man, what we, actively or complicitly, sometimes choose to do.

The third of Sartre's insights is that by being at a distance from ourselves we have the capacity to conceive of things as other than they are, or as they are not. Sartre (my pages 87-88) characterizes it as a capacity for negation but, more simply or more complicatedly, we might call it imagination, the capacity to bring into the world meanings, truths and even realities which otherwise would not have been in it, and which can be positive as well as negative. For all that the imagination was Sartre's first great philosophical interest,[309] his own capacity for conceiving of things as other than they are seems at times to have been in conflict with his propensity for conceiving of things as his doctrine required. The conflict is apparent in, for example, his analysis of the anti-Semite. Sartre has no trouble convincing us that the anti-Semite lives in a state of hate, is terrifying to others, and mediocre. But again he overstates his argument, now by insisting that the anti-Semite has consciously chosen to be an anti-Semite, which we cannot believe literally because it denies the evidence that racist bigotry is at least in part driven by unconscious impulses. At exactly this point, however, we sense that Sartre's imagination has outwitted his dogmatism and brought into the world the truth that was about to be lost in the doctrine: the truth that the anti-Semite is not an anti-Semite man but an anti-Semite-thing, and that anti-Semitism, like all bigotries, is an attempt to return the world itself to a state of thingness. The moral of the story is that it is imagination, not necessarily consciousness, which keeps us from the massiveness and impenetrability of stone in all its manifestations, including dogma. We should trust to imagination, Sartre is saying in spite of himself, and be prepared to catch ourselves off guard, take ourselves by surprise.

Although I have quoted Sartre more often and at greater length, I really began this essay with Plato and I can't help feeling that we have come full circle back to Plato. He said that the world we inhabit, the visible, tangible, changeable world, is made up of objects of sensation and opinion which come into being and go out of being. Moreover, two millennia before quantum physicists demonstrated that the act of observing a subatomic particle changes its behaviour and, in action-at-a-distance experiments (my page 21), effectively determines the reality of its properties, Plato said that the existence or degree of reality of objects is inseparable from our sensations and opinions: objects come to be and cease to be, he suggested (pages 14-15), *because of* the sensations and opinions we have about them. For Plato, this inseparability of object and opinion rendered the contents of the world of change less than 'fully real', mere 'likenesses' or 'moving shadows' of the perfect and unchanging forms that did exist fully on a higher plane of reality. The world of change, and with it everything that we have ever brought and will ever bring into it, is imperfect, ephemeral and therefore worthless. So Plato pronounced, and as a result he introduced (or lent his philosophical-patriarchal authority to) a jaundiced, dismissive, defeatist strain of thinking that has blighted the world ever since. Closer to our own day, Kafka and Sartre have tipped defeatism into despair by telling us that the world is also *absurd*, its meanings dependent upon the judgements and choices that we ourselves make, randomly – 'chance determines where one stops reflecting', as Kafka put it (page 73) – and without any basis or qualifications for doing so – 'without justification and without excuse', as Sartre put it (page 50).

If it is true, as I think it is, that our everyday world consists of objects of sensation and opinion, then it is all the more true that its meanings are the meanings we apprehend in it – they come *from* us, not *to* us. According to Sartre, some of the meanings we apprehend give rise to negative realities such as 'brokenness' and 'destruction', which are, he says, objective facts and yet only enter the world through human consciousness: even if we had never actively caused damage and destruction ourselves, 'brokenness' and 'destruction' would still have come into the world through our capacity to conceive of what is not, 'what is not working' or 'what is not whole', for example. Just sometimes, however, the meanings we apprehend have the effect not of *dividing* the world into opposing properties or qualities but of *connecting* seemingly unconnected properties and qualities, and not of denying mysteries and doubts but of bringing mysteries and doubts into the world as new realities. For every brokenness and destruction potentially there is a connectedness, a coming together of people and things and places and events that would have passed each other by unentangled had we not been there to entangle them. I shall not attempt to speculate as to whether these realities are objective facts, or suggest that there is any one way of bringing them into being, for there are as many ways of apprehending their meanings as there are apprehenders and, as Arvo Pärt said of the perceptions of his listeners (page 124), they are all justified. But I believe that, though we may exercise it in spite of ourselves and for the briefest of moments in a whole lifetime, we all have a capacity to bring about realities so positive that I can only think to call them varieties of love for the world. And it is a capacity we would not have if, as Plato would seem to have preferred, we were never born but subsisted as ethereal ideas of ourselves in a realm of eternal perfection. The world of change, and the contents that we bring into it *by being part of it ourselves*, are imperfect and ephemeral, but not worthless. Plato is wrong. Unless, that is, we have misjudged him, or he misjudged himself:

Poor Plato, look, you've been misunderstood,
it's change we thought had always been your foe.
You hated change, and yet your hate sprang from
a greater, lesser, unacknowledged love:
love for that world of likenesses
you'd banished to a lower realm.
You loved the crooked thing for all that you decried
the defect of its crookedness.
It's love of children`s games, not fear,
that had you carve their rules in stone.
And man you loved, botch-job of minor gods,
irrational, impetuous and gross,
but still the source of all that you would save.
No handbook for dictators, then, but foot-
notes to your sadness wrought, like rules, in stone.

Poor us, in turn, compelled forever to
repeat what you had tried to warn against:
attachments to the world and choices made
in thoughtfulness, or barely made at all;
gyrations of our souls in space that guide,
misguide and guide haphazardly.
The chance events that might have passed unfixed
we fix in place and time and consequence.
A strobe-lit, rainbowed arc of Devon gulls,
or fireworks on a bow-shaped Izu beach;
the startled gasp as Lowna's woods come to
a tumbled wall, which almost but not quite connects
the fields ahead to dreamt-of fields within.
Haphazardly arrived at, yes, but such
the moments, meanings, worlds that we would save.

7. POSTSCRIPT

The quantum leap, it seems to me, is one of the greatest affronts to our idea of the reasonableness of the cosmos. We can make no sense of things that come and go as they please, discontinuously, without rhyme or reason. And yet at the Big Bang – which, for all we know currently, may have started as some sort of quantum phenomenon – the cosmos itself blinked into existence out of nothing, discontinuously, without rhyme or reason. At the more sedate pace of terrestrial evolution, the first life forms and then we ourselves likewise blinked into existence, again without any obvious necessity for our having done so.

Does some *principle* explain this fact that everything and everyone has come into being, however briefly and however contingently, when they might just as easily, just as logically, not have come into being? An impersonal principle that says *there shall always be something rather than nothing*, an unnamed, metaphysical principle describable only in terms of what it is not. [310] Not a knowable law of physics, for it is meaningless to conceive of physical laws operating 'before' the universe and causing it to appear: even if they existed, what they were 'before' is undiscoverable because the Big Bang denotes an absolute boundary (or 'singularity', as cosmologists call it) at which all laws and predictions break down and through which no information could ever reach us. And not God, or not God in the sense of a personal, supernatural creator who has designed the universe down to its minutest details: whether we allow six days, six thousand years or 13.7 billion years for it to have happened, divine creation is patently a device to mask the limitations of our capacity for the intelligible, of our language and, ultimately, of our imagination.

I had thought to dispense with so many old explanations of why the world and we ourselves exist, but in the end I seem to have reinstated them all, bereft of their names, as one metaphysical principle. 'Archaic' man's denial of linear time and his trust in the cyclical making and remaking of reality; Plato's Form of the Good, personified as a benevolent creator who, lacking in envy, wants to share out his goodness and then, in Plotinus's One, depersonalized once more into an abstract principle; and sufficient reason and perfection, the principles by which Leibniz assures us not only that there is a God who made the world but a God bound by an objective standard of completeness and bestness – a God, in other words, answerable to an abstraction above His own authority. All these and other explanations I have tried to leave behind, only to find them back again; perhaps God back again, albeit no longer a personal entity, no longer called God, and no longer credited with the design or aeon-to-aeon running of the universe. All back again because in their different ways they all represent the hope, or call it faith, that there is something outside and beyond the realm of that which comes into being and goes out of being: the hope that even the end of our universe [311] is nothing to fear because a new Big Bang will create a new universe and, in time, new forms of life will evolve within it. Those forms that develop consciousness (or other, unimaginable modes of self-awareness) may be beset by all the uncertainties that trouble us and, we have to assume, may replicate all that we would call bad and hateful – new stupidities, new cruelties, new Holocausts for new worlds. And of course everything and everyone we have ever found good, ever loved, in good faith and in bad, lucidly and in our obsessions, illusions and delusions, will be long gone, left on the wrong side of the boundary through which no memory will pass. But somewhere in that brave new universe the probability, maybe the certainty, of goodness and love will return.

Acknowledgements

I would like to thank the following publishers for permitting me to quote, at some length in several cases, from their copyright material:

Harvard University Press for excerpts from *The Great Chain of Being: A Study of the History of an Idea* by Arthur O. Lovejoy © 1936, 1964 by the President and Fellows of Harvard College, reprinted by permission of the publisher.

The Medici Society Limited and Encyclopædia Britannica for extracts from *The Six Enneads* of Plotinus (translated by Stephen MacKenna and B.S. Page), reprinted from Great Books of the Western World © 1952, 1990 Encyclopædia Britannica, Inc.

Nature Publishing Group for extracts from Bernard d'Espagnat's article 'The Quantum Theory and Reality' in the November 1979 issue of *Scientific American*.

The New York Times Company for an excerpt from an article in *The New York Times* of 7 August 1955, which may have been responsible for popularizing the phrase "energy too cheap to meter". The article is 'Nuclear History Due to Be Made in Geneva Parley' © 1955 *The New York Times*. All rights reserved. Used by permission and protected by the copyright laws of the United States. The printing, copying, redistribution, or retransmission of this content without express written permission is prohibited.

Open Court Publishing for excerpts from *Albert Einstein: Philosopher-Scientist* edited by Paul A. Schilpp (1970) © 1949, 1951, 1969, 1970 by the Library of Living Philosophers, Inc., reprinted by permission of Open Court Publishing Company, a division of Carus Publishing Company, Chicago, IL.

Penguin Group for excerpts from David Magarshack's translation of *The Brothers Karamazov* by Fyodor Dostoyevsky © the estate of David Magarshack 1958, from Robert Baldick's translation of *Nausea* by Jean-Paul Sartre © Penguin Books Ltd 1965, and from the Richard Wilhelm/Cary Baynes translation of part of the *Hui Ming Ching* included in *The Secret of the Golden Flower.* All three reprinted by permission of Penguin Books Ltd.

Philosophical Library and Taylor & Francis Books UK for permission to reproduce passages from the Hazel Barnes translation of *Being and Nothingness* by Jean-Paul Sartre © 1956, 1984 Philosophical Library, Inc.

Princeton University Press for excerpts from Mircea Eliade's *The Myth of the Eternal Return or, Cosmos and History* (translated by Willard Trask), and Henri-Charles Puech's essay 'Gnosis and Time' (translated by Ralph Manheim) in *Man and Time: Papers from the Eranos Yearbooks*, both originally published by the Bollingen Foundation.

Random House Group for extracts from three titles in *The Standard Edition of the Complete Psychological Works of Sigmund Freud* (translated and edited by James Strachey), namely *The Ego and the Id*, *Civilization and its Discontents* and *Totem and Taboo*, all published by Vintage Books and reprinted by permission of The Random House Group Limited.

Random House Group again for material from three titles by Franz Kafka, *The Castle* (translated by Willa and Edwin Muir, published by Vintage Books), 'Aphorism 86' from *Shorter Works of Franz Kafka* (translated by Malcolm Pasley, published by Secker & Warburg), and *In the Penal Settlement* (translated by Ernst Kaiser and Eithne Wilkins, published by Secker & Warburg), all reprinted by permission of The Random House Group Limited.

Springer Science+Business Media B.V. for excerpts from Bernard d'Espagnat's essay 'Quantum Logic and Non-Separability' in *The Physicist`s Conception of Nature* edited by Jagdish Mehra (1973).

Sources and notes to pages 2-7

1. PREFACE

[1] In Robert Gittings, editor, *Letters of John Keats* (Oxford: Oxford University Press, 1990 reprint), p. 43.
[2] From Mary Guggenheim`s translation of *Portrait de l`antisémite* in *Partisan Review*, Vol. XIII, No. 2 (Spring 1946), pp. 166-167. Sartre`s essay was republished under the title *Réflexions sur la question juive*, translated as *Anti-Semite and Jew* by George Becker (New York: Shocken Books, 1995 reprint). Generally Becker`s is much the better translation, I think, but just here Guggenheim has the defter touch.
[3] First published in German in 1912-13; translation by James Strachey reprinted in Albert Dickson, editor, *The Pelican Freud Library* (Harmondsworth: Penguin Books, 1985), Vol. 13, p. 154.

2. THE STAY OF THE WHOLE WORLD

Wonted motions and the government of the universe

[4] As recorded in the first century AD by Plutarch; Fragment 94, p. 284 in the translation by G.S. Kirk (*Heraclitus: The Cosmic Fragments*, Cambridge: Cambridge University Press, 1962 reprint). Karl Popper takes a dim view of Heraclitus, whose 'failure to distinguish between legal laws or norms on the one hand and natural laws or regularities on the other is characteristic of tribal tabooism: both kinds of law alike are treated as magical …' (*The Open Society and Its Enemies*, Princeton: Princeton University Press, fifth edition, 1971, Vol. I, pp. 14-15).
[5] *Of the Laws of Ecclesiastical Polity*, Book I, Chap. 3; reproduced on p. 925 of *The Literature of Renaissance England*, edited by John Hollander and Frank Kermode (New York: Oxford University Press, 1976).
[6] E.M.W. Tillyard, *The Elizabethan World Picture* (Harmondsworth: Penguin Books in association with Chatto & Windus, 1972 reissue), especially the chapter 'Order'.
[7] Or that every true proposition is 'analytic', meaning that the predicate of a subject-predicate proposition can be shown through 'analysis' (a process of substituting definitions) to be included in the subject. My

main sources are Nicholas Rescher`s *The Philosophy of Leibniz* (Eaglewood Cliffs, New Jersey: Prentice-Hall, 1967, pp. 22-27) and Arthur Lovejoy`s *The Great Chain of Being* (Cambridge, Massachusetts: Harvard University Press, 1964, pp. 174-175).

[8] *On the Ultimate Origination of Things* (*De rerum originatione radicali*); pp. 136-44 in *Leibniz: Philosophical Writings*, translated by Mary Morris and G.H.R. Parkinson (London: Dent, Everyman Classics, 1984 reprint).

[9] As Rescher puts it (*The Philosophy of Leibniz*, pp. 28-29), God 'freely subscribes' to this objective standard of perfection and 'it is only because God [does so] in selecting a possible world for actualization that possible substances come to have (figurative) "claim" to existence.' Rescher intends a rebuke to Lovejoy, who observes (*The Great Chain of Being*, pp. 177-178) that, even within the terms of Leibniz`s own system, God seems redundant because 'essence in itself tends towards existence' (*On the Ultimate Origination of Things*; p. 137 in *Leibniz: Philosophical Writings*).

[10] From *New Essays on the Human Understanding*; p. 158 in *Leibniz: Philosophical Writings*.

[11] From a letter published in 1753, quoted by Lovejoy on pp. 144-145 of *The Great Chain of Being*. A source for the German-language text of the letter is included in Lovejoy`s notes.

[12] Niels Bohr, 'Discussion with Einstein on Epistemological Problems in Atomic Physics' in P.A. Schilpp, editor, *Albert Einstein: Philosopher-Scientist* (La Salle, Illinois: Open Court/Library of Living Philosophers, third edition, 1970), pp. 201-202. This collection of essays, hereafter referred to as Schilpp, was first published in 1949 to celebrate Einstein`s seventieth birthday.

[13] Heisenberg gave the lecture at the University of Chicago in the spring of 1929; his German text is translated by Carl Eckart and Frank Hoyt as *The Physical Principles of the Quantum Theory* (New York: Dover Publications, 1930). My reference is to equation (1) on p. 14 of the translation. While I do not pretend to understand the mathematics by which Heisenberg arrives at the equation, his text is clear enough: 'Any use of the words "position" and "velocity" with an accuracy

exceeding that given by equation (1) is just as meaningless as the use of words whose sense is not defined.' Elaborating on this comment in terms similar to those later expressed by Bohr (my main text page 11 and note 16 below), Heisenberg urges caution in the use of 'reality', 'actually' and other everyday words that 'very often' lead to statements of a kind which 'do not involve any consequences and which therefore have no content at all – in spite of the fact that [such statements] produce some kind of picture in our imagination' (footnote on p. 15 of the translation).

[14] *Zeitschrift für Physik*, Vol. 43; translated by John Wheeler and Hubert Zurek in their jointly edited *Quantum Theory and Measurement* (Princeton: Princeton University Press, 1983), p. 83. Equation (1) of the 1927 paper (translation p. 65) says that the product of the uncertainties in position and momentum is *roughly* equal to *h*; this limit becomes *greater than or* equal to *h* in Heisenberg`s Chicago lecture of 1929.

[15] From *A Philosophical Essay on Probabilities*, translated by F.W. Truscott and F.L. Emory (New York: Dover Publications, 1951 reprint), p. 4.

[16] 'As a more appropriate way of expression,' Bohr recalled later ('Discussion with Einstein ...' in Schilpp, pp. 237-238), 'I advocated the application of the word *phenomenon* exclusively to refer to the observations obtained under specified circumstances, including an account of the whole experimental arrangement. In such terminology, the observational problem is free of any special intricacy since, in actual experiments, all observations are expressed by unambiguous statements referring, for instance, to the registration of the point at which an electron arrives at a photographic plate.' While it may be incorrect to describe Bohr himself as a logical positivist, his terminology does seem close to that of the Vienna Circle of positivists, whose theory of knowledge was founded on verifications likewise expressed in terms of readings on laboratory instruments. Compare, for example, this passage from 'Causality in Contemporary Physics', an essay written in 1931 by Moritz Schlick, leader of the Vienna Circle: 'As is well known, only the individual propositions derived from a

natural law are testable, and these always have the form: "Under such and such circumstances this indicator will point to that mark on the scale", "Under such and such circumstances there occurs a darkening on this point of the photographic plate", and the like. The verifiable propositions are of this nature and of this nature is every verification.' I quote from p. 98 of the translation of Schlick's essay in Stephen Toulmin, editor, *Physical Reality: Philosophical Essays on Twentieth-Century Physics* (New York: Harper Torchbooks, 1970). The volume edited by Toulmin I refer to hereafter as Toulmin.

[17] My remarks on experimental observation are based particularly on the last few paragraphs of John Gribbin's 'Quantum Rules, OK!', a *New Scientist* offprint (Inside Science No. 25, 16 September 1989), and more generally on chapter eight of his book *In Search of Schrödinger's Cat* (London: Black Swan, 1992 reprint). I am indebted to Gribbin, whose skill at non-mathematical, conceptual explanation makes him a democratizer of knowledge that would otherwise be inaccessible to a layperson such as myself.

[18] 'Discussion with Einstein ...' in Schilpp, p. 210.

[19] Max Born, 'Einstein's Statistical Theories' in Schilpp, p. 176. Born's context relates to field theory. The full quote is as follows: 'What [Einstein] is aiming at is a general field-theory which preserves the rigid causality of classical physics and restricts probability to masking our ignorance of the initial conditions ... of all details of the system considered.'

[20] Reprinted together with Bohr's reply (a key document in the Copenhagen interpretation) in Toulmin, pp. 122-142. The two papers were originally published in 1935 in *Physical Review*, Vols. 47 and 48 respectively.

[21] To the best of my understanding, these measurements are possible because they involve values that commute (produce the same mathematical results regardless of the order in which they are calculated), whereas the values involved in the uncertainty relations do not commute.

[22] My account of the EPR reasoning is based on pp. 455-456 of Abraham Païs`s *'Subtle is the Lord ...' : The Science and the Life of Albert Einstein* (Oxford: Oxford University Press, 1982).
[23] Page 130 in Toulmin. Italics as in the original.
[24] Bernard d`Espagnat, 'The Quantum Theory and Reality' in the November 1979 edition of *Scientific American* (Vol. 241, No. 5, pp. 128-140). According to d`Espagnat, Einstein locality is one of three unproven but 'obvious or natural' assumptions in 'local realistic' theories of nature. The other two are realism ('the doctrine that regularities in observed phenomena are caused by some physical reality whose existence is independent of human observers') and the validity of inductive inference ('[which] can be applied freely, so that legitimate conclusions can be drawn from consistent observations').

Leave nothing to chance

[25] *Timaeus* 27-29 and 52; pp. 40-41 and 71-72 in the translation by H.D.P. Lee (*Timaeus and Critias*, Harmondsworth: Penguin Classics, 1977 reprint).
[26] As I understand it, Lee has chosen 'therefore' as an abbreviated way of saying 'therefore [belong to the order of things that] change and come into being.' For comparison, a more recent translation by Donald Zeyl (in John Cooper, editor, *Plato: Complete Works*, Indianapolis, Indiana: Hackett Publishing, 1997, p. 1235) has 'perceptible things are grasped by opinion, which involves sense perception. As such, they are things that come to be, things that are begotten.' Referring to the same passage, Francis Cornford (*Plato`s Cosmology: The* Timaeus *of Plato translated with a running commentary*, London: Routledge & Kegan Paul, 1966 reprint, p. 24) comments: 'As having a visible and tangible body, [the world] is an object of perception and of judgments based on perception. Accordingly, it belongs to the realm of "things that become and can be generated".'
[27] *Laws* 797; p. 284 in the translation by Trevor J. Saunders (Harmondsworth: Penguin Classics, 1975 reprint). Like many other passages in Plato`s dialogues, this one is an object of opinion. On the one hand, it is a key piece of evidence in Popper`s thesis that 'Plato

teaches *that change is evil, and that rest is divine*' (*The Open Society and Its Enemies*, Vol. I, p. 37). On the other hand, in his monumental counterblast to Popper (*In Defense of Plato*, Cambridge, Massachusetts: Harvard University Press, 1953, Appendix XV, pp. 630-631), Ronald Levinson retorts that a close reading of this passage in its context reveals that 'Plato`s maxim is not "all change is bad" but "all change which endangers greater values than itself is bad".' On the basis of translations of the dialogues themselves, personally I find it difficult to avoid the conclusion that Plato is generally hostile to change.

[28] For example, in *Republic* 424 (p. 169 in H.D.P. Lee`s translation, Harmondsworth: Penguin Classics, 1970 reprint), Plato`s discussion of the beneficial effects of education in the ideal community suggests a virtuous rather than a vicious cycle of change. Levinson cites the same passage to support his argument that, far from hoping to abolish change as alleged by Popper, Plato believes that 'change will remain a permanent element in human affairs' (*In Defense of Plato*, p. 464).

[29] *The Great Chain of Being*, pp. 148-149.

[30] *On the Ultimate Origination of Things*; p. 139 in *Leibniz: Philosophical Writings*.

[31] *The Great Chain of Being*, p. 168.

[32] From the *Theodicy*, translated by Lovejoy on his pp. 166-167.

[33] From p. 352 of Wheeler`s 'Beyond the Black Hole' in Harry Woolf, editor, *Some Strangeness in the Proportion* (Reading, Massachusetts: Addison-Wesley, 1980), the proceedings of a symposium held in Princeton to celebrate the centenary of Einstein`s birth. Wheeler credits the Swiss theologian Hans Küng with drawing special attention to Spinoza`s influence on Einstein.

[34] My sources are 'On Scientific Truth' in Einstein`s *Essays in Science*, translated by Alan Harris (New York: The Wisdom Library, 1934, p. 11), and 'Einstein Believes in "Spinoza`s God"', an article in *The New York Times* of 25 April 1929, p. 30. Rabbi Goldstein had cabled Einstein, who was in Düsseldorf at the time, to ask whether he believed in God. Translation of Einstein`s German as in the original *New York Times* article.

[35] 'Discussion with Einstein ...', p. 206 in Schilpp. The italics are mine.
[36] 'I consider it quite possible that physics cannot be based on the field concept, i.e., on continuous structures. In that case, *nothing* remains of my entire castle in the air, gravitation theory included, [and of] the rest of modern physics.' As reflected in this letter to his friend Michele Besso (10 August 1954, reproduced on p. 467 of Païs`s *'Subtle is the Lord ...'*), in his last years even Einstein had come to doubt the feasibility of a unified field theory, which did indeed elude him to the end.
[37] Letter (13 October 1945) from Einsten to Ilse Rosenthal-Schneider, as paraphrased on pp. 144-145 of her 'Presuppositions and Anticipations in Einstein`s Physics' in Schilpp. Einstein`s expression 'a world of qualitatively different lawfulness' is believed to allude to Kant.
[38] From Einstein`s 1917 paper in *Physikalische Zeitschrift*, quoted by Wolfgang Pauli in his 'Einstein`s Contributions to Quantum Theory' in Schilpp, p. 156. The translation is by Schilpp himself.
[39] Letter (7 November 1944) translated by Born on p. 176 of his 'Einstein`s Statistical Theories' in Schilpp. Born`s phrase 'aloof and sceptical' occurs on p. 163 of the same essay.
[40] From pp. 123-124 in Toulmin. Italics as in the original.

Teetering on the brink of probability

[41] Article by James Gleick in *Science Times Supplement*, 21 October 1986, pp. C1 and C4. The three teams of scientists, at the University of Washington, Seattle, the University of Hamburg, and the National Bureau of Standards in Boulder, Colorado, were the first ever to observe and demonstrate the existence of quantum jumps. Their journal reports, which are highly technical, are in *Physical Review Letters*, Vol. 56, No. 26 (30 June 1986, pp. 2797-2799) and Vol. 57, No. 14 (6 October 1986, pp. 1696-1698 and 1699-1702). Direct observation of quantum jumps was achieved by the University of Washington team using an improvised microscope.

Sources and notes to page 21

[42] Strictly speaking, the ten tests have been of Bell`s inequality, a mathematical theorem which enables experimenters to interpret observed correlations between two spatially separated systems that have interacted. The theorem, formulated by the British physicist John Bell in 1964, in effect makes it possible to evaluate the EPR conception of physical reality against that of the Copenhagen interpretation because it shows that each predicts a different, and now testable, experimental outcome. A result known as a violation of Bell`s inequality is interpreted as an endorsement of the predictions of quantum mechanics and therefore, as I understand it, as an indirect if not a direct endorsement of the Copenhagen interpretation. My main source on Bell`s inequality is d`Espagnat`s *Scientific American* article. The technical report on the third Paris test is in *Physical Review Letters*, Vol. 49, No. 25 (20 December 1982, pp. 1804-1807).

[43] I. Marcikic, H. de Riedmatten, W. Tittel, H. Zbinden, M. Legré, and N. Gisin, 'Distribution of Time-Bin Entangled Qubits over 50 km of Optical Fiber' in *Physical Review Letters*, Vol. 93, No. 18 (29 October 2004, 180502-1 to 180502-4).

[44] Referring to one of the earlier and less restrictive tests (the only one to measure proton spins, conducted in 1976 at the Saclay Nuclear Research Centre in France), d`Espagnat argues that its violation of Bell`s inequality implies that at least one of the three premises of local realistic theories (my note 24 above) must be false, and that Einstein separability is 'the most plausible candidate'. He goes on to qualify the mechanism apparently at work in distant-correlation experiments as follows: 'No event that causes another event can be linked to it through this mechanism; the instantaneous influences can pass only between events that are related by a common cause. Hence the concept of a signal could be redefined in such a way that only those means of communication that transmit useful information would be called signals. The principle of the finite velocity of signals would then be preserved.' (*Scientific American* article, pp. 138, 140.)

[45] As d`Espagnat points out with some vehemence, the fact that 'non-separability is now one of the most certain general concepts in physics' has educational and cultural (his word) implications as well as

philosophical implications. He regrets that elementary scientific teaching still 'implicitly propagates' separability as one premise in a view of the world that is nothing but 'a crude model *tailored to specified purposes of ours*', a 'mutilation of the truth [which] throws undue discredit on the concept of *unity*', and a falsehood that 'should not be spread'. These quotes are from d`Espagnat`s essay 'Quantum Logic and Non-Separability' in Jagdish Mehra, editor, *The Physicist`s Conception of Nature* (Dordrecht, Holland: D. Reidel, 1973), pp. 734-735. Italics as in the original.

[46] As Lovejoy puts it (*The Great Chain of Being*, p. 330), 'there could be no conceivable rational ground for the world`s having popped into existence – in however rudimentary a form – at one instant rather than at an earlier one ... Perhaps the world *may* suddenly have burst into being one fine day; but if so, it is a world which just as logically might not have been, and it is in that sense a colossal accident, with no necessity of reason behind it.' These observations would apply more obviously to what we now know as the Big Bang theory of the creation of the universe (to which Lovejoy does allude by implication). Philosophically speaking, however, I think that they apply equally well to the reality of a universe pervaded with quantum uncertainty (which Lovejoy does not discuss at all).

[47] From Bohr`s reply to the EPR paper, p. 132 in Toulmin.

[48] 'On Scientific Truth' in *Essays in Science*, p. 11.

3. ALL THESE PASSIVE EXPECTATIONS OF THE REAL

The best building in Cambridge

[49] C. Nakane, *Japanese Society* (Harmondsworth: Pelican Books, 1977 reprint), pp. 29-30. Nakane`s source is an undated article from the *Asahi Shimbun*, a well respected daily newspaper.

[50] The *Analects* (sayings of Confucius, compiled by disciples after his death in about 479 BC) are said to have been brought to Japan in AD 405 by a Korean scholar named Wani. The Japanese expression *chō-yō-no-jo* (長幼の序) originated in another early Chinese text, the *Mencius*, which consists of dialogues and teachings attributed to

Mencius (who died in about 289 BC and is regarded as second only to Confucius in terms of ideological influence). Alluding to the five human relationships that are central to the Confucian tradition, the text reads: 'between father and son, there should be affection; between sovereign and minister, righteousness; between husband and wife, attention to their separate functions; between old and young, a proper order [長幼有序]; and between friends, fidelity.' This translation comes from Book III, Pt. I, Chap. IV, para. 8 of James Legge`s *The Works of Mencius*, first published by Clarendon Press in 1895; I have used the edition reprinted in Taiwan in 1994 (Taipei: SMC Publishing, combined Vols. I & II of *The Chinese Classics*). It seems reasonable to assume that the *Mencius* would have been introduced into Japan at about the same time as the *Analects*, either by Wani or perhaps another incoming Confucian scholar.

[51] Nakane`s thesis also helps make sense of some otherwise puzzling aspects of historical Japan, particularly in the Tokugawa period (1603-1868). On the basis of neo-Confucian principles as interpreted in Japan, Tokugawa society was stratified into four classes, warriors, farmers, artisans and merchants, ranked in that order according to the supposed value of their respective roles. It was largely an elaborate fiction, maintained despite the fact that the supposed value corresponded less and less with the actual content and significance of the role (especially in the case of the merchants, who dominated economic activity and whose loans were indispensable to financially indebted members of the warrior class). Moreover, the seemingly horizontal alignment of each tier of the official stratification belied the reality that most social relations were aligned vertically. This was even true among outcastes, who did not exist for the purposes of the warrior-farmer-artisan-merchant classification but who did exist for the purposes of civil and criminal law and were ranked in descending order into five main groups: outcaste farmers; tea-whisk makers; monkey-keepers (entertainers who put on monkey shows); *hinin* (非人, 'non-humans', typically beggars and itinerants, including commoners who had fallen into destitution); and *eta* (穢多, 'much filth', hereditary outcastes associated in particular with defiled occupations such as

butchering and leather-working). Customary authority occasionally flowed upwards as well as downwards – for instance, the recognized head of the *eta* in Edo (modern Tokyo) controlled fifteen monkey-keeper households and had powers over the *hinin* of the city – but the point remains that; even beyond the pale of official society, relations operated hierarchically and not in a horizontal plane. All of which is consistent, I think, with Nakane`s thesis in its historical context. My source on Tokugawa customary law is a short paper of my own, 'The *eta* and *hinin* in late Tokugawa and early Meiji Japan: outcastes and their notional emancipation', published in the *Proceedings of the British Association for Japanese Studies* (Sheffield: University of Sheffield Centre of Japanese Studies, 1979, Vol. Four, Part One, pp. 10-24).

[52] *Japanese Society*, p. 31. My note 55 below is thematically linked.

[53] I know of one incident (atypical and again semi-historical, dating back at least forty years) in which a conflict with seniority-based order did indeed occur, not because the junior party deliberately set out to defy the order but because, neither Japanese nor a former student of the senior party, he had no sense of being locked into it in the first place. He was an American academic, an authority on Japanese economic history, who got into an exchange on some point of contention (details unknown) with an eminent Japanese professor. Correspondence went back and forth until it came to an abrupt end with a letter from the Japanese side, which said more or less directly: 'I am a full professor. You are an assistant lecturer. You do not have the right to criticize me.' Sketchy as it is, I think this revealing little incident is worth preserving for social-anthropological posterity.

[54] The phenomenon of 'year clubs' (*dōki no kai*, 同期の会) is closely related to the aversion to merit-based differentiation that I referred to earlier (page 27): if one individual from a particular year`s intake is promoted, others in the corresponding 'year club' feel justified in demanding promotion too on the grounds that they joined the company at the same time (not necessarily, or not at all, on the grounds that they have the same or greater *ability*). I would even say that 'year clubs'

give concrete expression to the Japanese proverb *deru kui wa utareru* (出る杭は打たれる). Word for word this translates as 'The post that sticks out will get hammered in', which suggests 'Mind you never step out of line' or some such injunction against insubordination and non-conformity in general. However, the original Japanese conveys something subtly different, closer to 'Don`t push yourself forward just because you think you`re better than everybody else', a sense that comes across very clearly from the following entry in a Japanese proverb dictionary:

> In the same way that a protruding post will be driven back in, so in human relations those who set themselves above the crowd will be envied and meet with misfortune. There is nothing wrong with outdoing other people, but human nature recoils from this simple logic [人情はこの理屈に反発する]. It is all the more intolerable when someone with no ability behaves in a bumptious manner.

My translation is from the *Kotowaza Jiten* compiled by M. Tajima (Tokyo: Gotō Shoin, tenth edition, 1981), p. 327. Because its purpose is, so to speak, to explain the Japanese to themselves, I regard this dictionary as an authentic voice of Japanese sensibilities.

[55] This sort of compartmentalized thinking was one factor in the management sclerosis that allowed Nissan, Japan`s second-largest carmaker, to slide to the brink of insolvency in 1999. Nissan was then effectively acquired by Renault of France. The new chief operating officer, Carlos Ghosn, Brazilian-Lebanese by birth and partly French-educated, has a very impressive reputation for succeeding in difficult, cross-cultural business situations. One of the first steps he took at Nissan was to create nine cross-functional teams, CFTs, that brought together managers (mostly middle managers, including some from Europe and North America) in a way that would have been unthinkable under the old regime. The teams had no decision-making powers of their own but, together with access to company-wide information, they

were given a three-month brief to review every aspect of Nissan`s operations and make recommendations for restoring growth and profitability. Including those drafted into sub-teams, more than five hundred Nissan employees participated in the exercise, which achieved its objective: ideas that had been evaluated by the CFTs provided the basis for major decisions – including factory closures, large-scale redundancies and other previously taboo measures – taken by Renault-Nissan`s executive committee. The story is a recent and almost perfect illustration of Nakane`s thesis (my page 27) that in Japan seniority-based ranking and, by extension, the whole apparatus of functional hierarchy, can only be changed by some drastic event or group disintegration (in this case, the threatened disintegration of the whole Nissan company). As it was, the CFT initiative got off to a hesitant start but if, hypothetically speaking, Nissan had been in slightly *less* dire straits in 1999, it might have met with such intractable resistance that it failed altogether. In other words, the degree of crisis probably made all the difference to the outcome. My narrative of events is based on David Magee, *Turnaround: How Carlos Ghosn Rescued Nissan* (New York: Harper Business, 2003), pp. 65-79.

[56] My own translation, from memory and I hope accurate (apart from the name of the academy, which is fictitious). Coincidentally, at about this same time my wife and I were invited to a wedding in Tokyo, a formal affair with the usual speeches in which elders and betters pass on their worldly wisdom to the young couple. In another strange conjunction of gender and the steering wheel, one of the guests ended his speech eulogizing the bridegroom with a punch line that translates absolutely literally as: 'Marriage is like a car, and our lucky bride now has a splendid driver.' The simile, delivered with not a trace of irony or humour, met with nodding approval from his audience.

[57] The unemployment rate in 2010 was 5.1%, low by international standards but high by postwar Japanese standards. More significantly, one third (17.5 million individuals) of the employed population in 2010 were classed as non-regular workers, defined as part-timers, agency-supplied staff and others hired on a short-term basis, compared with one fifth (8.8 million individuals) in 1990. The vast majority of these

non-regular workers are women but, given that women have long had second-class status in most aspects of employment in Japan, I suspect that the greatest sense of dislocation is felt by the five million men who find themselves – some but not all by choice – in part-time, inequitably paid and sometimes menial occupations. They include men now in or nearing their forties who first entered the job market during the economic malaise of the 1990s, when Japanese corporations were taking on non-regular workers rather than regular employees as a way of saving on wages and social security costs. At the age when many of them might once have expected to be rising up the rungs of a corporate career ladder, these men move from one job to another in a shiftless existence that offers none of the certainty of an assured place, and little prospect of ever finding such certainty. By this definition theirs is a lost generation and Japan`s suicide statistics suggest that it may be a generation prone to despair. Is it coincidence that in 2003, when men of this generation would have been in their late twenties to early thirties, suicide was the leading cause of death for Japanese men aged 20-44, accounting for 42% of deaths in the 25-29 group and 39% in the 30-34 group? These were the highest proportions by age among male suicides and, while many complex factors would have been at work, changes in corporate recruitment practices were surely in the mix. For comparison, in 2003 suicide was the leading cause of death among Japanese women aged 15-34, with the highest proportions in the 20-29 groups. In 2010, across both sexes and all ages total suicides in Japan were probably at the 30,000-level (my own estimate based on National Police Agency data), down from the 2003 peak of 32,109 but still an appalling average of up to sixty male suicides and more than twenty female suicides *per day*. My main source on trends in Japan`s labour market is the *Economic Survey of Japan 2011* published by the Organisation for Economic Co-operation and Development (Overview with main conclusions available at www.oecd.org/eco/surveys/japan). My source for the analysis of suicide statistics is the Japanese Ministry of Health, Labour and Welfare (www.mhlw.go.jp: searching the Japanese-language pages by 自殺 死亡統計 brings up exhaustively detailed figures to 2003); rudimentary data to 2008 can be found in

English on the World Health Organization website (www.who.int/mental_health/media/japa.pdf).

[58] The missing link is the woman`s husband. Unless my memory is to blame, the magistrate made no mention of him and I can only think that she must have been divorced or separated.

The doers and the done-to

[59] Poem 82 in R.T. Davies, editor, *Medieval English Lyrics: A Critical Anthology* (London: Faber and Faber, 1968 reprint), pp. 171-173. According to Davies`s notes, the refrain 'I say algate' means 'I say always, at all events'.

[60] My source is Johan Huizinga`s *The Waning of the Middle Ages*, translated by F. Hopman (Harmondsworth: Peregrine Books, 1976 reissue), pp. 57-58.

[61] *The Waning of the Middle Ages*, p. 60.

[62] *The Road to Wigan Pier* (Harmondsworth: Penguin Books, 1967 reprint), p. 123. *Ain`t We Got Fun*, lyrics by Raymond Egan and Gus Kahn, music by Richard Whiting, was first performed in 1920. The lyrics, which differ slightly from Orwell`s version, together with a recording made by Billy Jones in 1921 are available at Wikisource (http://en.wikisource.org/wiki/Ain`t_We_Got_Fun), although you may wish to think twice before clicking the link as the copyright position is unclear.

[63] *The English People*, reprinted in Sonia Orwell and Ian Angus, editors, *The Collected Essays, Journalism and Letters of George Orwell* (Harmondsworth: Penguin Books in association with Secker & Warburg, 1970), Vol. 3, p. 37.

[64] The same train of associations might take us to a letter that Wilfred Owen wrote to his mother from Scarborough, Yorkshire, where he was assigned light duties (at a hotel-cum-barracks) following treatment for shellshock at Craiglockhart War Hospital near Edinburgh. The letter is dated 31 December 1917 :

> Last year, at this time, (it is just midnight, and now is the intolerable instant of the Change) last year I lay awake in a windy tent in the middle of a vast, dreadful encampment. It seemed neither France nor England, but a kind of paddock where the beasts are kept a few days before the shambles. I heard the revelling of the Scotch troops, who are now dead, and who knew they would be dead. I thought of this present night, and whether I should indeed – whether we should indeed – whether you would indeed – but I thought neither long nor deeply, for I am a master of elision.
>
> But chiefly I thought of the very strange look on all faces in that camp; an incomprehensible look, which a man will never see in England, though wars should be in England; nor can it be seen in any battle. But only in Étaples.
>
> It was not despair, or terror, it was more terrible than terror, for it was a blindfold look, and without expression, like a dead rabbit`s.
>
> It will never be painted, and no actor will ever seize it. And to describe it, I think I must go back and be with them.
>
> From Letter 578 in Harold Owen and John Bell, editors, *Wilfred Owen: Collected Letters* (London: Oxford University Press, 1967), p. 521.

[65] *Gosford Park*, made in 2001, was directed by Robert Altman. Julian Fellowes won an Oscar for his original screenplay in the 2002 Academy Awards.

[66] Are we to intuit an oblique reference to the Battle of Trafalgar in the detail that the chief petty officer, Walter Hardy, shares his surname with the captain of the *Victory*, Thomas Hardy, the man immortalized in Lord Nelson`s legendary last words, 'Kiss me, Hardy'?

[67] *The Lion and the Unicorn: Socialism and the English Genius*, in *The Collected Essays, Journalism and Letters*, Vol. 2, pp. 118-119.
[68] 'London Letter' to *Partisan Review* dated 15(?) August 1945, in *The Collected Essays, Journalism and Letters*, Vol. 3, pp. 446-447.
[69] The phrase 'real shove from below' comes from p. 125 of *The Lion and the Unicorn.*

The spirit of the age

[70] This quotation is from a manuscript that Bentham wrote in the 1780s, cited under the abbreviated title **Reward* in Ross Harrison, *Bentham* (London: Routledge & Kegan Paul, 1983), p. 247. By then Bentham had already identified equality as one of four 'subordinate ends' by which legislators should aim to achieve the greatest happiness of the greatest number in society; although there were circumstances in which equality would have to yield to 'the pre-eminent object', security, it is clear that for Bentham equality followed ineluctably from his 'greatest happiness principle', which itself followed from the application of reason. In his *Principles of the Civil Code*, intended as a practical handbook for legislators, Bentham wrote:

> In an arrangement designed to give to all men the greatest possible sum of good, there is no reason why the law should seek to give more to one individual than to another. There are abundance of reasons why it should not; for the advantages acquired on one side, never can be an equivalent for the disadvantages felt upon the other. The pleasure is exclusively for the party favoured; the pain for all who do not share the favour.
>
> *Principles of the Civil Code*, Chap. II; translation from the French by R. Hildreth reproduced in *Jeremy Bentham: Selected Writings on Utilitarianism* (Ware, Hertfordshire: Wordsworth Classics, 2000), pp. 316-317.

While Bentham believed in rights based on rational, utilitarian principles, he did not believe in the doctrine of natural rights and his *Anarchical Fallacies* ridiculed France`s revolutionary Declaration of the Rights of Man and of the Citizen (adopted by the National Assembly in August 1789 and included as a preamble to the Constitution of 1791) as 'nonsense upon stilts'. Originally published only in French, a later English edition of *Anarchical Fallacies* is reprinted on pp. 383-459 of *Jeremy Bentham: Selected Writings on Utilitarianism*; the famous phrase occurs on p. 405.

[71] From a manuscript dated 1809, quoted in John Dinwiddy`s *Bentham* (Oxford: Oxford University Press, 1989), p. 81.

[72] Harrison (pp. 212-213) and Dinwiddy (pp. 82 and 110) agree that Bentham fully accepted the principle of female suffrage but hesitated to include it in his reform proposals for fear that, in the social and political conditions of early nineteenth-century Britain, he would be so ridiculed that his arguments for broadening *male* suffrage would not be taken seriously.

[73] *Lettres philosophiques*, translated by Leonard Tancock as *Letters on England* (Harmondsworth: Penguin Books, 1980); Letter 12, 'On Chancellor Bacon', p. 59.

[74] 'Lord Bacon' in *The Works of Lord Macaulay: Essays and Biographies*, Vol. II (London: Longmans Green, 1906), pp. 616. Macaulay`s phrase 'mingled contempt and admiration' appears on p. 646.

[75] *In Bluebeard`s Castle: Some Notes towards the Redefinition of Culture* (New Haven: Yale University Press, 1971), p. 8.

[76] The passage from which these phrases come reads as follows:

> … an ideal social being may be conceived as so constituted that his spontaneous activities are congruous with the conditions imposed by the social environment formed by other such beings. … I have argued that conformably with the laws of evolution in general, and conformably with the laws of organization in particular, there has been, and is, in

> progress an adaptation of humanity to the social state, changing it in the direction of such an ideal congruity. And the corollary ... is that the ultimate man is one in whom this process has gone so far as to produce a correspondence between all the promptings of his nature and all the requirements of his life as carried on in society. If so, it is a necessary implication that there exists an ideal code of conduct formulating the behaviour of the completely adapted man in the completely evolved society.
>
> *The Data of Ethics* (London: Williams & Norgate, 1907), pp. 237-238.

[77] Letter from Marx to Ferdinand Lassalle dated 16 January 1861, translated by I. Lasker in *Karl Marx and Frederick Engels: Selected Correspondence* (Moscow: Progress Publishers, 1965), p. 123.

[78] I have an old debt here to a British Broadcasting Corporation (BBC) Radio 4 *Analysis* documentary broadcast on 26 January 1995 (transcript may still be available from BBC News and Current Affairs Department archives). Produced by Michael Blastland and presented by Peter Kellner, its title, 'The End of Enlightenment?', speaks for itself.

[79] The origins of this tendency doubtless had something to do with the universalism of the Enlightenment, or what Lovejoy in *The Great Chain of Being* (full citation in my note 7) calls its 'uniformitarianism'. Because, as he puts it (pp. 288-289), 'in nearly all the provinces of thought in the Enlightenment the ruling assumption was that Reason – usually conceived as summed up in the knowledge of a few simple and self-evident truths – is the same in all men and equally possessed by all', universal intelligibility and acceptability constituted the 'decisive criterion' by which the validity or worth of any matter of serious human concern came to be judged. In short, Lovejoy continues (pp. 292-293), the Enlightenment was 'an age devoted, at least in its dominant tendency, to the simplification and the standardization of thought and life', a process which translated into a 'general attack upon the *differentness* of men and their opinions and valuations and

institutions'. He goes on to argue that Romanticism was a 'diversitarian' reaction against the 'uniformitarianism' of the Enlightenment: see my note 123 and note 241 below.

80 It is beyond the scope of this essay to speculate on how far Spencer and Marx should be held responsible for everything that has been done in their names. But it is hard to believe that the brutally matter-of-fact content and tone of some of their writings would have had no effect on those they influenced, whether of a capitalist or a communist persuasion. In Spencer`s case I would cite the following passage from *The Man versus the State*, first published in 1884, in which he explains why the weakest and least adapted members of society will suffer, and *must* suffer, as humanity is 'moulded into harmony' with the necessities of the social state:

> To become fit for the social state, man has not only to lose his savageness, but he has to acquire the capacities needful for civilized life. Power of application must be developed; such modification of the intellect as shall qualify it for its new tasks must take place; and, above all, there must be gained the ability to sacrifice a small immediate gratification for a future great one. The state of transition will of course be an unhappy state. Misery inevitably results from incongruity between constitution and conditions. All these evils which afflict us, and seem to the uninitiated the obvious consequences of this or that removable cause, are unavoidable attendants on the adaptation now in progress. Humanity is being pressed against the inexorable necessities of its new position – is being moulded into harmony with them, and has to bear the resulting unhappiness as best it can. The process *must* be undergone, and the sufferings *must* be endured. No power on earth, no cunningly-devised laws of statesmen, no world-rectifying schemes of the humane, no communist

> panaceas, no reforms that men ever did broach or ever will broach, can diminish them one jot. Intensified they may be, and are; and in preventing their intensification, the philanthropic will find ample scope for exertion. But there is bound up with the change a *normal* amount of suffering, which cannot be lessened without altering the very laws of life.
>
> From 'The Sins of the Legislators' in *The Man versus the State* (London: Williams & Norgate, 1884), pp. 67-68.

In Marx`s case I would cite *The Communist Manifesto,* co-authored with Engels and first published in German in 1848, which reads in part as an open invitation for succeeding generations of Party inquisitors, secret police, youth brigades, misguided or ill-intentioned busybodies and other informers to detect and denounce 'class enemies' wherever they might be known, or imagined, to lurk:

> The lower middle class, the small manufacturer, the shopkeeper, the artisan, the peasant, all these fight against the bourgeoisie, to save from extinction their existence as fractions of the middle class. They are therefore not revolutionary, but conservative. Nay more, they are reactionary, for they try to roll back the wheel of history....
>
> The 'dangerous class' [by which Marx means the *Lumpenproletariat*], the social scum, that passively rotting mass thrown off by the lowest layers of old society, may, here and there, be swept into the movement by a proletarian revolution; its conditions of life, however, prepare it far more for the part of a bribed tool of reactionary intrigue.
>
> *The Communist Manifesto* (Harmondsworth: Penguin Books, 1969 reprint of Samuel Moore`s 1888 translation), pp. 91-92.

[81] As recorded by the Earl Cowper in his preface to *Lord Melbourne`s Papers*, edited by Lloyd Sanders (London: Longmans, Green & Co., 1889), p. xii. Although Cowper does not explain when or in what circumstances Melbourne made this remark, in his biography of Melbourne, *Lord M* (London: The Reprint Society, 1955, single-volume edition including *The Young Melbourne*, p. 342), David Cecil suggests that it would have been during the period when Macaulay, serving as Secretary at War in Melbourne`s 1839-1841 administration, 'at once dazed and dazzled his colleagues by the uninterrupted flow of his discourse.' Sadly, Cecil too fails to cite any documentary source for the remark.
[82] Lewis Strauss, Chairman of the US Atomic Energy Commission, as quoted in *The New York Times* of 7 August 1955 (pp. 1, 3, 'Nuclear History Due to Be Made in Geneva Parley'). The wording is probably from a speech that Strauss had made to the National Association of Science Writers the previous year (*New York Times*, 17 September 1954, 'Abundant Power from Atom Seen'). As indicated in my *Acknowledgements* (page 148), The New York Times Company issues stern warnings against the unauthorized use of its copyright material and you are advised not to reproduce it without formal permission.
[83] *Nineteen Eighty-Four* (Harmondsworth: Penguin Books, 1980 reprint), p. 51.

All these passive expectations of the real

[84] *Being and Nothingness: An Essay on Phenomenological Ontology*, translated by Hazel Barnes (London: Routledge, 1993 reprint), p. 571. Sartre subscribes to the phenomenological view that consciousness is always 'intentional', that is, directed upon some object. As I understand his terminology, *comprendre* is associated with 'unreflective' consciousness or 'the pre-reflective *cogito*', the mode of consciousness which is immediately aware of the object and at the same time implicitly aware of its own awareness (as, for example, we are immediately aware of watching a film and implicitly aware of ourselves watching it). By contrast, *connaître* is associated with the 'reflective' consciousness which, in a deliberate (as opposed to an

implicit) act of reflection, directs its attention on itself as an object of study. In my opinion, however, none of this changes the fact that Sartre`s denial of the unconscious simply does not ring true with our everyday experience.

85 *Being and Nothingness*, p. 412. See also my note 183 below.

86 Sartre`s footnote 14 on p. 412. *Cahiers pour une morale* (written in 1947, translated by David Pellauer as *Notebooks for an Ethics*), a collection of aphoristic comments, arguably does not count because it remained unpublished until 1983, three years after Sartre`s death. In *L`existentialisme est un humanisme* (published in 1946, translated by Philip Mairet as *Existentialism and Humanism*) Sartre tries to find a way out of the despairing tangle of human relations by invoking a principle of ethical universalization: it would be inconsistent, he argues, to choose freedom for ourselves without also choosing freedom for others. The problem is that this argument directly contradicts everything Sartre has said in *Being and Nothingness* about our relations with other human beings. The last of Sartre`s major philosophical works to be published in his lifetime, Vol. 1 of *Critique de la raison dialectique* (1960, translated by Alan Sheridan-Smith as *Critique of Dialectical Reason*) is the greatest disappointment because evidently it is the result of the 'radical conversion' referred to in *Being and Nothingness*, which turns out to be Sartre`s own conversion to Marxism. His aim, it seems, is to recast Marxism so that it treats the individual as an active agent and not exclusively as an 'inert object' or 'passive product' determined 'entirely … by prior circumstances – that is, in the final analysis, by economic conditions' (from the Barnes translation of *Question de méthode*, effectively the preface to the *Critique,* in *The Problem of Method*, London: Methuen, 1963, pp. 85-87). But the task is doomed from the outset for it attempts an impossible fusion of existentialism, which is a philosophy of spontaneous consciousness and 'anguished' individual freedom, with Marxism, a deterministic theory of history and society according to which the individual acts only as a member of a group or class. For the record, I have not read the *Critique of Dialectical Reason* itself and nor am I likely to.

[87] 'The being of consciousness qua consciousness is to exist *at a distance from itself* [*à distance de soi*] as a presence to itself, and this empty distance which being carries in its being is Nothingness.' *Being and Nothingness*, p. 78; the corresponding passage in *L`être et le néant* (Librairie Gallimard, 1943) is on p. 120. Sartre`s italics.

[88] 'Human freedom precedes essence in man and makes it possible; the essence of the human being is suspended in his freedom. .... Man does not exist *first* in order to be free *subsequently*; there is no difference between the being of man and his *being-free*.' *Being and Nothingness*, p. 25. Sartre`s italics.

[89] Sartre`s phrase 'condemned to be free' occurs on p. 439 of *Being and Nothingness*. Elsewhere he describes anguish in terms of the nightmarish unpredictability of our own future decisions and actions. To say, for example (p. 36), that 'I await myself in the future' is to say that 'I "make an appointment with myself on the other side of that hour, of that day, or of that month." Anguish is the fear of not finding myself at that appointment, of no longer even wishing to bring myself there.' Anguish and fear are not synonymous and to distinguish between them Sartre imagines (p. 29) the vertigo we might feel crossing a narrow path along the top of a dangerous precipice: 'Vertigo is anguish to the extent that I am afraid not of falling over the precipice, but of throwing myself over. A situation provokes fear if there is a possibility of my life being changed from without; my being provokes anguish to the extent that I distrust myself and my own reactions in that situation.'

[90] *Being and Nothingness*, pp. 37-38.

[91] *Being and Nothingness*, p. 38.

[92] *Being and Nothingness*, p. 39.

[93] *Being and Nothingness*, p. 37.

[94] *Being and Nothingness*, p. 39. The 'nihilated' of 'nihilated by the consciousness of my freedom' comes from *néantir*, a word coined by Sartre, which Barnes (Key to Special Terminology, p. 632) glosses as follows: 'Consciousness exists as consciousness by making a nothingness ... arise between it and the object of which it is consciousness. Thus nihilation is that by which consciousness exists. To nihilate is to encase with a shell of non-being.'

[95] 'There is … no question of expelling anguish from consciousness nor of constituting it in an unconscious psychic phenomenon; very simply I can make myself guilty of bad faith while apprehending the anguish which I am, and this bad faith, intended to fill up the nothingness which I *am* in relation to myself, precisely implies the nothingness which it suppresses.' *Being and Nothingness*, p. 44.

[96] Unlike a conventional lie directed towards other people, bad faith does not set up a duality between the deceiver and the deceived: 'the one to whom the lie is told and the one who lies are one and the same person, which means that I must know in my capacity as deceiver the truth which is hidden from me in my capacity as the one deceived' (*Being and Nothingness*, p. 49). This paradox is another consequence of Sartre`s insistence that there is no such thing as an unconscious which, as Freudians would say, enables us to deny something consciously while knowing it unconsciously.

[97] *Being and Nothingness*, p. 59.

[98] *Being and Nothingness*, pp. 39-40. My italics.

[99] *Being and Nothingness*, p. 626. Sartre`s italics.

The proof of the pudding

[100] In Japanese, *ichi o kiite jū o shiru* (一を聞いて十を知る). The proverb originated in China (in the *Analects* of Confucius, I believe).

[101] To interpret *Being and Nothingness* as demolishing 'them-and-us' barriers is, I appreciate, perverse because Sartre would probably say that 'them and us' denotes the reality that human relations consist in irreconcilable conflicts – or irremovable barriers – between own our consciousness and the consciousnesses of all the other people we share the world with.

[102] Conscription provides a particularly good illustration of what Sartre means by insisting that, condemned to be free, we have unlimited responsibility not just for our own choices but for everything that happens around us in the world:

> there are no *accidents* in a life; a community event which suddenly bursts forth and involves me in it does not come from the outside. If I am mobilized in a war, this war is *my* war; it is in my image and I deserve it. I deserve it first because I could always get out of it by suicide or by desertion .... For lack of getting out of it, I have *chosen* it. This can be due to inertia, to cowardice in the face of public opinion, or because I prefer certain other values to the value of the refusal to join in the war (the good opinion of my relatives, the honor of my family, *etc*.). Anyway you look at it, it is a matter of choice. This choice will be repeated later on again and again without a break until the end of the war. ... If therefore I have preferred war to death or to dishonor, everything takes place as if I bore the entire responsibility for this war. Of course others have declared it, and one might be tempted perhaps to consider me as a simple accomplice. But this notion of complicity has only a juridical sense, and it does not hold here. For it depended on me that for me and by me this war should not exist, and I have decided that it does exist.

Being and Nothingness, p. 554. Sartre`s italics.

[103] For many people, Kynaston writes, 1945 remains ‘the great, good date of the 20th century’, the year when Britain turned away from ‘the cruel, unplanned, capitalist miseries of the past’. Against this ‘uplifting orthodoxy’, however, he sets the evidence that even in 1945 the expectations of progressive politicians and planners were far removed from those of most ‘ordinary people’, predominantly working-class, whose ‘individualistic, acquisitive’ tendencies came to be reflected much more accurately in the ‘Thatcherite socio-economic settlement’ of the 1980s (which, he suggests, was then broadly endorsed by New Labour under the leadership of Tony Blair). My references are to Kynaston`s essay ‘Dual Britannia’ in the *FT* [*Financial Times*]

Magazine of 19/20 May 2007, pp. 17-19. In *Austerity Britain 1945-51* (London: Bloomsbury Publishing, 2008, pp. 178-179 and 605), Kynaston acknowledges the work of three other historians, Steven Fielding, Peter Thompson and Nick Tiratsoo, who have examined the mismatch between the collectivist expectations of what we would now call Old Labour and the individualist expectations of the working-class electorate Old Labour claimed to represent. *Austerity Britain* is the first of four volumes in Kynaston`s ongoing social history of Britain from 1945 to 1979.

[104] In *Simone de Beauvoir and Jean-Paul Sartre: The Remaking of a Twentieth-Century Legend* (Hemel Hempstead: Harvester Wheatsheaf, 1993, especially pp. 98-121), Kate Fullbrook and Edward Fullbrook present circumstantial and textual evidence to support their claim that Sartre was heavily influenced by a late draft of *L`invitée* of which he had read more than half in February 1940, five months before he began work on *Being and Nothingness*. *L`invitée* (translated by Yvonne Moyse and Roger Senhouse as *She Came to Stay*) was published in 1943, the same year as *Being and Nothingness*. See also my note 183 below.

4. THE AMBIVALENCE OF STAR DUST

[105] Pages 79-80 in the edition paired with *The Floating Opera* (New York: Anchor Books, 1989). *The End of the Road* was first published in 1958.

[106] From *The Fall of Man*, published in 1616, quoted by Tillyard in *The Elizabethan World Picture* (full citation in my note 6), p. 89.

[107] Unless I am mistaken, Goodman`s notion of the proper state of man and his understanding relates closely to what Francis Bacon, writing at about the same time, called 'that pure light of natural knowledge': my main text p. 76 and note 151 below.

The old affliction and where it came from

[108] The age of the universe has been narrowed down to 13.7 billion years, plus or minus 120 million years (i.e. the margin of uncertainty is

within one per cent), on the basis of data obtained from the Wilkinson Microwave Anisotropy Probe (WMAP), a spacecraft launched in 2001. Developed jointly by the National Aeronautics and Space Administration (NASA) Goddard Space Flight Center and Princeton University, WMAP detects temperature differences in the microwave background radiation left over from the Big Bang; the measurement of these microwave patterns across the sky now enables accurate testing of theoretical models of the cosmos. My main, non-technical source is the WMAP Project website (http://wmap.gsfc.nasa.gov). One of the extremely technical papers that report the dating and other results is G. Hinshaw et al., 'Five-Year Wilkinson Microwave Anisotropy Probe Observations: Data Processing, Sky Maps, and Basic Results' in *The Astrophysical Journal Supplement Series*, Vol. 180, No. 2 (February 2009), pp. 225-245.

[109] The Milky Way`s estimated age of 13.6 billion years, plus or minus 800 million years, is based on observations made in 2003 using one of the instruments (a high-performance optical spectrograph) of the Very Large Telescope array operated by the European Southern Observatory (ESO) in Chile. The observations focused on two so-called 'turnoff' stars in the globular cluster NGC 6397, which are very old but which contain chemical elements that could only have been synthesized in an even older generation of more massive stars that had exploded as supernovae after relatively short lives. By measuring the amount of beryllium in the two 'turnoff' stars, it was possible to determine how much time had elapsed between the demise of these earlier stars and the formation of the 'turnoff' stars. Adding the elapsed time of 200-300 million years to the estimated age of the NGC 6397 cluster, 13.4 billion years, produces the figure of 13.6 billion years for the Milky Way as a whole. The margin of uncertainty of 800 million years (almost six per cent) relates to the age of NGC 6397, which is derived from stellar evolutionary modelling. Non-technical source: ESO press release dated 17 August 2004 (www.eso.org/public/outreach/press-rel/pr-2004/pr-20-04.html). Technical paper: L. Pasquini et al., 'Beryllium in turnoff stars of NGC 6397: Early Galaxy spallation, cosmochronology and cluster

formation' in the journal *Astronomy and Astrophysics*, Vol. 426, No. 2 (November 2004), pp. 651-657.

110 Radiometric dating (measurement of the decay of naturally occurring radioactive isotopes) of meteorite fragments suggests that they formed 4.58 to 4.53 billion years ago, which, on the assumption that all the solid bodies in the solar system formed at the same time, is also taken as the likely age range for the solar system itself. Analysis of lead isotopes gives an age for meteorites and the earth of 4.54 billion years, with an uncertainty of less than one percent. The oldest rocks so far found on earth (in Canada) date to about 4.03 billion years ago; the oldest mineral grains (of zircon, found in Australia) are thought to be about 4.4 billion years old. For comparison, the oldest samples brought back from the moon (which, unlike the earth, has not had its earliest rocks destroyed or recycled by tectonic forces) have estimated ages of 4.5 to 4.4 billion years. Non-technical source: online article 'Age of the Earth' maintained, and last updated in July 2007, by the US Geological Survey (http://pubs.usgs.gov/gip/geotime/age.html). Technical papers with abstracts reasonably accessible to the general reader: J. Baker et al., 'Early planetesimal melting from an age of 4.5662 Gyr [Gigayears = billion years] for differentiated meteorites' in the journal *Nature*, Vol. 436, No. 7054 (25 August 2005), pp. 1127-1131; and S. Wilde et al., 'Evidence from detrital zircons for the existence of continental crust and oceans on the Earth 4.4 Gyr ago' in *Nature*, Vol. 409, No. 6817 (11 January 2001), pp. 175-178.

111 I have purloined the phrase 'from chemical evolution to Darwinian evolution' from the notice announcing a virtual seminar at the NASA Astrobiology Institute on 3 November 2008 in which Jack Szostak, a professor of genetics at Harvard Medical School, was to report on experimental progress towards building synthetic cells as a way of understanding how life might have begun on earth. The announcement (under Director`s Seminars at http://astrobiology.nasa.gov/events) reads in part: 'Through our efforts to synthesize extremely simple artificial cells, we hope to discover plausible pathways for the transition from chemical evolution to Darwinian evolution. We view the two key components of a primitive cell as a self-replicating nucleic acid

genome, and a self-replicating boundary structure.' Together with Alonso Ricardo, Szostak wrote a very readable account of developments in their field for the September 2009 edition of *Scientific American* (Vol. 301, No. 3, pp. 54-61). Another Harvard colleague, George Church, who is working on synthetic ribosomes (the protein-making machinery within a cell), describes his goal as the creation of an artificial genome of 151 genes, thought to be the minimum required to produce a functioning, self-replicating cell: Church`s results are outlined in a HarvardScience article dated 7 March 2009, 'Taking a stride toward synthetic life', included in the interdisciplinary Origins of Life Initiative (www.harvardscience.harvard.edu/directory/programs). Astonishingly, there are fossil remains of what may have been the first cellular organisms, microbe-like prokaryotes (cells that lack a distinct nucleus), but their dating is controversial because they are so minute and difficult to distinguish from objects produced by non-biological processes. The controversy, or at least a varying degree of caution in interpreting data, is illustrated by two papers in the same journal, *Philosophical Transactions of the Royal Society: B*, Vol. 361, No. 1470 (29 June 2006): in one, 'A fresh look at the fossil evidence for early Archaean cellular life' (pp. 887-902), Martin Brasier and others warn that 'structures older than about 3.0 Gyr [i.e. three billion years] should not be accepted as of biological origin until alternative hypotheses for their abiogenic origin have been tested and falsified'; by contrast, in 'Fossil evidence of Archaean life' (pp. 869-885), J. William Schopf reviews data relating to seventy-five fossil deposits and 'geologic units' and asserts they 'support the view that life`s existence dates from more than or equal to 3500 Myr [Million years] ago.' Whatever the precise age of the earliest prokaryotes, they in turn must have evolved from something even older and more primitive (whether genetic molecules within fatty-acid membranes or some other 'protocells'), which suggests a plausible age for the very first life forms in excess of 3.5 billion years. For comparison, in their *Scientific American* article (p. 54) Szostak and Ricardo speak of 'life first [arising] from nonliving matter around 3.7 billion years ago'.

[112] Fossilized *Ardipithecus ramidus* remains were first found by Tim White in 1992 in the Afar Rift region of Ethiopia; a dossier of papers summarizing almost two decades of research on these and other remains, including the partial skeleton of a female nicknamed 'Ardi', was published in the journal *Science* on 2 October 2009 (Vol. 326, Issue 5949, pp. 1-188). *Homo habilis* was identified as a species by Louis Leakey and others in 1964 from fossils discovered at the Olduvai Gorge in Tanzania; the recent discovery in Kenya of a 1.44 million-year-old *Homo habilis* skull suggests that the species survived longer than previously recognized and coexisted with *Homo erectus*, which upsets the earlier assumption that *Homo erectus* had evolved after *Homo habilis*: see F. Spoor, M.G. Leakey et al., 'Implications of new early *Homo* fossils from Ileret, east of Lake Turkana, Kenya' in *Nature*, Vol. 448, No. 7154 (9 August 2007), pp. 688-691. The oldest known fossil remains of anatomically modern humans – our most direct ancestors, that is – have been found in Ethiopia. The Omo I and Omo II fossils of early modern humans were discovered at sites in the Kibish Formation in 1967; argon dating analysis of volcanic ash layers at the sites has since confirmed the age of Omo I and II at about 195,000 BP [Before Present]. Remains found at the Herto site in 1997 have been dated to about 160,000 BP; although classified as *Homo sapiens idaltu* rather than *Homo sapiens sapiens*, the Herto fossils provide further evidence of the transition from archaic humans to fully modern humans. My latter sources are: I. McDougall et al., 'Stratigraphic placement and age of modern humans from Kibish, Ethiopia' in *Nature*, Vol. 433, No. 7027 (17 February 2005), pp. 733-736; J.G. Fleagle et al., 'Paleoanthropology of the Kibish Formation, southern Ethiopia: Introduction' in the *Journal of Human Evolution*, Vol. 55, Issue 3 (September 2008), pp. 360-365; and T.D. White et al., 'Pleistocene *Homo sapiens* from Middle Awash, Ethiopia' in *Nature*, Vol. 423, No. 6941 (12 June 2003), pp. 742-747.

[113] Absolute brain size is an incomplete or misleading evolutionary measure for at least three reasons: it is less meaningful than brain size relative to body mass, later changes have involved *reduction* in brain size as well as enlargement, and the most significant changes are those

that take place in the neocortex and related structures in particular. Nevertheless, one puzzle is what to make of the Neanderthals, whose average brain size is thought to have been larger than that of most modern humans today (albeit Neanderthals appear less big-brained when their bulkier bodies are taken into consideration). Recent research indicates that, contrary to earlier findings, there was some interbreeding between early modern humans and Neanderthals – perhaps during the thousands or tens of thousands of years they coexisted in the Near East – and that as a result Neanderthal genetic material accounts for up to four percent of the DNA of many non-African human populations living now. As I understand it, this probably represents interbreeding between two separate species, *Homo sapiens* and *Homo neanderthalensis*, that originated in common ancestors but then evolved separately. And yet the very fact that we are cousins and not descendants of the Neanderthals suggests some intriguing questions: What if we had descended directly from the Neanderthals? Would the quality of our consciousness somehow be different? Would we be troubled by free will? Would Sartre have written *Being and Nothingness*? Would there have been a Sartre to write it? My factual sources include: J.H. Kaas, 'From mice to men: the evolution of the large, complex human brain' in the *Journal of Biosciences*, Vol. 30, No. 2 (March 2005), pp. 155-165; G.L. Roth, 'The evolution of consciousness' in Roth and M.F. Wullimann, editors, *Brain Evolution and Cognition* (New York: Wiley, 2001), pp. 555-582; C. Sherwood et al., 'A natural history of the human mind: tracing evolutionary changes in brain and cognition' in the *Journal of Anatomy*, Vol. 212, Issue 4 (April 2008), pp. 426-454; and M. Ponce de León et al., 'Neanderthal brain size at birth provides insights into the evolution of human life history' in *Proceedings of the National Academy of Sciences*, Vol. 105, No. 37 (16 September 2008), pp. 13764-13768. Recent findings relating to Neanderthal/early modern human interbreeding are in R.E. Green et al., 'A Draft Sequence of the Neandertal Genome' in *Science*, Vol. 328, No. 5979 (7 May 2010), pp. 710-722; the full paper can be accessed online, together with a press release ('The Neandertal in us') and supporting material, on the website of the Leipzig-based Max Planck Institute for Evolutionary Anthropology (www.eva.mpg.de/neandertal/index.html). Despite the immense technical challenges involved, the research team headed by Svante Pääbo hopes to decode the remaining parts of the Neanderthal genome, which may well mean more surprises to come.

[114] *Timaeus* 41; p. 58 in the Lee translation (full citation in my note 25 above). The creation of the soul of the universe is described in 34-37; Lee pp. 46-51.

[115] *Timaeus* 43; Lee p. 59.

[116] *Timaeus* 41; Lee p. 57.

[117] As described in *Timaeus* 69 (Lee p. 97), the mortal parts of man`s soul were put in by the lesser gods, who

> took over from [the creator] an immortal principle of soul, and, imitating him, encased it in a mortal physical globe [the skull], with the body as a whole for vehicle. And they built on to it another mortal part, containing terrible and necessary feelings: pleasure, the chief incitement to wrong, pain, which frightens us from good, confidence and fear, two foolish counsellors, obstinate passion and credulous hope. To this mixture they added irrational sensation and desire which shrinks from nothing, and so gave the mortal element its indispensable equipment.

[118] *Laws* 904; pp. 438-439 in the Saunders translation (my note 27).

[119] *Republic* 617-618; pp. 397-398 in the Lee translation (my note 28).

[120] *Republic* 619; Lee p. 399. Sartre has his own take on the myth of Er, which he refers to in *Being and Nothingness*: see my text page 118.

[121] *Timaeus* 41-42; Lee p. 58.

[122] *Timaeus* 43; Lee p. 59.

[123] I have borrowed the phrase from Lovejoy`s *The Great Chain of Being*, p. 326. Lovejoy`s broader but related context is his history of the idea of creation as a 'great chain' of being, which he starts in the fourth century BC with Plato and ends in the mid-nineteenth century

with the German philosopher Friedrich Schelling. It turns out to be a history of *two* contradictory ideas of God (or of the Good, which tends to be synonymous with God) and man`s perplexity as to which he should imitate. At its beginning is the passage in the *Timaeus* (29-30; Lee p. 42) which purports to explain why 'this universe of change' was framed in the first place, namely that the framer, the creator, was 'good, and [since] what is good has no particle of envy in it … he wished all things to be as like himself as possible.' The problem is that in Plato`s age a 'good' creator is a self-sufficient creator, perfect and complete in himself, and yet at the same time we are asked to believe that a 'good' creator would be guilty of envy, and not perfect or complete at all, unless he created beings other than himself. The consequence of this contradiction, Lovejoy argues, is that for centuries man was torn between two images and ideals of the Good: the 'otherworldiness' represented by a truly self-sufficient being 'out of time … [and] needing no world of lesser beings to supplement or enhance his own eternal self-contained perfection' (p. 315); and the 'this-worldliness' represented by a generative creator who, far from keeping existence to himself alone, has produced a bewildering diversity and fullness of lesser beings. If the Good lay in the contemplation or imitation of God, it required, 'on the one hand, a transcendence and suppression of the merely "natural" interests and desires, a withdrawal of the soul from "the world" the better to prepare it for the beatific vision of the divine perfection; and … on the other hand, a piety towards the God of things as they are, an adoring delight in the sensible universe in all its variety, an endeavor on man`s part to know and understand it ever more fully, and a conscious participation in the divine activity of creation' (p. 316). Lovejoy traces his history through many twists and turns until, in its later phases, God and the 'great chain' are 'temporalized' (in the sense that, in a metaphysical anticipation of later theories of evolution, fullness comes to be seen as something realized over time and not all at once in a single act of creation) and 'this-worldliness' finally prevails. The attributes of the second image of Plato`s creator – 'insatiable generativeness, the tendency to produce diversity, the necessity of the realization of the greatest possible "fullness" of being' – are the attributes of the world of Romantic philosophers such as Schelling. But, Lovejoy concludes (p. 326),

> the generativeness is now that of an insufficiency striving unconsciously for richer and more various being; and the fullness is not the permanent character but the flying goal of the whole of things.

In broad-brush terms, it seems to me, Lovejoy`s description of the conflict between two visions of the Good, self-contained stasis on one side and restless generativeness on the other, also works as a description of the fundamental difference between the two worlds that I am trying to differentiate – the old, pre-Enlightenment world and the new, post-Enlightenment world respectively. In more precise terms, however, I am in danger of oversimplifying or even garbling Lovejoy`s argument, for his contention is that the 'flying goal' ideal did not come directly out of the Enlightenment itself but out of the Romantic reaction to the Enlightenment, which he characterizes as a revolt of 'diversitarianism' against 'uniformitarianism'. I touch on 'uniformitarianism' in my note 79 above and, in relation to the Neoplatonist philosopher Plotinus, again in my note 241 below.

[124] From p. 151 of Coplestone`s pamphlet *A Reply to the Calumnies of the Edinburgh Review against Oxford*, printed in Oxford in 1810. As is clear from his title, Coplestone`s main target was the *Edinburgh Review*, the literary and political magazine founded by Francis Jeffrey, Sydney Smith and Henry Brougham in 1802; generally associated with Whig opinion, it argued forcefully in favour of political, social and other reforms. For example, in its October 1809 edition (Vol. XV, p. 50, spelling and punctuation here modernized) the *Edinburgh Review* complained:

> There is a timid and absurd apprehension on the part of ecclesiastical tutors of letting out the minds of youth upon difficult and important subjects. They fancy that mental exertion must end in religious

> scepticism; and to preserve the principles of their pupils they confine them to the safe and elegant imbecility of classical learning. A genuine Oxford tutor would shudder to hear his young men disputing upon moral and political truth, forming and pulling down theories, and indulging in all the boldness of youthful discussion. He would augur nothing from it but impiety to God and treason to kings. And yet, who vilifies both more than the holy poltroon who carefully averts from them the searching eye of reason, and who knows no better method of teaching the highest duties than by extirpating the finest qualities and habits of the mind? If our religion is a fable, the sooner it is exploded the better. If our government is bad, it should be amended.

Coplestone`s riposte (*A Reply to the Calumnies*, pp. 150-151), perhaps written with this very passage before him, was that Oxford`s 'greater and more solid good to the nation' was to 'send out into the world an annual supply of men, whose minds are imbued with literature according to their several measures of capacity, impressed with what we hold to be the soundest principles of policy and religion, grounded in the elements of science, and taught how they may best direct their efforts to farther attainments in that line'. However, he continued:

> Let not this be construed into an admission that speculation is discouraged. The fact is not so. But it is not, and it ought not to be the business of a body. It is for us to execute an established system; to teach and to recommend what is thoroughly approved. Individuals may engage in the task of discovery; and they are better fitted for that task, if they be well informed in what is already known. In case they should be rewarded for their honourable search, "if truth shall have spoken to them before other men", let

> them in the name of truth not withhold the secret; it will be eagerly listened to here as elsewhere; and if, after due probation, it be found to be indeed the voice of truth which spake it, our system will thankfully receive the wholesome aliment. But to expect that every crude opinion or untried theory shall enter as soon as it demands admission, and take its place amongst us, while we rise up and make room to receive it, is against all reason and the analogy of things. Let the experiments be tried, and repeatedly tried, in some insignificant spot, some corner of the farm: but let us not risk the whole harvest of the year upon a doubtful project.

According to Newman White`s biography of Percy Bysshe Shelley (*Shelley*, London: Secker & Warburg, 1947, Vol. I, p. 74), the university conferred an honorary degree on Coplestone as a reward for his defence against the *Edinburgh Review*. White goes on (pp. 110-115 of Vol. I) to tell of Coplestone`s role in ending Shelley`s days as an undergraduate at Oxford: it was probably Coplestone who unmasked Shelley and his friend Thomas Hogg as authors of *The Necessity of Atheism*, the pamphlet that got them both expelled from University College in March 1811.

[125] *Reflections on the Revolution in France*, edited by Conor Cruise O`Brien (Harmondsworth: Pelican Classics, 1968), p. 119. For Burke, 'innovation' evidently denotes gratuitous change while 'reform' denotes meaningful change. In his notes O`Brien links this passage with the new proverb that Burke coined in his *Letter to a Noble Lord* of 1796: '*To innovate is not to reform*. The French revolutionists complained of everything; they refused to reform anything; and they left nothing, no, nothing at all, *unchanged*.' The latter quotation is reproduced more fully in O`Brien`s *The Great Melody: A Thematic Biography and Commented Anthology of Edmund Burke* (London: Sinclair-Stevenson, 1993 reprint, p. 537), in which O`Brien also defends Burke against Isaiah Berlin`s charge that he was a 'reactionary

thinker' out to attack the Enlightenment. 'Burke nowhere attacks the Enlightenment as a whole. He was himself, intellectually, a child of the early Enlightenment, that of Locke and Montesquieu,' O`Brien argues (p. 595), adding for good measure (Appendix, p. 608) that 'In reality, Burke was no more a reactionary that Isaiah Berlin. He was a liberal and pluralist opponent of the French Revolution.' Berlin`s charge is contained in his essay 'Alleged Relativism in Eighteenth-Century European Thought' in *The Crooked Timber of Humanity: Chapters in the History of Ideas* (London: Fontana Press, 1991, p. 78); O`Brien`s defence of Burke in his review of Berlin`s book in the April 1991 edition of *The New York Review of Books* (edited and reproduced with correspondence between O`Brien and Berlin in the Appendix to *The Great Melody*). Plainly I am treading on eggshells here but, on the evidence of Burke`s own utterances relating to tradition, ancestral values and other subjects, I still feel justified in choosing him as a spokesman for the old world.

[126] *The Faerie Queen*, Book III, Canto vi, stanza 30; p. 255 in *The Literature of Renaissance England* (see my note 5 for full citation). Hollander and Kermode suggest 'seed nursery' to convey the meaning of Spenser`s word 'seminarie'.

[127] *The Faerie Queen*, Mutability Cantos, Canto viii (unfinished, dated 1609), stanzas 1-2; pp. 319-320 in *The Literature of Renaissance England.* 'God of Sabbaoth' = 'God of Hosts', 'hight' = 'named'. Hollander and Kermode gloss 'Sabaoths sight' as follows: 'Spenser may mean "grant me sight of the Lord on the last day", but more probably he means *Sabbath* in the sense of eternity – the stillness that will follow the tumult of the six days of the world`s history.' As a religious, philosophical or poetic conceit, the idea that change is ultimately contained within a greater changelessness seems wholly benign in a melancholy sort of way, for it invites quiet acceptance in the face of life`s vicissitudes and all the other regrets of the world. This was true for Spenser no less than for Boethius, who in AD 524, while awaiting execution for alleged involvement in a plot against the Ostrogoth king Theodoric, comforted himself with the paradoxical thought that the very fact Fortune appeared to have changed towards

him was proof of the constancy of her changefulness (*The Consolation of Philosophy*, Book II; p. 23 in the translation by Victor Watts [Harmondsworth: Penguin Classics, revised edition 1999]). However, it is a conceit that also has more sinister ideological potential, as Popper argues in Vol. II of *The Open Society and Its Enemies* (full citation as for Vol. I in my note 4), which mounts a systematic attack on the historicist philosophies of Hegel and Marx. The following passage comes from Popper`s p. 212:

> Like the philosophies of Heraclitus and Plato, and like those of Comte and Mill, Lamarck and Darwin, [Hegel`s and Marx`s] are philosophies of change, and they witness to the tremendous and undoubtedly somewhat terrifying impression made by a changing social environment on the minds of those who live in this environment. Plato reacted to this situation by attempting to arrest all change. The more modern social philosophers appear to react very differently, since they accept, and even welcome, change; yet this love of change seems to me a little ambivalent. For even though they have given up any hope of arresting change, as historicists they try to predict it, and thus to bring it under rational control; and this certainly looks like an attempt to tame it. Thus it seems that, to the historicist, change has not entirely lost its terrors.
>
> In our own time of still more rapid change, we even find the desire not only to predict change, but to control it by centralized large-scale planning.... Plato`s will to arrest change, combined with Marx`s doctrine of its inevitability, yield, as a kind of Hegelian ‘synthesis’, the demand that since it cannot be entirely arrested, change should at least be ‘planned’, and controlled by the state whose power is to be vastly extended.

Popper began *The Open Society and Its Enemies* in 1938 and finished it in 1943. Although he makes no explicit references to the war against Nazism or any other contemporary events, it is clear that Popper`s target in this passage is the Stalinist model of totalitarian state control. As he later explained with exquisite understatement, 'The expectation that Marxism would become a major problem [after the war had been won] was the reason for treating it at some length' (from his Preface to the second edition of 1950, reproduced in Vol. I, pp. viii-ix). My note 137 below is thematically related.

[128] Ecclesiastes 1:9.

[129] *Laws* 797; Saunders p. 283.

[130] Online galleries of European Palaeolithic cave/rock paintings can be viewed by accessing the Bradshaw Foundation (www.bradshawfoundation.com). Links from there include INORA [International Newsletter On Rock Art] Online. Palaeolithic paintings are, it seems, very difficult to date accurately using conventional methods. But an ongoing project conducted by Alistair Pike of Bristol University and other archaeologists, who apply the uranium-series dating technique to thin calcite layers that have formed over the painted surfaces, may significantly improve the dating of some of the most important cave paintings on the Iberian Peninsula. As of April 2012, their findings have yet to be published in the peer-reviewed literature; meantime the project is reliably, if briefly, described in the press release 'Bristol archaeologists delve into secrets of Ice Age cave art' dated 6 October 2008 on the Bristol University website (www.bristol.ac.uk/news/2008/5934.html).

[131] Although Neanderthals and anatomically modern humans probably evolved as two separate species (my note 113 above), the evidence suggests that both intentionally buried at least some of their dead, and may have started to do so as early as the Middle Palaeolithic. For example, the presence of flower pollen in soil around a Neanderthal skeleton at the Shanidar cave in northern Iraq (dated to about 50,000 BP, which puts it in the late Middle Palaeolithic) has been interpreted as evidence that the body was scattered with flowers or laid to rest on a bed of flowers: an instance of ritualized behaviour or of some other

symbolic expression that is difficult to explain if we assume the body was buried for purely utilitarian reasons (such as to avoid attracting the attention of large predators)? It has to be said, though, that another explanation for the pollen could be that it was introduced into the site by burrowing rodents – more bathos than pathos if so. Even older ages for *Homo sapiens sapiens* interments are indicated by the Mugharet es-Skhūl and Qafzeh cave burials in Israel, which are now dated (on the basis of ESR [electron spin resonance] and thermoluminescence analysis) at 119,000-81,000 BP and 115,000-92,000 BP respectively. My main sources: M.P. Pearson, *The Archaeology of Death and Burial* (Stroud, Gloucestershire: The History Press, 2009 reprint), pp. 148-149; J. Riel-Salvatore and G.A. Clark, 'Middle and Early Upper Paleolithic Burials and the Use of Chronotypology in Contemporary Paleolithic Research', published with ten critical commentaries and a reply by the authors in the journal *Current Anthropology*, Vol. 42, No. 4 (August-October 2001), pp. 449-479; and J. Sommer, 'The Shanidar IV "Flower Burial": a Re-evaluation of Neanderthal Burial Ritual' in the *Cambridge Archaeological Journal*, Vol. 9, Issue 01 (April 1999), pp. 127-129. The question of when intentional burials first began seems to be central to the even more contentious question of when symbolic behaviour in general first began: my source here is J.M. Lindly and G.A. Clark, 'Symbolism and Modern Human Origins', with twelve critical commentaries and reply in *Current Anthropology*, Vol. 31, No. 3 (June 1990), pp. 233-261.

[132] *The Myth of the Eternal Return or, Cosmos and History*, translated from French by Willard Trask (Harmondsworth: Penguin Group/Arkana, 1989); Foreward, p. vii. As Eliade himself acknowledges in the Preface added in 1959 (p. xi), *The Myth of the Eternal Return* is a misleading title because, although his book does deal with the Greek myth of that name (my note 137 below), its overall scope is far broader.

[133] *The Myth of the Eternal Return*, p. 48.

[134] *The Myth of the Eternal Return*, p. 5. But what of *new* objects fashioned by the industry of man? What meaning did premodern man attach to the first bronze tool that he made, for instance, and then the

first iron tool? Did he convince himself that he was reinventing an artefact that some god, hero or ancestor had invented in the distant past? And if not, how did he avoid recognizing that he had created something that undeniably had value and reality and yet for which there was no exemplary model? As I go on to say, Eliade's 'original ontology' is very convincing as an explanation of why our ancestors were averse to change in general but, paradoxically, this makes it all the more difficult to understand how they would have accommodated technological change in particular.

[135] *The Myth of the Eternal Return*, pp. 27-28.

[136] *The Myth of the Eternal Return*, p. 35.

[137] *The Myth of the Eternal Return*, p. 34. Eliade makes another Greek connection when he discusses regeneration and cyclical recurrence, which reveal, he says (pp. 89-90), 'an ontology uncontaminated by time and becoming. Just as the Greeks, in their myth of eternal return, sought to satisfy their metaphysical thirst for the "ontic" and the static (for, from the point of view of the infinite, the becoming of things that perpetually revert to the same state is, as a result, implicitly annulled and it can even be affirmed that "the world stands still"), even so the primitive, by conferring a cyclic direction upon time, annuls its irreversibility.' In a footnote Eliade quotes from an essay by the French historian of religion Henri-Charles Puech, 'Gnosis and Time' (translated by Ralph Manheim, in *Man and Time: Papers from the Eranos Yearbooks*, London: Pantheon Books, 1957, pp. 40-41). I reproduce the Puech quotation in full because it is both a beautiful piece of writing and directly relevant to my theme:

> Dominated by an ideal of intelligibility which finds authentic and full being only in that which is in itself and remains identical with itself, in the eternal and immutable, the Greeks regarded movement and change as inferior degrees of reality, in which, at best, identity can be apprehended in the form of permanence and perpetuity, hence of recurrence. The circular movement which assures the survival of the

> same things by repeating them, by bringing about their continuous return, is the perfect and most immediate expression (hence that which is closest to the divine) of the absolute immobility at the summit of the hierarchy. According to the famous Platonic definition [a reference to *Timaeus* 37-38; Lee pp. 50-52], the time which is determined and measured by the revolution of the celestial spheres is the mobile image of immobile eternity which it imitates by moving in a circle. Consequently both the entire cosmic process and the time of our world of generation and decay develop in a circle or according to an indefinite succession of cycles, in the course of which the same reality is made, unmade, and remade, in conformity with an immutable law and determinate alternations. The same sum of being is preserved; nothing is created and nothing lost ... ; moreover, certain thinkers of dying antiquity – Pythagoreans, Stoics, Platonists – went so far as to maintain that within each of these cycles of time ... the same situations recur that have already occurred in the preceding cycles and will occur in subsequent cycles – and so *ad infinitum*. No event is unique, nothing is enacted but once (for example the condemnation of Socrates); every event has been enacted, is enacted, and will be enacted perpetually; the same individuals have appeared, appear, and will appear at every turn of the circle. Cosmic time is repetition and *anakuklosis*, eternal return.

Whether it is called 'annulling the irreversibility of time' or 'the myth of the eternal return', this old conception of reality may help to explain the historicist's urge, as Popper sees it (my note 127 above), to tame change as the next best thing to arresting it altogether.

[138] *The Myth of the Eternal Return*, p. 75. Eliade digresses briefly into the phenomenon of religious confession – 'magical in structure' and of interest primarily for what it says about 'primitive man`s need to free himself from the recollection of sin, i.e., of a succession of personal events that, taken together, constitute history.'
[139] *The Myth of the Eternal Return*, pp. 157-158.
[140] Hobson`s choice because there are objections to both names, for complex historical, cultural and other reasons. Reference source: Alan Barnard, *Anthropology and the Bushman* (Oxford: Berg, 2007), pp. 4-6.
[141] From 'Old K"xau', based on Biesele`s doctoral thesis of 1975, in Joan Halifax, editor, *Shamanic Voices: A Survey of Visionary Narratives* (Harmondsworth: Penguin Group/Arkana, 1991), pp. 54-62. As Halifax observes in her introductory note, woven into K"xau`s narrative are references to his own initiation as a healer invested with the power of *n/um* and to his trance journeys into the bodies of those he seeks to cure. The !Kung, or Northern Bushmen/San, mostly live in desert regions of Botswana, Namibia and Angola.

Evolution`s gift to metaphor

[142] My source once again is *The Literature of Renaissance England*, pp. 28-34, which compares seven versions of 1 Corinthians 13.
[143] *The Castle*, translated by Willa and Edwin Muir, with additional material translated by Eithne Wilkins and Ernst Kaiser (Harmondsworth: Penguin Books in association with Martin Secker & Warburg, 1957), pp. 214-216.
[144] In our own day, Michael Frayn`s play *Copenhagen* has turned the uncertainty relations, complementarity and other elements of quantum physics into brilliant metaphorical devices to explore the mystery of a real historical event involving Heisenberg and Bohr: the visit Heisenberg paid to Bohr, his old mentor and friend, at a time (September 1941) when Denmark was occupied and Heisenberg was working as a scientist of the Third Reich. Meeting as spirits in a dramatic afterworld, Heisenberg, Bohr and Bohr`s wife, Margrethe, relive the visit over and over again in the hope, as Bohr puts it, that 'this time we shall get it right' and understand Heisenberg`s motives.

Bohr is a fatherly-priestly figure to Heisenberg, so one possibility is that Heisenberg has come to seek absolution for making his scientific knowledge available to the Nazis. Or rather, as Margrethe observes, has he come to show off to his foster-parents how well he has done for himself in a resurgent, triumphant Germany? Has Heisenberg been sent to pick Bohr`s brains about the Allies' project, already the subject of rumour in 1941, to develop an atomic bomb? Or has he come of his own accord in a desperate attempt to save the world from nuclear weapons – by persuading the Allies, via Bohr, and Germany, through his own power to influence Nazi research priorities, that the technical requirements of building such weapons in time to be used in the war are so disproportionate that it makes no sense for either side to divert resources to their development? The possibilities continue to split and scatter with the bewildering speed of colliding particles. Could it be that Heisenberg is *unconsciously* sabotaging Nazi nuclear weapons research, or evading an even more acute moral dilemma for himself, by not thinking to do one fundamental calculation (the diffusion equation for the U-235 isotope of natural uranium) that Allied scientists – scientists Hitler had driven out of Germany and Austria because they were Jews – have thought to do? If so, perhaps the profoundest of Margrethe`s observations is that the last and greatest demand that Heisenberg made upon his friendship with her husband, and in effect the purpose of his visit, was to 'be understood when he couldn`t understand himself', and that Bohr`s last and greatest act of friendship towards Heisenberg was to 'leave him misunderstood'. By the end of the play we have many possible explanations for Heisenberg`s visit, but no agreed version of events. It seems that *all* the explanations exist simultaneously, like waves and particles that are everywhere and nowhere, until someone – Bohr, Margrethe, each of us in the audience, *but not Heisenberg himself* – makes an observation and then one explanation is specified for that one observation. Even in principle, however, it cannot be a definitive explanation because some factors, especially nature and nurture in their complementary relationship with the 'entirely inscrutable whims' of the person observed, could only be explained by other, mutually exclusive observations. Our 'extraordinary peregrinations' through life, Frayn has Heisenberg say, 'are not fully objective aspects of the universe'; they exist 'only partially', through the efforts of those who observe us. But then, as Frayn suggests through Heisenberg`s closing lines, historical events are not fully objective aspects of the universe either and it may, or may not, be true that Europe (unlike Japan) was spared atomic bombing during the Second World War by 'one short moment in Copenhagen. By some event that will never quite be located or defined. By that final core of uncertainty at the heart of things.' My direct quotations are from the Methuen edition of *Copenhagen* (London: Methuen Drama Modern Classics, 2009 reprint), pp. 53, 89, 69-70, and 94.

145 H. Yamanouchi, *The search for authenticity in modern Japanese literature* (Cambridge: Cambridge University Press, 1980), pp. 93-94. *Yabu no naka*, translated by Jay Rubin as *In a Bamboo Grove*, can be found in *Rashōmon and Seventeen Other Stories* (Harmondsworth: Penguin Classics, 2006), pp. 10-19. Akutagawa`s device of narrating a single story from different viewpoints, probably inspired by Robert Browning`s novel-length poem *The Ring and the Book* (based on the true case of a seventeenth-century Italian murder trial, retold partly through dramatic monologues) has in turn been adopted by the contemporary British author David Peace in his novel *Occupied City* (a fictionalized account of the mass poisoning of employees of a Tokyo bank in 1948).

146 The Tokyo war crimes trial was properly called the International Military Tribunal for the Far East (IMTFE). Pal`s dissenting opinion is reproduced in full in Vol. II of B.V.A. Röling and C.F. Rüter, editors, *The Tokyo Judgment: The International Military Tribunal for the Far East, 29 April 1946 - 12 November 1948* (Amsterdam: APA University Press, 1977); my quotations are from pp. 540 and 982. Röling, who had served as the Dutch judge on the international tribunal, issued a dissenting opinion of his own: where Pal concluded that all the accused should be acquitted, Röling called for the acquittal of only five of them but his fundamental point was that 'It is well-nigh impossible to define the concept of initiating or waging a war of aggression both accurately and comprehensively' (Vol. II, p. 1061). For a recent

Japanese perspective, see K. Ushimura, 'Pal`s "Dissentient Judgment" Reconsidered: Some Notes on Postwar Japan`s Responses to the Opinion' in the English-language journal *Japan Review*, Vol. 19 (2007), pp. 215-223. Ushimura speculates (p. 218) that one of the reasons why Pal`s opinion was not translated into Japanese until 1952, the year the allied Occupation formally ended, was that no Japanese publisher would have 'dared' to negotiate with the Occupation authorities for the rights: the two condensed translations published that year both suggested by their titles that Pal argued for Japan`s 'innocence [*muzai*, 無罪]', a word that does not appear in the title of Pal`s published opinion ('Judgment [sic] of Mr Justice Pal, member from India'). Most of the text of the official judgement of the Tokyo tribunal, excluding the dissenting opinions, is available online via the HyperWar Project (www.ibiblio.org/hyperwar/PTO/IMTFE: scanned from authentic documents but reformatted, with the result that page numbering may not correspond with that in Röling and Rüter). Even after sixty years, it is very difficult to know what sort of justice was done in Tokyo, particularly given the lax standards of evidence that the IMTFE Charter (Annex 5) permitted the tribunal to apply. Section IV, Article 13 reads in part: 'The Tribunal shall not be bound by technical rules of evidence. … and shall admit any evidence which it deems to have probative value. All purported admissions or statements of the accused are admissible.' Admissible evidence was to encompass any document, 'regardless of its security classification and without proof of its issuance or signature, which appears to the Tribunal to have been signed or issued by any officer, department, agency or member of the armed forces of any government', and diaries, letters or other documents, 'including sworn or unsworn statements, which appear to the Tribunal to contain information related to the charge.'

Uncertain knowing: light enough to see by, and never enough

[147] Donne`s sermon, which takes verse 12 of 1 Corinthians 13 as its text, is reproduced in *The Literature of Renaissance England*, pp. 558-564.

[148] From *John Milton: Complete English Poems, Of Education, Areopagitica*, edited by Gordon Campbell (London: Dent, fourth Everyman edition, 1990), p. 557.
[149] *Complete English Poems, Of Education*, p. 564.
[150] *Complete English Poems, Of Education*, pp. 558 and 564.
[151] Or so I interpret the annotated text in the *Milton Reading Room* (www.dartmouth.edu/~milton/reading_room/of_education/text.shtml), an online library of Milton`s poetry and selected prose created by Thomas Luxon and his students at Dartmouth College, New Hampshire. The annotation to which I refer links to the phrase 'ruines of our first Parents', which in the *Milton Reading Room* edition, based on the reprint of 1673, appears at the beginning of the second paragraph. In turn, Luxon`s annotation links to an online text of Bacon`s *Valerius Terminus of the Interpretation of Nature*, an unfinished work probably dating from about 1603, in which the key passage reads: 'it was not that pure light of natural knowledge, whereby man in paradise was able to give unto every living creature a name according to his propriety, which gave occasion to the fall' (http://fly.hiwaay.net/~paul/bacon/valerius/ch1.html, from Vol. III of *The Works of Francis Bacon* collected by James Spedding et al. in 1876, Cap. 1, paragraph seven). Milton's purpose in writing *Of Education* was partly to dismiss the views of Johann Comenius, a Moravian educational reformer who had visited England in the winter of 1641-42 and who, unlike Milton, advocated a system of universal education. For all that he had a different sense of the direction reform should take, however, Comenius evidently agreed with Milton that the ultimate end of education was to undo the Fall: every 'universal teacher' or 'universal cultivator of men`s minds', Comenius wrote, 'must bear in mind [that] the goal of all universal human culture … is restoration to the lost image of God, or to the lost perfection of free will'. My source is *Pampaedia*, a posthumous work in Latin, translated by A.M.O. Dobbie as *Comenius`s Pampaedia or Universal Education* (Dover, Kent: Buckland Publications, 1986), pp. 80-81.
[152] Bacon, *Valerius Terminus*, Cap. 1, paragraphs three and seven.

[153] From 1639 Milton was entrusted with the education of his two young nephews. One of them, Edward Phillips, has left a record of the curriculum Milton had them study from the ages of ten to about sixteen: more than half of their texts, in Latin, Greek, Hebrew, Chaldee, Syriac, Italian and French, are recommended in *Of Education.* (The relevant extract from Phillips`s 'The Life of Mr John Milton' of 1694 is reproduced as an appendix in the *Complete English Poems, Of Education, Areopagitica*, pp. 570-571.) While the curriculum itself seems daunting to us, probably it did not seem unreasonable to scholar-gentlemen of the late English Renaissance, whose feelings of inadequacy, if any, would have been more theological in nature: the effort to regain to know God aright was difficult, they believed, because the apparatus of man`s understanding had been damaged by the Fall. The Fall was thought to have impaired both the understanding (or wit) and the will, which together constituted the reason at the top of a triple hierarchy of the mind; the hierarchy descended through the common sense, the fancy and the memory in the middle, to the five senses at the base. My source is *The Elizabethan World Picture*, pp. 78-81: I am assuming that the notions Tillyard describes (or at least the association of the Fall with defects of the understanding) were still current in the first half of the seventeenth century.

[154] *The Brothers Karamazov*, translated by David Magarshack (Harmondsworth: Penguin Classics, 1985 reprint), pp. 298-299.

[155] 'Aphorism 86' of 'The Collected Aphorisms' in *The Great Wall of China and Other Short Works*, translated and edited by Malcolm Pasley (Harmondsworth: Penguin Books, 1991), p. 93.

[156] A literal rendering of *shiran kao o suru* (知らん顔をする), which is used in situations where in English we might speak of pretending not to notice or 'turning a blind eye to' the misfortunes of others.

[157] In an attempt to answer this question, the political philosopher Michael Walzer insists that the extreme human rights violations that justify and 'perhaps even require' armed intervention are qualitatively different from other violations and not just more of the same. 'The common brutalities of authoritarian politics [and] the daily oppressiveness of traditional social practices' do not justify outside

intervention, he says, because essentially they are local issues that have to be dealt with locally. 'I don't mean to describe a continuum that begins with common nastiness and ends with genocide but rather a radical break, a chasm, with nastiness on one side and genocide on the other. We should not allow ourselves to approach genocide by degrees.' He goes on to argue that 'the most successful interventions' over the thirty years to 2001 were acts of war by neighbouring states – Vietnam's invasion of Cambodia and ousting of the Khmer Rouge in 1978, India's military support for the secession of East Pakistan (Bangladesh as it became) in 1971, and Tanzania's overthrow of the Idi Amin regime in Uganda in 1979. Walzer argues too that it may be a practical advantage if the motives for such interventions are 'not wholly (or even chiefly) altruistic', as in the case of India's intervention in East Pakistan, motivated partly by the need to stem the cross-border flood of refugees that was putting an unsustainable burden on India's resources and economy. Is this an answer, or the answer, to another question: who, if anybody, should intervene when the international community as a whole chooses not to? It is surely controversial at best, and dangerous at worst, to suggest that it is up to neighbouring states to step in when the world fails to act in a man-made humanitarian crisis. But unless and until there is some formalized mechanism for multilateral intervention (a United Nations-mandated force, say, kept on permanent standby), does anyone have a better suggestion? My references are all to Walzer's essay 'The Argument about Humanitarian Intervention', first published in the journal *Dissent* (Winter 2002, pp. 29-37) and available online (http://them.polylog.org/5/awm-en.htm).

[158] As of March 2011 UNAMID, a joint African Union/United Nations peacekeeping mission, had almost eighteen thousand military personnel and more than five thousand police officers in Darfur. But from 2004 until 2008 the only peacekeeping operation on the ground in Darfur, mounted by the African Union alone, seems to have had no more than seven thousand troops at its disposal, poorly equipped, hampered by funding issues, and largely ineffective. Main source: UNAMID website (http://unamid.unmissions.org: Background and other links).

Uncertain knowing: two ideas of history

159 From 'Prologue to an Autobiography' in Naipaul's *Finding the Centre* (Harmondsworth: Penguin Books, 1985), pp. 51-52.
160 'Prologue to an Autobiography', p. 52.
161 *An Area of Darkness* (Harmondsworth: Penguin Books, 1970 reprint), pp. 167, 41 and 30.

The secret of brute matter

162 *Being and Nothingness*, pp. xli-xlii in the Barnes translation. The corresponding expressions in *L`être et le néant* (pp. 32-34) are *l`être est en soi; l`être est ce qu`il est;* and *l`être est.*
163 *Being and Nothingness*, p. xlii.
164 Mary Warnock (*The Philosophy of Sartre*, London: Hutchinson University Library, 1966, pp. 107, 109) is good on the particularity of things and why we find it so disturbing: 'If I suddenly cease to be able to see a hammer, for instance, as just the thing I need to knock a nail in, which I want to do for some very good, statable purpose – if I suddenly see it instead just as a collection of physical properties which I have no reason to expect ever to see conjoined with one another again – then there is the fear that all my plans and projects themselves, as well as the things I had been accustomed to regard as means to their fulfilment, will melt and dissolve, and become indescribable and particular as well.' Nausea, she says, is one of the consequences of this 'unmanageableness of things, our failure wholly to possess them'.
165 *Nausea*, translated by Robert Baldick (Harmondsworth: Penguin Books, 1971 reprint), p. 180.
166 *Nausea*, p. 186.
167 *Nausea*, pp. 189-190. I have corrected a typographical error, 'beasts' for 'beats', on p. 189. The corresponding passages in the original French of *La nausée* (Paris: Librairie Gallimard, 1938) are on pp. 182-183.
168 *Being and Nothingness*, p. 84.
169 *Being and Nothingness*, p. 81.
170 *Being and Nothingness*, p. 620.

[171] I am indebted to Joseph Catalano (*A Commentary on Jean-Paul Sartre`s "Being and Nothingness",* New York: Harper Torchbook edition, 1974, pp. 45-46) for his clarification of how a collection of disparate existences can 'become' a chestnut tree, for example, only in relation to consciousness. Most of all, I am indebted to Catalano (specifically his p. 101) for the whole idea that a consciousness-creation myth is embedded in *Being and Nothingness*, although I hasten to add that Catalano does not describe it in terms of a creation myth.

[172] *Being and Nothingness*, p. 619. As I understand it, Sartre`s assertion of the 'ontological primacy' of the in-itself is consistent with his rejection of all forms of philosophical idealism, which holds that the existence of things consists in our knowledge of them.

[173] I am referring to the distinction that Sartre makes between ontology (strictly speaking, *Being and Nothingness* is an ontological essay concerned only with describing being) and metaphysics (which, according to Sartre, is the discipline that speculates on *why* there is being). The origin of the for-itself, he says (*Being and Nothingness*, pp. 620-621), is a question for metaphysics. 'Ontology will therefore limit itself to declaring that *everything takes place as if* the in-itself in a project to found itself gave itself the modification of the for-itself. It is up to metaphysics to form the *hypotheses* which will allow us to conceive of this process as the absolute event which comes to crown the individual venture which is the existence of being.' See also my note 277 below.

[174] *Being and Nothingness*, pp. 620 and 81-82.

[175] *Being and Nothingness*, p. 79.

[176] In keeping with his description of consciousness as a 'nothingness' and a 'lack', Sartre says (*Being and Nothingness*, p. 85) that 'the for-itself is perpetually determining itself *not to be* the in-itself. This means that it can establish itself only in terms of the in-itself and against the in-itself.'

[177] *Being and Nothingness*, p. 7.

[178] *Being and Nothingness*, p. 9. Not all negative realities (*négatités*) that arise through the human capacity for negation are of this 'objective' kind, as is clear from Sartre`s meditation on the significance

of finding that Pierre is not in the café (*Being and Nothingness*, pp. 9-11). He contrasts the 'objective' quality of Pierre`s absence (which, through his 'real expectation' of seeing Pierre, Sartre has caused '*to happen* as a real event concerning this café') with the 'abstract' quality of the absences of Paul Valéry and the Duke of Wellington (which, arising from judgements that Sartre may make to amuse himself, fail to establish 'a *real* relation between the café and Wellington or Valéry').

[179] *Being and Nothingness*, p. 8. Sartre`s italics.

[180] What we would regard as natural calamities Sartre describes (*Being and Nothingness*, p. 9) as 'agencies' of destruction: 'destruction is an essentially human thing and ... *it is man* who destroys his cities through the agency of earthquakes or directly, who destroys his ships through the agency of cyclones or directly.'

[181] *Being and Nothingness*, pp. 59-60.

[182] *Being and Nothingness*, pp. 59.

[183] *Being and Nothingness*, pp. 55-56. Sartre`s tableau of the woman, her companion and the disembodied hand bears a striking resemblance to a scene in *L`invitée*, which Kate and Edward Fullbrook (*Simone de Beauvoir and Jean-Paul Sartre: The Remaking of a Twentieth-Century Legend* [full citation in my note 104], pp. 98-100) highlight as evidence of Sartre`s 'unattributed use' of ideas and material from de Beauvoir`s novel. Their larger claim (pp. 101-102) is that *L`invitée* 'articulates a philosophical system that in its basic structure differs almost not at all from the one found in *Being and Nothingness* ... Beauvoir had already produced a full statement of "Sartrean" existentialism by 1940.' This larger claim includes Sartre`s formulation of being-for-others (*l`être-pour-autrui*), a third dimension of being (in addition to being-for-itself and being-in-itself) in which we perceive other people, are perceived by them, and may perceive ourselves, as objects to be possessed. In Sartre`s words, the 'original meaning' of being-for-others is *conflict* because '[w]hile I attempt to free myself from the hold of the Other, the Other is trying to free himself from mine; while I seek to enslave the Other, the Other seeks to enslave me' (*Being and Nothingness*, p. 364). He categorizes the forms of the conflict into love, language and masochism on one side and indifference, desire, hate and sadism on the

other – the two groups of 'fundamental attitudes' between which we are 'indefinitely tossed' (*Being and Nothingness*, p. 412; my main text pages 46-47). According to Kate and Edward Fullbrook (their p. 111), all of this is 'a condensed version' of the analysis of human relations that de Beauvoir had already worked out in *L`invitée*.
[184] Exodus 20:1-17.
[185] John 8:24.

All at once and right away: a meaning of the Holocaust

[186] See my note 2 for publication details of the English translations by Guggenheim, *Portrait of the Antisemite*, and by Becker, *Anti-Semite and Jew*.
[187] Writing in October 1944, Sartre (*Anti-Semite and Jew*, p. 71) specifically mentions 'the gas chambers at Lublin', a reference to the first major concentration camp to be discovered, Lublin/Majdanek, which was liberated by the Soviet army in July 1944. Although the fleeing Nazis destroyed other evidence of the camp`s purpose, they failed to demolish the gas chambers. Estimates of how many people died at Majdanek between 1941 and 1944 range from 360,000 (including about 120,000 Jews) to 78,000 (including 59,000 Jews). I have used three online sources: the *Concise Encyclopedia of the Holocaust* maintained by Israel`s official Holocaust memorial authority (www1.yadvashem.org/education/entries/English/41.asp), which cites the highest estimates, first made in 1948; 'Majdanek Victims Enumerated. Changes in history textbooks?' on the official website of the Auschwitz-Birkenau Memorial and Museum (http://en.auschwitz.org.pl/m/index: search by exact phrase 'Majdanek Victims'), which cites the lowest figures, published in 2005 by Tomasz Kranz, a director of research at the Majdanek Museum; and 'Lublin/Majdanek Concentration Camp: Areas of Research' on the United States Holocaust Memorial Museum site (www.ushmm.org/wlc/en/: search by 'Lublin/Majdanek'), which estimates that a minimum of 95,000 to 130,000 people (including 89,000 to 110,000 Jews) died at Majdanek and its subsidiary camps up to January 1945 (sic).

[188] *Anti-Semite and Jew*, p. 7.
[189] *Anti-Semite and Jew*, p. 25. In his Preface to this translation (p. vi), Michael Walzer takes Sartre`s class analysis as evidence that, despite his denials, Sartre was already moving towards Marxism in the 1940s. If true, this lends weight to the interpretation that Sartre had his own conversion to Marxism in mind when he made his veiled reference to 'an ethics of deliverance' in that puzzling footnote in *Being and Nothingness* (my main text page 47 and note 86).
[190] *Anti-Semite and Jew*, p. 17.
[191] Sartre`s word, which appears on p. 22 of *Réflexions sur la question juive* (Paris: Éditions Gallimard, 1954).
[192] Page 167 in *Portrait of the Antisemite* (quoted more fully as the second epigraph on my page 2); pp. 21-22 in *Réflexions sur la question juive.* As Walzer suggests in his Preface to the Becker translation (p. x), what Sartre describes as the anti-Semite`s fear of truth is very like the 'intolerance of ambiguity' examined in Theodor Adorno`s social-psychological study *The Authoritarian Personality*, a product of a programme of research initiated in 1944 by the American Jewish Committee. 'Intolerance vs. tolerance of ambiguity' is one of the measures used by Adorno, Else Frenkel-Brunswik and others in quantitatively scoring the cognitive 'personality orientation' of the subjects they interviewed under clinical conditions. The authors themselves were struck by the parallels with Sartre`s essay, which came to their attention after they had collected and analyzed their data: 'There is marked similarity between the syndrome which we have labeled the authoritarian personality and "the portrait of the anti-Semite" by Jean-Paul Sartre. … That his phenomenological "portrait" should resemble so closely, both in general structure and in numerous details, the syndrome which slowly emerged from our empirical observations and quantitative analysis, seems to us remarkable.' Adorno and his colleagues conducted their interviews with one hundred and fifty subjects (men and women studied separately in four 'statistical groupings') selected from among more than two thousand who had earlier filled in questionnaires; typically aged between twenty and thirty-five and categorized 'almost exclusively' as middle-class,

most lived in the San Francisco Bay area. For methodological reasons, members of 'minority groups' were deliberately excluded from the calculations, which is another reason why, as Adorno observes in the Introduction, 'The findings of the study may be expected to hold fairly well for non-Jewish, white, native-born, middle-class Americans.' My references are to the original 1950 edition of *The Authoritarian Personality* (New York: Harper & Brothers, Studies in Prejudice series), pp. 461-464, 971 and 22-27.

193 *Anti-Semite and Jew*, pp. 20-21.

194 *Portrait of the Antisemite,* pp. 168-169. Sartre`s analysis gives an interesting existential edge to the Japanese proverb 'The post that sticks out will get hammered in' (my note 54 above).

195 *Portrait of the Antisemite*, p. 169. The anti-Semite, Sartre argues, has no understanding of money, securities or any form of wealth other than inherited property: he can conceive only of 'one type of primitive and land-owning appropriation, based on a veritable magical connection with possession, in which the object possessed and its possessor are linked by a [bond of] mystical participation'.

196 *Portrait of the Antisemite*, p. 169. Sartre on Frenchness is very reminiscent of Eliade on premodern man`s 'ceaseless repetition of gestures initiated by others' (my main text page 68).

197 *Portrait of the Antisemite*, pp. 177-178. The three editorial changes in [square brackets] are mine: 'consciousness' rather than 'conscience' for Sartre`s French word *conscience* (*Réflexions sur la question juive*, p. 64), 'the Good' for *le Bien* and 'the human condition' for *la condition humaine* (both p. 65 of *Réflexions*).

198 *Portrait of the Antisemite*, pp. 175-176.

199 Walzer Preface, p. vii. By his own account, Sartre did no original research before writing the essay, which Walzer (p. vi) describes as 'a philosophical speculation variously supported by anecdotes and personal observations.'

200 From Fromm`s Foreword to *The Fear of Freedom* (London: Routledge & Kegan Paul, 1960 paperback edition), pp. ix-x.

201 'There is one factor in the relationship of the sadistic person to the object of his sadism,' Fromm says (*The Fear of Freedom*, pp. 124-125),

'which is often neglected and therefore deserves especial emphasis here: his dependence on the object of his sadism. ... The sadist needs the person over whom he rules, he needs him very badly, since his own feeling of strength is rooted in the fact that he is the master over someone. This dependence may be entirely unconscious.' Adorno and his co-authors (*The Authoritarian Personality*, pp. 451-452) also take account of unconscious processes, defining one of the categories that they use to measure ambivalence, for instance, as follows: 'Category 51b deals with the mechanisms which help to circumvent ambivalence or to keep it on an unconscious level. The most outstanding of these mechanisms consist in a thinking in terms of dichotomies, i.e., in terms of pairs of diametrical opposites, and in an inclination toward displacement. Thus, glorification of the ingroup and rejection of the outgroup, familiar from the sphere of social and political beliefs, can be found as a general trend in some of our clinical data'. In common with Fromm, Adorno was associated with the Frankfurt School of philosophy and social (or 'critical') theory.

5. THE FEAR OF EXTINCTION

The sustaining illusion

[202] *Nostromo: A Tale of the Seaboard* (Harmondsworth: Penguin Modern Classics, 1967 reprint), p. 409.
[203] *Nostromo*, p. 231.
[204] *Nostromo*, pp. 235-236.
[205] *Nostromo*, pp. 412-413.
[206] *Nostromo*, p. 252.
[207] *Nostromo*, p. 235.
[208] *Nostromo*, p. 224.
[209] *Nostromo*, pp. 345-346.
[210] *Nostromo*, p. 430.
[211] *Nostromo*, pp. 344-345.
[212] *Nostromo*, p. 13.
[213] In existential terms, it is easy enough to portray Nostromo as a man in bad faith, an exotic version of Sartre`s café waiter. Where the waiter

plays at *being* a waiter, Nostromo plays at *being* the Capataz de Cargadores (with the difference that, through the very extravagance of his behaviour, Nostromo himself creates the expectations to which he conforms, whereas the waiter conforms passively to the conventional expectations of the world around him). But this is familiar stuff and something more interesting comes out if we compare Nostromo with the principal character in Kafka`s dialogue 'Conversation with [a] Suppliant', who confesses that 'it is the aim of my life to get people to look at me. … There has never been a time in which I have been convinced from within myself that I am alive. You see, I have only such a fugitive awareness of things around me that I always feel they were once real and are now fleeting away.' Nostromo and the Suppliant, it seems to me, are affected by the same condition: a terror of ceasing to be, of losing the last of their fugitive awareness, of going out of existence in a dissolution of all their familiar realities. Lacking a sense of existence on their own account, both must look to others for a reflected assurance of their own being, and hence both require a permanent audience. For all the magnificence of Nostromo`s exploits, nothing but bravado distinguishes them from the Suppliant`s technique of attracting attention to himself by praying sprawled full-length on the church floor. In *The Divided Self: An Existential Study in Sanity and Madness* (Harmondsworth: Pelican Books, 1965, pp. 108-110), the psychiatrist R.D. Laing considers Kafka`s Suppliant a clear example of a man suffering from 'ontological insecurity', a term which perhaps we could also apply to Nostromo. My Kafka quotations are from the fragments translated by Ernst Kaiser and Eithne Wilkins in the collection *In the Penal Settlement* (London: Secker & Warburg, 1973 reprint, pp. 6 and 8); the fragments, first published in a German-language periodical in 1909, came from *Description of a Struggle*, a story that was thought to have been destroyed or lost. There are significant differences of wording in the complete translation by Tania and James Stern in *Description of a Struggle and The Great Wall of China* (London: Secker & Warburg, 1960, pp. 48-49), which, as Max Brod explains in his postscript (pp. 334 and 338-339), is based on a manuscript that he rediscovered by chance in 1935.

[214] From 'Prologue to an Autobiography' (full citation in my note 159), p. 63.
[215] 'Prologue to an Autobiography', p. 71.
[216] 'Prologue to an Autobiography', p. 63.
[217] 'Prologue to an Autobiography', p. 64. There is a particularly bitter irony in that word 'vacancy', which recalls the subject of one of his father`s *Trindidan Guardian* pieces – an old Negro gatekeeper who for thirty-six years opened and closed the Chaguanas railway crossing at most four times daily and who 'lived in absolute harmony with the long vacancies of his calling' (p. 61).
[218] 'Prologue to an Autobiography', p. 62.
[219] 'Prologue to an Autobiography', p. 70.
[220] 'Prologue to an Autobiography', p. 72.
[221] *An Area of Darkness* (full citation in my note 161), pp. 42-43.
[222] *An Area of Darkness*, pp. 266-267. Naipaul`s italics.
[223] *Nobody Nowhere* (London and Philadelphia: Jessica Kingsley Publishers, 1999), p. 27.
[224] *Nobody Nowhere*, p. 13.
[225] *Nobody Nowhere*, p. 45.
[226] *Nobody Nowhere*, p. 97.
[227] *Nobody Nowhere*, p. 38.
[228] *Nobody Nowhere*, pp. 45 and 185.
[229] Her ways of making things 'slow down' were to blink rapidly or turn the lights on and off, which had 'the effect of strobe lights without the control being taken out of your hands' (*Nobody Nowhere*, pp. 46 and 185).
[230] 'I rejected much interactive contact,' she elaborates (*Nobody Nowhere*, p. 180), 'because [it] robbed me of the security I found in my ability to lose myself through colour, sound, pattern and rhythm.' These are references to the semi-hypnotic state in which she could lose all sense of self in the pattern of her bedroom wallpaper, monotonous work, or even the voice of her supervisor at university.
[231] *Nobody Nowhere*, p. 60.
[232] *Nobody Nowhere*, p. 190.

233 *Nobody Nowhere*, p. 189. Some of the things Donna Williams did as a child, such as swinging upside down by her knees from the highest branch of tree, were not just embarrassing but downright dangerous. There is another uncanny echo here – this time with Kafka`s Suppliant and his confession that 'it is the aim of my life to get people to look at me … I have only such a fugitive awareness of things around me' (my note 213 above).

234 *Nobody Nowhere*, p. 186.

This body, not that; me, not you

235 William Hazlitt said all there is to say about death (death as an inescapable fact, that is, as opposed to dying, the mechanics of how and when the inescapable fact finally catches up with us) almost two hundred years ago: 'Perhaps the best cure for the fear of death is to reflect that life has a beginning as well as an end. There was a time when we were not: this gives us no concern – why, then, should it trouble us that a time will come when we shall cease to be? I have no wish to have been alive a hundred years ago, or in the reign of Queen Anne: why should I regret and lay it so much to heart that I shall not be alive a hundred years hence, in the reign of I cannot tell whom?' From 'On the Fear of Death', written in about 1822, in *Selected Essays of William Hazlitt*, edited by Geoffrey Keynes (London: Nonesuch Press, 1970 reprint), p. 160.

236 *Timaeus* 41-42; Lee translation p. 58. The same passage is reproduced more fully on pages 63-64 of my main text.

237 From the *Fourth Ennead*, Tractate VIII.4, translated by Stephen MacKenna and B.S. Page in *Plotinus: The Six Enneads* (Chicago: Encyclopædia Britannica Great Books of the Western World series, 1988), p. 203.

238 Plotinus seems to use 'the Good' interchangeably with 'the One' but, confusingly, he also says that the One 'precedes' the Good (*Fifth Ennead*, Tractate V.12; p. 234 in the MacKenna/Page translation [hereafter abbreviated to MacKenna]). For Plotinus it is a matter of finding the least-worst option: properly speaking no name is right because, as I understand his objection (*Fifth Ennead*, Tractate III.13;

MacKenna p. 223), a name implies a duality of subject and predicate, which does not and cannot apply to the absolutely first principle of his metaphysics.

239 *Republic* 508-509; p. 273 in the Lee translation.

240 *Fifth Ennead*, Tractate III.14; MacKenna p. 224.

241 Generativeness is one of several strands in Lovejoy`s *The Great Chain of Being* that lead back to Plotinus. The generative aspect of Plotinus`s One flows from the motive that Plato had adduced for the creation of the world of change, namely that the creator was good and lacking in envy and therefore wanted all things to be as like himself as possible (*Timaeus* 29-30; Lee translation quoted in my note 123). Hence Plotinus describes the One in language very similar to Plato`s: 'The One is perfect because it seeks for nothing, and possesses nothing, and has need of nothing; and being perfect, it overflows, and thus its superabundance produces an Other' (*Fifth Ennead*, Tractate II.1; translated by Lovejoy on his p. 62). Indirectly a product of this 'superabundance' (or 'exuberance', the word chosen by MacKenna, p. 214), the world, Plotinus says, 'is a sort of Life stretched out to an immense span, in which each of the parts has its own place in the series, all of them different and yet the whole continuous, and that which precedes never wholly absorbed in that which comes after' (*Fifth Ennead*, Tractate II.2; Lovejoy translation, p. 63). Just as the theologies and philosophies of later centuries turned Plotinus`s 'immense span' into a great scale or 'chain' of being, so they elaborated his notion of the One, ambiguously, into other metaphysical principles, notably continuity and plenitude. On the one hand, continuity manifests itself in Leibniz`s law of continuity (my main text page 8), which banishes disorder and irregularity from the world, while the principle of plenitude (so named by Lovejoy, his p. 52) manifests itself in Leibniz`s principle of perfection, which, as parodied by Voltaire, provides a basis for believing that all is for the best in the best of all possible worlds. In these guises, continuity and plenitude are static ideals which hold that the world could not and should not be other than as it is. But, Lovejoy argues (his Chapter X), plenitude is also a major factor in the philosophical, religious and aesthetic ideas of

Schelling and other German Romantic writers who, in their 'diversitarian' revolt against the 'uniformitarianism' of the Enlightenment (my note 79 and note 123 above), see the world in terms of dynamic life forces struggling and *continuing* to produce the maximum possible diversity and fullness of being. Given the complex irony of Lovejoy`s history, which itself mirrors the ambiguity at the heart of Plato`s and Plotinus`s metaphysics, it is no surprise that the 'uniformitarian' tendency harks back to the absolute and self-sufficient aspect of the One – the aspect in which the One is perfect because 'it seeks for nothing, and possesses nothing, and has need of nothing'.

[242] *Fifth Ennead*, Tractate I. 7; MacKenna pp. 211-212.

[243] *History of Western Philosophy* (London: Unwin University Books, fifth impression, 1969), p. 293. In *The Cambridge History of Later Greek and Early Medieval Philosophy* (Cambridge: Cambridge University Press, 1980 reprint, pp. 239-240), A.H. Armstrong cautions that Plotinus`s fondness for sun/sunlight and similar imagery should not be misinterpreted as meaning that *Nous* (or Soul) is produced by an automatic or even necessary process of 'emanation': 'There is no deliberate action on the part of the One,' Armstrong writes, 'and no willing or planning or choice or care for what is produced.'

[244] I base my interpretation here on Lloyd Gerson`s article on Plotinus in the online *Stanford Encyclopedia of Philosophy* (http://plato.stanford.edu/entries/plotinus: The Three Fundamental Principles of Plotinus` Metaphysics). Starting from a reference to *Timaeus* 30 (Lee translation p. 43), Gerson says that the role of Intellect (*Nous*) is 'to account for the real distinctness of the plethora of Forms, virtually united in the One. … Intellect is the principle of essence or whatness or intelligibility as the One is the principle of being.'

[245] *Fourth Ennead*, Tractate VIII.3; MacKenna p. 202.

[246] *Fourth Ennead*, Tractate VII.13(18); MacKenna p. 200.

[247] *Fifth Ennead*, Tractate I. 2; MacKenna p. 208.

[248] *Fourth Ennead*, Tractate VIII. 4; MacKenna p. 202.

[249] Armstrong (*Cambridge History* cited in note 243 above, especially pp. 242-243 and 255) suggests that the wilful reaching of individual souls towards the lower realm is a 'development' of the 'illegitimate

self-assertion' or *tolma* by which *Nous* first came to be engendered from the One, and Soul engendered from *Nous*: 'All existence, in this way of looking at it, depends on a kind of radical original sin, a wish for separation and independence, of which Plotinus says explicitly in one passage [*Third Ennead*, Tractate VIII.8; MacKenna p. 133] that it would have been better if it had never been.' According to Armstrong, Plotinus makes no explicit attempt to resolve the contradiction in his metaphysics between this *tolma*-affected, downward tendency towards separation and independence and the sublime, upward tendency towards union with the One. Armstrong also has some extremely interesting things to say about Plotinus`s conception of the nature of man, which is double or, more correctly, triple. 'Our true self,' Armstrong interprets (p. 224), 'the "man within", is our higher soul which exists eternally close to and continually illumined by Intellect. This does not sin or suffer and remains essentially free and unhampered in its rational and intellectual activities by the turbulence of the body and its world, into which the higher soul does not "come down". What enters the lower world is only an irradiation from the higher soul, an image or expression of it on the lower level, which joins with the bodily organism to form the "joint entity", the "composite"; it is this "other man" or lower self which sins and suffers and is ignorant and emotionally disturbed, and in general is the subject of what most people regard as ordinary human experience.' As Armstrong observes, a doubleness of nature is consistent with Plato`s description [*Timaeus* 69; Lee translation quoted in my note 117] of the human soul as both immortal and, in some respects, mortal. However, Armstrong then translates (p. 225) from two passages [*Second Ennead*, Tractate IX.2 and *Fifth Ennead*, Tractate III.3; pp. 67 and 217 in MacKenna] in which Plotinus speaks of a 'middle' part of the human soul and identifies it as the reasoning 'we', our true self, midway between the superior power of intellect (associated with *Nous*) and the inferior power of sense-perception (associated with the lower, visible world). What this third element adds, or symbolizes, is the possibility of *choice*: we can choose to live on the level of our higher and rational self, close to the oneness of *Nous* (and, through *Nous*, ultimately of the

One); we can choose to sink into separateness and partialness on the level of the visible world and there, as Armstrong puts it (pp. 255-256), 'busy ourselves with the petty concerns of our particular body'; or most characteristically, we might say, we can 'fluctuate between the two' (Armstrong p. 226). Plotinus`s conception of the piggy-in-the-middle nature of man and his soul seems to have been among the most enduring ideas that he bequeathed to later thought and literature. It is surely one of the influences at work in Alexander Pope`s image of man as a god-beast 'Placed on this isthmus of a middle state, / …. In doubt his mind or body to prefer' (*Essay on Man*, Epistle II, lines 1-18). Is it at work too in Freud`s conceptualizations of the mind, according to which the so-called, or so-translated, *ego* – our sense of 'I-ness' or 'me-ness', which conventionally we regard as our true self – exists in a state of dynamic tension between the internalized moral strictures of the *ego ideal* or *super-ego* 'above' and the irrational, unruly and amoral urges of the *id* 'below'? Issues relating to the translation, or mistranslation, of Freud`s German are touched on in my notes 252, 254 and 310 below.

[250] *Fourth Ennead*, Tractate VIII.4; MacKenna pp. 202-203. The 'casting of the wings' is a reference to the allegory of the soul as a winged charioteer in Plato's *Phaedrus* 246-250.

[251] Compare, for example, this passage from the *Hui Ming Ching*, a Taoist-Buddhist meditation text, which in its written form dates from 1794 but which stems from a tradition of esoteric Chinese learning that had long been passed down orally:

> Before this our body is born of our parents, at the time of conception, [the] seed [of a 'germinal vesicle'] is first created and human nature and life dwell therein. The two are intermingled and form a unity, inseparably mixed like the sparks in the refining furnace, a combination of primordial harmony and divine law. Therefore it is said: 'In the state before the appearance [i.e. before our birth into the world, or before the creation of the world itself?] there is an inexhaustible breath.' Furthermore it is

> said: 'Before the parents have begotten the child, the breath of life is complete and the embryo perfect.' But when the embryo moves and the embryo vesicle is torn, it is as if a man lost his footing on a high mountain: with a cry [an allusion to the first cry of a new-born baby?] the man plunges down to earth, and from then on human nature and life are divided. From this moment human nature can no longer see life nor life human nature. And now fate takes its course: youth passes over into maturity, maturity into old age, and old age into woe.
>
> *Hui Ming Ching: The Book of Consciousness and Life*, English translation by Cary Baynes included in *The Secret of the Golden Flower: A Chinese Book of Life* (San Diego: Harvest/HBJ, revised edition 1962), p. 70. Editorial additions within [square brackets] are mine.

I hesitate to make too much of this source, mainly because of the history of how it came to be known outside China. The first few pages originally appeared in German in 1926; the translation was by L.C. Lo but it was revised by Richard Wilhelm, who is better known as the translator of another Chinese text, *The Secret of the Golden Flower*, that came out in 1929 accompanied by (and in the German edition preceded by) a commentary by Carl Jung. In 1961 Cary Baynes translated the Lo/Wilhelm *Hui Ming Ching* into English and included it in the new edition of her 'authorized' version of *The Secret of the Golden Flower*, which she had translated under Jung`s supervision. In turn, this version has found its way into other languages, including a Japanese edition (which, although still essentially an exposition of Jung`s ideas, at least attempts to get closer to the texts themselves by translating them directly from the Chinese and not the German). In other words, in translation the *Hui Ming Ching* and *The Secret of the Golden Flower* are heavily associated with the Jungian school of psychology, which brings us to the bigger issue. Identifying 'human nature' with consciousness and its separation from 'life' as an 'aberration, or deracination' of consciousness, Jung interprets these texts as guides to achieving 'reunion with the unconscious laws of being, and the purpose of this reunion [as] the attainment of conscious life or, expressed in Chinese terms, the bringing about of the Tao' (from Jung's commentary in the Baynes volume, pp. 98-99; pp. 101-102 refer to the passage from the *Hui Ming Ching* that I have quoted above). But what exactly is going on here? Have Wilhelm and Jung, in a collaborative exercise of great cross-cultural insight, demonstrated that 'just as the human body shows a common anatomy over and above all racial differences, so, too, the psyche possesses a common substratum [the collective unconscious] transcending all differences in culture and consciousness' (Jung's commentary, p. 87). Or, by turning the language and concepts of Taoism into the language and concepts of analytical psychology, have they in fact perpetrated an act of cross-cultural bodysnatching? As I simply do not know the answer, I shall confine myself to observing that the imagery of the *Hui Ming Ching* – a state of perfect unity ended by an abrupt splitting-apart and, through birth, *embodiment in the world* – is strikingly similar to Plotinus's. The publication history of the German and English translations can be pieced together from the prefaces to the Baynes volume (pp. vii-xvi). The Japanese translation is by Y. Yuasa and A. Sadakata, in *Ōgon no hana no himitsu* (Tokyo: Jimbun Shoin, 1990 reprint), pp. 281-282.

[252] I am persuaded by Bruno Bettelheim's argument that *ego* has none of the immediacy that Freud intended by using the pronoun *ich* as a noun, *das Ich*: 'Where Freud selected a word that, used in daily parlance, makes us feel vibrantly alive, the translations present us with a term from a dead language that reeks of erudition precisely when it should emanate vitality.' I quote from Bettelheim's *Freud and Man's Soul* (Harmondsworth: Pelican Books, 1989, p. 55), which suggests (Preface, pp. vii-viii) that the main reason why this and many other deficiencies of the English translations have never been systematically corrected is not because of the practical difficulties, great as they would be, but because 'criticizing the translations has come to seem almost like criticizing the venerated master himself.' Most of the translations were done in Freud's lifetime and were, according to Bettelheim,

'accepted or, at the very least, condoned by him'. The chief editor of the English-language *Standard Edition of the Complete Psychological Works of Sigmund Freud*, James Strachey, was a trusted follower, while the co-editor was Freud`s daughter, Anna. More broadly, Bettelheim is surely saying something very important about the nature of the trust that we put in translations and translators: we would do well, he warns, to distinguish clearly between *technical* translations of texts – instruction manuals, to take an extreme example – that are amenable to more or less literal and neutral rendering into other languages, and *interpretive* translations of texts – including, or especially, religious and other works with canonical status – that are not so amenable. However skilfully and conscientiously it is done, translating the latter sort of text from one language into another, especially when, as with the *Hui Ming Ching*, the linguistic differences are compounded by huge cultural differences, has the potential to turn it into a thing of specious certainty. What I mean is that, particularly when faced with an obscurity or key concept or difficult nuance in the original language, the translator has to choose one word or phrase rather than another to convey it. That choice then takes on an authority of its own, even though another translator, or the indeed same translator, might have chosen a different word or phrase. And in the case of the Freud canon it seems that, effectively having usurped the authority of the German texts in the English-speaking world, the collected *Standard Edition* attracted a variety of champions each with some vested interest, intellectual, doctrinal, professional, commercial, in *preserving* its authority.

[253] *The Ego and the Id*, German edition first published in 1923; the Joan Riviere translation, as revised and edited by Strachey in the *Standard Edition*, is reprinted in *The Pelican Freud Library*, Vol. 11, pp. 364-365. In the same passage Freud likens the 'bodily *ego*' to the cortical homunculus (the distorted 'little man' image by which, as I understand it, the human brain represents anatomical features in proportion to the motor-sensory information associated with them) that 'stands on its head in the cortex, sticks up its heels, faces backwards and, as we know, has its speech-area on the left-hand side.'

[254] *Civilization and its Discontents*, 1930; Riviere/Strachey translation in *The Pelican Freud Library*, Vol. 12, pp. 254-255. Freud explains (pp. 251-253) that his reflections on the 'shrunken residue' were occasioned partly by a letter from the French writer and mystic Romain Rolland, to whom Freud had sent a copy of his essay on religion, *The Future of an Illusion.* Rolland wrote back agreeing with Freud`s judgement that religion is an illusion but chiding him for failing to appreciate 'the true source of religious sentiments', which Rolland described as a sensation of 'eternity' or 'oceanic' feeling and Freud reformulated as 'a feeling of an indissoluble bond, of being one with the external world as a whole'. Freud`s response, which sets the tone of *Civilization and its Discontents*, was that he could not discover any such feeling in himself but would try to offer a psychoanalytic or 'genetic' (sic) explanation for its seemingly widespread experience by other people: personally speaking, I cannot decide whether this response displays an endearing humility and open-mindedness on Freud`s part, or proves that he completely missed Rolland`s point – which may be that some experiences are beyond explanation, psychoanalytic, 'genetic' or otherwise. Freud had already discussed 'inside' and 'outside' in several earlier writings, including his 1915 paper *Instincts and their Vicissitudes*: see the C.M. Baines/Strachey translation in Vol. 11 of *The Pelican Freud Library*, p. 115. (For reasons he explains on pp. 98-101 and 105-106 of *Freud and Man`s Soul*, Bettelheim proposes *The Uneasiness Inherent in Culture* and *Drives and Their Mutability* as more appropriate English titles for these two works. While we`re about it, he would also say that *The I and the It* works much more meaningfully as a title than *The Ego and the Id.*)

[255] Donna Williams`s ambivalence about being in 'the world' was mirrored in her ambivalence about being in her own body, experienced variously as a vehicle for her first tentative steps out of 'my world' ('From a body to a room': my page 106), as a wall between the two worlds (*Nobody Nowhere*, p. 94) and as a prison (*Nobody Nowhere*, p. 137: 'I wanted desperately to get out of my own body. To leave it there to be stomped on, used and abused as its invaders so chose'). In some autistic and other conditions it seems that the body may be perceived

not as something solid and constricting but as so flimsy that it is liable to fall apart at any moment: in her *Autistic States in Children* (London: Tavistock/Routledge, revised edition, 1992, pp. 35-36), the child psychotherapist Frances Tustin suggests that this sense of bodily fragility is characteristic of autistic children who, operating in 'manipulative' terms because they 'lack the creative notion of *growing*', feel that their limbs are stuck onto them and may easily come off; likewise they may be afraid of baths and showers because they are convinced that the water will peel off their skin or wash away their hair. Tustin bases these observations both on her own work with autistic children and on the writings of other clinical specialists cited in her text and bibliography.

[256] *Being and Nothingness*, p. 259; Sartre`s italics.

[257] *Being and Nothingness*, p. 261; my italics. Needless to say, Sartre`s conception of bodies as things is closely related to his conclusion that the 'fundamental attitudes' behind human relations are all despairing variations of sadism or masochism (my main text pages 46-47). The body is also of central importance to Sartre because it gives concrete expression to what he terms our *facticity*, the condition of being born into a particular set of social and other circumstances which, though random and contingent, are yet the raw materials out of which we have to make our conscious choices. On facticity, see also my page 118.

Plato meets the jazz age

[258] If so, Roquentin is mistaken in thinking her a black singer: Sophie Tucker was in fact white, born into a Jewish family in pre-Revolutionary Russia. The recording of the song that she made with Ted Lewis and his band in 1926, which technically (and perhaps metaphysically, depending on your perception) fits Roquentin`s description, can be heard by clicking the link on www.sfmuseum.org/hist2/days.html (Virtual Museum of the City of San Francisco: copyright position unclear). *Some of These Days* was written by Shelton Brooks.

[259] *Nausea*, pp. 36-37.

[260] *Nausea*, pp. 37-38.

[261] *Nausea*, pp. 38-39.
[262] *Nausea*, p. 191.
[263] *Nausea*, pp. 247-248.
[264] *Nausea*, p. 60.
[265] *Nausea*, p. 248.
[266] *Nausea*, p. 184.
[267] Towards the end of his life, Sartre was asked by Simone de Beauvoir what he thought he had been trying to say at the time he wrote *Nausea*, to which he replied: 'I saw it as a metaphysical essence; I had created a metaphysical object. It was like a Platonic idea, you might say, but a particularized idea and one that the reader would discover as he read the book. I began *Nausea* believing that, and by the end I no longer believed it.' While Sartre`s reply does not endorse my interpretation that Roquentin yearns for a reality of perfect forms, it does confirm that, at least initially, Sartre himself conceived of *Nausea* in Platonic terms. 'A writer has only one subject,' he declares in the same conversation, 'and that`s the world. ... There`s no doubt that the subject of *Nausea* is primarily the world.' He agrees explicitly with de Beauvoir`s suggestion that it is 'a metaphysical dimension of the world that has to be revealed' and implicitly with her suggestion that the 'metaphysical dimension' is contingency. The conversation was part of a series of exchanges tape-recorded in Rome and Paris in 1974, published by de Beauvoir after Sartre`s death in 1980, translated by Patrick O'Brian as *Adieux: A Farewell to Sartre* (London: André Deutsch and Weidenfeld & Nicolson, 1984); pp. 204-207.
[268] *Nausea*, p. 184. Sartre`s italics.
[269] *Nausea*, p. 191
[270] *Nausea*, pp. 184-185. Sartre elaborates on suicide, and on death in general, in *Being and Nothingness*. If it is a freely chosen act, suicide may seem to have the potential for meaningfulness but in fact, Sartre argues (p. 540), it is 'an absurdity which causes my life to be submerged in the absurd': by Sartre`s reckoning suicide could only be meaningful if it *failed*, because our acts only have meaning in relation to the future towards which they project us and a successful suicide would cut us off from that future. Death itself is an aspect of the

fundamental contingency (or 'facticity': my main text page 118) of human reality: *just there* without reason or justification, it is, says Sartre (p. 545), 'a pure fact as is birth; it comes to us from outside and it transforms us into the outside. At bottom it is in no way distinguished from birth, and it is the identity of birth and death that we call facticity.' And because it is contingent, Sartre insists (p. 533), above all death is absurd: 'It has often been said that we are in the situation of a condemned man among other condemned men who is ignorant of the day of his execution but who sees each day that his fellow prisoners are being executed. This is not wholly exact. We ought rather to compare ourselves to a man condemned to death who is bravely preparing himself for the ultimate penalty, who is doing everything possible to make a good showing on the scaffold, and who meanwhile is carried off by a flu epidemic.'

[271] *Nausea*, pp. 38 and 247.

[272] *Nausea*, p. 124; *La nausée*, pp. 120-121. Much of the language of *Nausea* is very Kafkaesque and this passage in particular reads as if penned by Kafka. On the evidence of *Adieux: A Farewell to Sartre* (p. 198), however, Sartre wrote *Nausea* before he had read Kafka.

[273] *Being and Nothingness*, pp. 82-83.

[274] *Being and Nothingness*, p. 83. On the myth of Er, see also my main text page 63.

[275] *Nausea*, p. 241.

[276] 'I can not doubt that I am. But in so far as this for-itself as such could also not be, it has all the contingency of fact. Just as my nihilating freedom is apprehended in anguish, so the for-itself is conscious of its facticity. It has the feeling of its complete gratuity; it apprehends itself as being there *for nothing*, as being *de trop*. … Facticity … simply resides in the for-itself as a memory of being, as its unjustifiable *presence in the world*.' (*Being and Nothingness*, p. 84; see my note 94 above for a definition of Sartre`s word 'nihilating'.)

[277] *Being and Nothingness*, p. 620. The context here is the passage, quoted in my note 173, in which Sartre distinguishes ontology (the description of being) from metaphysics (speculation as to why there is being). According to his distinction, the origin of consciousness is a

question for metaphysics to hypothesize about; ontology will say only that everything happens *as if* the in-itself had fallen into consciousness in an attempt to justify its own existence. This still strikes me as a sleight of hand to get around the objection that there is no good reason for the in-itself to want a justification for its own existence. Whether a sleight of hand or not, it enables Sartre to insist that, while the origin of consciousness is a matter of hypothesis, its project of 'attaining to the dignity of the in-itself-for-itself' – the impossible union of inanimate being and animate nothingness – is a matter of *fact*.

[278] *Being and Nothingness*, pp. 89-90.

[279] *Being and Nothingness*, p. 566.

[280] *Being and Nothingness*, p. 615; *L`être et le néant*, p. 708.

6. SOME POINT OF THE PENDULUM`S SWING

Why the many are so many

[281] Unlike Coleridge, who, according to Keats`s letter to his brothers of December 1817 (full citation in my note 1), 'would let go by a fine isolated verisimilitude caught from the Penetralium of mystery, from being incapable of remaining content with half knowledge.'

[282] 'Postscript' in *The Spirit Level* (London: Faber and Faber, 1996), p. 70.

[283] I have referred here to Philip Borg-Wheelers`s programme note to the 1993 recording of *Cantus* by the Bournemouth Sinfonietta, directed by Richard Studt (coupled with other instrumental works on EMI Classics for Pleasure CD 7243 5 73117 2 4).

[284] All the passages that follow are from the Estonian daily newspaper *Postimees* of 12 June 1998; English translation by Alan Teder made available via David Pinkerton`s Arvo Pärt Information Archive (www.arvopart.org/article.php?id=40). Immo Mihkelson is an Estonian music journalist and radio broadcaster.

[285] Some of Pärt`s metaphors in this interview are as rich as his music, as when he is asked which of his compositions is most important to him:

> This is a very personal thing. I don`t wish to speak about it. All the compositions are like my own children. It is not necessarily [the case] that the healthiest or most beautiful child is the most precious. Some piece which has not succeeded and which may never be finished may still be the closest to one`s heart.

[286] The key passage from Bohr`s reply to the EPR paper (pp. 138-139 in Toulmin [full citation in my note 16]) reads as follows:

> From our point of view we now see that the wording of the … criterion of physical reality proposed by Einstein, Podolsky and Rosen contains an ambiguity as regards the meaning of the expression "without in any way disturbing a system". Of course there is … no question of a mechanical disturbance of the system under investigation during the last critical stage of the measuring procedure. But even at this stage there is essentially the question of *an influence on the very conditions which define the possible types of predictions regarding the future behavior of the system.* Since these conditions constitute an inherent element of the description of any phenomenon to which the term "physical reality" can be properly attached, we see that the argumentation of the … authors does not justify their conclusion that quantum-mechanical description is essentially incomplete. On the contrary this description … may be characterized as a rational utilization of all possibilities of unambiguous interpretation of measurements, compatible with the finite and uncontrollable interaction between the objects and the measuring instruments in the field of quantum theory. In fact, it is only the mutual exclusion of any two

experimental procedures, permitting the unambiguous definition of complementary physical quantities, which provides room for new physical laws, the coexistence of which might at first sight appear irreconcilable with the basic principles of science. It is just this entirely new situation as regards the description of physical phenomena that the notion of *complementarity* aims at characterizing.

[287] My source is David Drachman, 'Do we have brain to spare?', an editorial in the journal *Neurology*, Vol. 64, Issue 12 (28 June 2005), pp. 2004-2005. Drachman`s estimate of the number of neurons in the human cortex seems relatively low: for comparison, Kaas ('From mice to men: the evolution of the large, complex human brain' [full citation in my note 113], p. 163) puts the figure at 10^{11} (one hundred billion), versus about ten million for a mouse. Drachman`s calculation for the length of nerve fibres relates to the brain of a person aged twenty: if we survive to the age of ninety, he observes, we are likely to lose anything up to fifty percent of these nerve fibres. He observes too that, while normal ageing (as opposed to degenerative diseases such as Alzheimer`s) is the commonest cause of the '"stealth" erosion of cerebral horsepower', the redundancy and plasticity of the brain provide 'considerable buffering' against the greater impairments that would otherwise occur even under normal ageing conditions.
[288] And equally graphically in the Chinese text the *Hui Ming Ching*: my note 251.
[289] Or like Kafka`s Suppliant: my note 213.
[290] Strictly speaking, Sartre`s myth says it is *as if* inanimate matter (the in-itself) had fallen into consciousness (the for-itself) to escape contingency: my note 173 and note 277.

Not in the nature of things

[291] Page 626. As indicated on my main text page 51, Sartre`s context is his call for the 'repudiation' of the spirit of seriousness.

[292] The woman`s name is Sue Cox. My source is her interview on Radio 4`s *Today* programme on 18 September 2010, available via the Archive link on the *Today* website (http://news.bbc.co.uk/today: skip to 0732).
[293] *Being and Nothingness*, pp. 32-33.

Some point of the pendulum`s swing

[294] Page 110 in the paperback edition (Harmondsworth: Penguin Books in association with William Heinemann Ltd, 1976 reprint).
[295] My main source for these reflections is Erwin Schrödinger`s *What is Life?*, especially pp. 10-14 in the edition paired with *Mind and Matter* (Cambridge: Cambridge University Press, 1989 reprint). According to Schrödinger, the statistical explanation of paramagnetism is attributable to the French physicist Paul Langevin, who died in 1946; Brownian motion is named after the Scottish botanist Robert Brown, who observed (but did not explain) the phenomenon in 1827 while examining microscopic particles of pollen suspended in water.
[296] Page 401 in *Christmas Books and Hard Times* (London: Chapman & Hall, 1894).
[297] The version of the oath set down in 1593 by Antonio Pérez, a one-time secretary and favourite of Philip II, translated in Ralph Giesey`s *If Not, Not: the Oath of the Aragonese and the Legendary Laws of Sobrarbe* (Princeton: Princeton University Press, 1968), p. 6 and Appendix I. Sadly, the oath may be an invention of Renaissance scholars: all four versions that Giesey quotes (and describes as 'fictitious') in his Appendix date from the late sixteenth century, supposedly recorded from earlier, oral sources. But there is no documentary evidence of the oath in surviving records of Aragonese coronations, despite claims that it was already in use in the thirteenth and fourteenth centuries, and even as early as the eighth century (Giesey pp. 6, 28).
[298] One instance of such unpredictable or irrational behaviour is provided by Algeria`s parliamentary elections of December 1991, the first multi-party poll at national level since independence from France in 1962. In the first round, by far the largest single proportion of votes

cast, 47.3%, went to the Islamic Salvation Front (known by its French-language acronym FIS), some of whose leaders had openly said that if elected they would ban non-Islamic parties – in other words, remove any possibility of secular, democratic opposition to themselves once elected. This is surely a textbook illustration of what Popper (*The Open Society and Its Enemies*, Vol. I, p. 123 and note 4 on p. 265) terms variously the 'paradox of freedom', 'paradox of tolerance' and 'paradox of democracy'. We have to wonder whether Popper would have approved of what happened next in Algeria, namely that the army, alarmed at the near-certainty of an FIS majority in the 430-seat National Assembly, effectively staged a coup d`état and cancelled the run-off elections due in January 1992, triggering a ferocious civil war that lasted a decade. One of my sources is the European Union-funded European Institute for Research on Mediterranean and Euro-Arab Cooperation (www.medea.be: 'FIS, The Islamic Salvation Front' via country index/Algeria), which comments drily that in FIS ideology the concept of democracy is 'assimilated to atheism, and the legalisation of parties "which recommend contradicting Islam" is condemned.'

[299] A word he uses in his essay 'The Pursuit of the Ideal' in *The Crooked Timber of Humanity* (London: Fontana Press, 1991), p. 9. The context is Berlin`s argument – in favour of 'pluralism', as he puts it, and not 'cultural or moral relativism' – that 'collisions of values are of the essence of what they are and what we are.' Liberty and equality, for example, are both 'among the primary goals pursued by human beings through many centuries; but total liberty for wolves is death to the lambs, total liberty of the powerful, the gifted, is not compatible with the rights to a decent existence of the weak and the less gifted' (pp.12-13).

[300] I refer to the recent changes to Britain`s counter-terrorism laws, and particularly to the 'control orders' introduced as an emergency measure under the Prevention of Terrorism Act 2005. In December 2011 a revised regime of 'terrorism prevention and investigation measures', individually limited to a maximum of two years, ended the powers of the Home Secretary to order the virtual house arrest and, as some would say, internal exile of terrorism suspects. Detention without

charge has been reduced to fourteen days from the former twenty-eight days, although the Home Secretary retains the option of authorizing twenty-eight days in an emergency. While the reforms have been broadly welcomed in the press and elsewhere, there is concern that the 'control orders' have been watered down and renamed rather than abolished altogether. For instance, an editorial in *The Guardian* ('Review of terror laws: New name for an old problem', available online at www.guardian.co.uk/commentisfree/2011/jan/27/review-terror-laws-liberty) judges that 'In general, the balance of anti-terror powers should shift as a result [of the review carried out by Lord Macdonald, a Liberal Democrat peer, on behalf of the coalition government] from the routine to the exceptional.' But the editorial also cautions that 'Unfortunately the government`s proposals sustain – and by removing the need for [annual] parliamentary renewal arguably entrench – the home secretary`s ability to restrict the liberty of citizens without putting a case against them or securing a prosecution.'

[301] '[W]e must go and work in the garden', the closing words of *Candide*; p. 144 in the translation by John Butt (Harmondsworth: Penguin Classics, 1947).

[302] From the translation by N.K. Sandars (Harmondsworth: Penguin Books, 1972 reprint with revisions), p. 102.

[303] Ecclesiastes 2:24 and 3:21-22.

[304] Quoted by Erik Erikson in his *Childhood and Society* (Harmondsworth: Penguin Books in association with the Hogarth Press, 1970 reprint), p. 256. In an essay entitled 'Apocryphal Freud: Sigmund Freud`s Most Famous "Quotations" and Their Actual Sources', Alan Elms, an American professor of psychology, reveals (p. 92) that no such saying is recorded in Freud`s own utterances or correspondence and that Erikson, queried about it in 1982, had replied: 'Oh, I simply don`t know. I heard it in Vienna and it impressed me. I`ve never seen it in print. And some people now have said I made it up. If I did, I`m proud.' Elms`s essay is contained in Jerome Winer and James Anderson, editors, *Sigmund Freud and His Impact on the Modern World* (Hillsdale, New Jersey: The Analytic Press, The Annual of

Psychoanalysis, Vol. XXIX, 2001), which can be read online using Google Book Search (caution: the copyright position is unclear if accessing from the United Kingdom, where the print edition of the same volume is published by Routledge).

305 *Being and Nothingness*, p. 77. My italics.

306 I have not forgotten that earlier (main text page 87) I criticized Sartre for his verbal sleight of hand – the same *as if* trick, in fact – so you may wish to accuse me of hypocrisy to boot.

307 I allude to Books IV.17 and II.5 of *The Meditations of Marcus Aurelius Antoninus*; pp. 26 and 11 in the translation by A.S.L. Farquharson (Oxford: Oxford University Press, 1998 reissue).

308 The observation that the sextant, an instrument still occasionally used to this day, perpetuates the pre-Copernican illusion is not mine, alas. It comes from the melancholy meditations of Jonathan Raban, who, in ‘Sea-Room’ in *Granta* Issue 10 (Cambridge: Granta Publications, Travel Writing, undated but probably 1985/1986; pp. 21-34), reflects that ‘the essence of celestial navigation turned out … to consist in a sort of universal egoism. The heavenly bodies had been pinned up in the sky to provide an enormous web of convenient lines and triangles. Wherever he was, the navigator was always the crux of the arrangement, measuring the solar system to discover himself on his ship, bang at the heart of the matter.’ Raban`s first attempt to take a noon sight with his own sextant, from the kitchen window of his flat in London, is not an unqualified success: using the fourth-floor typing pool of a nearby office block as a notional horizon, he finds his latitude to be 45°30′ N. ‘Had I only been in Milan or Portland, Oregon,’ he muses, ‘it would have been spot-on. As it was, it did at least put a precise figure on the complaint from which I`d been suffering for the last few months: I was just six degrees and one minute out of kilter with where I was supposed to be.’ ‘Sea-Room’ later became *Coasting*, Raban`s full-length account of his voyage around Britain in a converted sailing trawler, the *Gosford Maid*.

309 Sartre`s short study on the subject, *L`imagination*, dates from 1936; his longer work, *L`imaginaire*, from 1940. The first has been translated

by Forrest Williams as *Imagination, a Psychological Critique*; the second by Bernard Frechtman as *The Psychology of the Imagination.*

7. POSTSCRIPT

310 If I had to call it something, up to a point my candidate would be Freud`s life principle, 'Eros'. On the one hand, in its favour is that fact that, unlike a personal 'God', an impersonal 'Eros' is very difficult to make in our own image and, to my knowledge, no wars have ever been fought in its name. On the other hand, the fit is not very good because Freud seems to conceive of 'Eros' as an earth-bound principle operating through human beings, whereas what I am struggling to imagine is a principle that operates in the first instance through the creation of elementary particles, galaxies and universes and only later, and perhaps incidentally, through the evolution of particular forms of life on particular planets. Freud first speculated on 'Eros, the preserver of life', and its relation to an opposing principle of death and destruction, in 1920 in *Beyond the Pleasure Principle* (Strachey translation in *The Pelican Freud Library*, Vol. 11, especially p. 327 and Freud`s long footnote on pp. 334-335). Three years later, in *The Ego and the Id* (under the section heading translated as 'The Two Classes of Instincts'; pp. 380-388 in Vol. 11 of *The Pelican Freud*), he developed his ideas more fully and observed (p. 387) that 'the death instincts are by their nature mute and … the clamour of life proceeds for the most part from Eros'. In 1930, in *Civilization and its Discontents* (*Pelican Freud*, Vol. 12, pp. 313-314), he concluded that civilization itself is 'a process in the service of Eros, whose purpose is to combine single human individuals, and after that families, then races, peoples and nations, into one great unity, the unity of mankind' and that 'the evolution of civilization … must present the struggle between Eros and Death, between the instinct of life and the instinct of destruction, as it works itself out in the human species.' As indicated at the end of my note 254, Bettelheim deplores the use of the English word 'instinct' to translate the *Trieb* of Freud`s German, most particularly in connection with the 'death instinct': 'Freud never spoke of a death instinct,' he

protests (*Freud and Man`s Soul*, p. 107), 'only of a mostly unconscious drive or impulse that provokes us to aggressive, destructive, and self-destructive actions.' Bettelheim, who consistently refers to 'Eros' as a 'life drive' and not a 'life instinct', offers his own translation (p. 111) of a passage from *Analysis Terminable and Interminable*, Freud`s last major paper on psychoanalysis, published in 1937: 'There can be no question of an antithesis between an optimistic and a pessimistic theory of life; only the simultaneous working together and against each other of both primordial drives, of Eros and the death drive, can explain the colorfulness of life, never the one or the other all by itself.' I see no point here in pursuing the idea of a death drive, for two reasons: firstly, in the sense that Freud and Bettelheim mean, it is another earth-bound, human-specific principle of great interest to us but not necessarily to the rest of the universe; and secondly, in the sense that I would mean, it would in any case be subordinate to the opposing principle – whether called 'Eros', 'the life drive', or left unnamed – which, so to speak, always had the last laugh. Metaphysically, if not in our experience, perhaps death *shall* have no dominion.

[311] The odds seem to be on a slow, cold death as the universe continues to expand forever under the influence of the 'dark energy' thought to make up more than seventy percent of the universe. The alternative scenario that it would end in a Big Crunch, another singularity in which the universe would collapse in upon itself under the force of its own gravity, now appears to be ruled out.

Index

The index is designed to be searched by name and/or theme. Macaulay's essay on Francis Bacon, for example, can be found both under Macaulay, Thomas Babington: 'Lord Bacon' (essay of 1837) and under the thematic heading progress/Progress: 'a philosophy which never rests … Its law is progress' (Macaulay). The index is comprehensive but not exhaustive: while all of my principal sources are directly referenced, few of my secondary sources are. Plain numbers (12, 140-141) refer to pages in my main text; numbers in italics (*n. 12, nn. 140, 141*) refer to my endnotes, *not* the pages on which the endnotes appear.

C

D

E

F

L

M

R

T

U

V

W

Y

www.ingramcontent.com/pod-product-compliance
Lightning Source LLC
Chambersburg PA
CBHW070626170726
48291CB00003B/898

* 9 7 8 1 9 1 6 0 6 2 2 3 8 *